ICE COLD VENGEANCE

A novel by

DeJon

Imagine DeJon Publications

An Urban Entertainment Company

Published by Imagine DeJon Publications
Copyright © 2015 by DeJon

ISBN: 978-0-9857933-3-3

First Printing May 2015
Printed in the United States of America

10 9 8 7 6 5 4 3 2

This is a work of fiction. It is not meant to depict, portray or represent any particular real persons. All the characters, incidents and dialogues are the products of the author's imagination and are not to be construed as real. Any references or similarities to actual events, entities, real people, living or dead, or to real locales are intended to give the novel a sense of reality. Any similarity in names, characters, entities, places and incidents is entirely coincidental.

Cover Copyright © 2015 by Imagine DeJon Publications all rights reserved
Cover Concept by: DeJon
Models Provided by: Starr Studded Imagine Studios
Editor: Dolly Lopez
Typeset: Linda Williams

Imagine DeJon Publications

To: KIM
Thanks for the support.
ReMeMber To AlwayS

Dedication

I dedicate this novel to Hideyoshi TakaMaro my spiritual advisor who showed me the true and righteous path.

StaY TRue to yourself!!!

DEJon
1Love

OCT-2018

CHAPTER ONE

Ice didn't know where the sudden surge of inhuman strength came from, nor did he give a fuck at this particular moment in time. He broke free of New York's Finests' clammy, fish-white hands that were desperately clutching at his clothes in every direction humanly possible. He realized he wasn't hurt as bad as he had previously thought. Surprisingly, he felt little pain in his shoulder, assuming now that the bullet must have only slightly grazed his flesh, stunning him momentarily.

The police were struggling to keep up with the young man as their strained lungs gave out from chain smoking stale Marlboro cigarettes and wolfing down too much free greasy deli food that the bodega owners gave to them when they made their rounds. Not to mention the fact that all New York City police officers knew that it was an unwritten rule in the streets that if a suspect made them run and got caught, their testicles would become the personal property of the New York City Police Department, so the majority of the force wasn't used to running after suspects.

Ice leaped a paint-chipped wooden fence as he turned the corner with the duffel bag filled with cash slung firmly over his good shoulder. He heard the all too familiar sounds of dogs barking wildly, and soon spotted a couple of ghetto-bred pit-bull who looked as if they were raised on steroids and raw bloody meat. The thick muscled canines eyed Ice hungrily, daring him to step into their territory as they bared their foam-covered fangs. Ice had a choice of either facing what the dogs had to offer him or catching a serious ass whopping from the Jakes, not to mention a possible life sentence due to all the carnage he was somehow connected to that same evening. The growling and muscle-bound pit-bull seemed a welcome alternative as Ice heard the static of police issued radios sounding closer and closer.

"Psst! In here! Come on and get your ass in here before they see you!" a voice coming from a cracked open doorway whispered hoarsely.

Ice hesitated for a split second before pushing his way into the back door and closing it quietly as not to attract any unwanted attention. He leaned with his back against the door, breathing heavily as he took in his new surroundings. He was in a somewhat clean but cluttered kitchen that was filled with old outdated appliances.

A split second later he turned towards his supposed savior. There standing a couple of feet away from him was a beautiful girl about nineteen, with her hair pulled back in a neat ponytail. She was wearing some tight Gap jean shorts that hugged her Coke bottle hips, and rocked a tiny matching navy blue wife-beater. The first thing that caught Ice's attention was that the woman's nipples resembled a couple of number 2 pencil erasers poking out through the fabric. Ice felt a slight stir in his groin area.

"Close your mouth and come down in the basement. You know how the po-po can get down and dirty sometimes," the girl said as she open another door that revealed a set of concrete steps which lead to the basement.

Just as Ice's foot touched the first step he heard a voice yell, "Hey, Jim! Watch the fucking dogs!" Then he heard a quick succession of gunfire followed by a yelp that only a dying canine would make while only trying to protect its master's property.

Ice tiptoed down the steps while tightly clutching the money bag, wondering what this pretty bitch's game plan was, while at the same time staring at the jean shorts that rode deep up in the crack of her apple-shaped ass.

The first thing Ice did was flop down a large beige sofa and light up a Newport while trying to control his racing heart.

The girl pulled a string that was hanging from the ceiling, causing a low watt lightbulb to flicker on. "So, why are so many police after you? Whatcha rob a bank or something?" she asked as she sat next to Ice and crossed her long, well-proportioned butterscotch legs.

"Yo, shorty, I appreciate the help and all that, but what I did or what I'm about to do is my business," he responded, still trying to figure out what this mysterious girl was really about.

"I feel you. I'm not trying to be all up in yours, but I had an older brother who was in a similar situation, except that he had some Blood niggas chasing him, and the Chinese motherfuckers locked the

2

doors causing him to get stabbed about twelve times. They didn't even open the door as he lay bleeding to death and calling out for help. Those razor-eyed pieces of shit finally opened up only when the cops knocked to ask if they saw anything," the girl said with her voice taking on a melancholic type of tone.

"Word?" Ice said before taking a long drag on his much needed cigarette.

"And the fucked up part about the whole thing was that my brother used to order shit from them at least three times a week," the girl replied as she lit up her own cigarette from Ice's pack.

After she helped bandage Ice's wound, he became a little more relaxed as time flew by, knowing the police looking for him were probably long gone and thinking that he probably made it to some another neighborhood.

For some reason Ice opened up to this stranger, telling her how he got mixed up in some wicked shit too soon after just coming home from jail. They both knew they were instantly attracted to each other as Ice lifted the shirt over her head and attacked her breasts like a newborn baby. Ice wasn't into too much foreplay for the simple fact that most girls just got wet from his looks and the knowledge that his long, light skinned dick would be up in them sometime that night.

Being from the hood, the thick girl recognized the look on Ice's face as she stepped out of her shorts, showing a thin airstrip of hair attached to a perfectly shaped pussy mound. A full grown camel toe had nothing on this young woman's private parts. Just like he knew it, shorty's pussy was dripping like a slum lord's leaky faucet as he roughly pushed her legs apart on the couch and took control of the situation. He positioned her coconut-colored legs on his shoulders for maximum advantage as he eased his swollen dick into her vagina as easily as a butcher would slice through a succulent tenderloin. Ice beat the pussy like his life depended on it, all the while never taking his eyes off the bag of money that rested on the floor by the sofa.

"*Boom! Boom! Boom!*" The thunderous knocks echoed throughout the kitchen and into the dimly-lit basement.

Ice was beyond caring who was at the door. The only thing that mattered right now was filling this ghetto bird up with hot sticky

3

cum that she so well deserved. The way he had her legs twisted up and spread so far apart, you would think the girl was a veteran gymnast trying to win the gold medal at the summer Olympics. Once Ice tamed the nappy dugout, he planned on shampooing this hood booger's throat with millions of his babies.

"*Boom! Boom! Boom!*" The knocks came once again, causing Ice to wake up. He quickly opened his eyes and realized that he was laid up in a hospital bed with a massive hard on that was poking up against the thin fabric of the starched white hospital sheet. It was just another dream that his mind conjured up, that maybe, just maybe he somehow escaped from the police with his hundred thousand dollar heist. Reality hit him full force in the face as he felt the steel police issued ankle bracelet cutting deeply into his skin and bone.

CHAPTER TWO

"Move the fuck over so I can see!" a teenage boy roughly barked as he nudged another guy his same age with a stiff elbow. "Slow up, nigga! I was the one who put you on, so chill!" a youth named Rock spat.

Four teenage guys were crammed in a tiny storage room, each trying to peep through a crudely made hole in the wall.

Meanwhile, on the other side of the hole was Laura Davenport, better known throughout the hood as Trina. All those who came in contact with her knew that Trina was no ordinary white girl roaming the ghetto in search of black dick and a little drama from their bleak unfulfilled lives. It's true, Trina loved having the African Mandingo spear slice into her alabaster ass every once in a while, but she loved that cash flow even more. Being that she was an extremely attractive woman in her mid-twenties with a ghetto laid out body that black women often hated on, she never had a problem with men of any race willing to spend that dough on her at any cost.

Trina stood butt ass naked in the staff locker room with one leg up on a chair. She slowly rubbed baby oil up and down her thighs while running her tongue over her red Revlon painted lips. Her curly brown pubic hair glistened under the bright lights as she turned her well-rounded ass in the direction of the supposedly secret peep hole and prepared to rub the soles of her feet. While she slowly bent over in a seductive manner, she knew for a fact that the horny teenage boys were harder than a roll of quarters and would blow their loads any minute now. All she had to do was "mistakenly" ease a stiff finger into her vagina while slowly spreading the baby oil, and the overly eager guys would lose their goddamn minds. The white girl wasn't a stranger on having men of all walks of life fall into her black widow spider's web of trickery and deceit.

Trina was very much aware of the hole because she discovered it approximately a week ago. She had gone to the storage room which was directly next door to the staff changing room to pick up some fresh linen. While moving some boxes she stumbled across the was accompanied by a cop who just took a quick look around the room and then went and stood over by the door.

"What do these assholes got on the menu today?" Ice asked as he took the lid off the plastic food tray.

"Nathaniel, don't talk like that. You're a very lucky young man that the bullet didn't hit any major arteries," she stated while looking at his medical chart that was located at the foot of the bed.

Ice stared at the contents on the tray that held some cold, slimy looking meat that they called "liver surprise", a small portion of green peas, a hard biscuit, a piece of fruit and a small carton of milk that a first grader could down in one shot. He thought something had to give sooner or later as he ignored the nurse's excessive chatter.

CHAPTER FOUR

"**I** told you before, nigga, you ain't gonna be slinging no rocks on this here corner!" Haitian Jack yelled at a guy about eighteen years old, spraying the youth's face with spit and chewed up pieces of goat meat.

The guy tried to answer back but his vocal cords were being tightly compressed by one of Jack's henchmen who had him in a rear naked choke hold that was eventually starting to take effect. Right before the young man's bulging eyes fully rolled into the back of his head, Jack added, "And this is just a little reminder so you know I ain't bullshitting with you young bitch ass niggas!"

A split second after that statement was made, a heavy black Israeli made nine flashed through the air, making direct contact with exposed teeth and gums.

"Ahhhh!" The unfortunate victim fell forward as four of his teeth were rudely dislodged while leaving a fifth tooth as a jagged bloody stump.

"After you finish seeing a dentist about your grille piece, come holler at me and I might find a place for you," Haitian Jack said with a hearty laugh as he jumped behind the wheel of his of classic candy-coated nickle clean 1995 BMW with the Lorenzo wheels.

Jackillya, better known as Crazy Haitian Jack, had recently relocated from Miami's over-populated Liberty City Projects to Queens, New York. Right before his drug and extortion empire was to have a solid concrete foundation. Everything eventually came crumbling down around his head like a wet house of cards. First, there was a coordinated joint effort by federal, local and state police agencies that rounded up most members of his bloodthirsty crew. Through trickery, deceit and blatant manipulation of facts, so-called stand up men on Jack's team started ratting each other out like they were auditioning for the TV show "The First 48 Hours". Jack barely escaped with a little money, a couple of guns and just the clothes on his back.

Haitian Jack was a tall, solidly built man in his late twenties who always kept a clean shaven bald head that blended in perfectly with his purple-black skin tone. He hated almost everything and everybody. He hated Americans, Jamaicans, any type of law enforcement, and white people just to name a few. He even disliked his fellow countrymen to a certain degree, saying that they'd stab you in the fucking back if presented with the right opportunity.

But the one thing he despised and hated the most and caused the veins in is neck to bulge out grotesquely was any young punk who felt like he was untouchable in the streets. When a situation of that caliber arose, Jack always made it his primary focus to prove that myth wrong. His dick actually became semi-hard when he had a so-called gangster in his presence and looked him dead in his terrified eyes as he shitted in his pants from pure fright. "What happened? I thought you said you couldn't be touched. Huh? I can't hear you, nigga!" Jack would say in a mocking tone before he made his victim just another memory and caused folks in the hood to say, "Damn! That's some fucked up shit! I never thought it would happen to him!"

A week later, the man would have been completely forgotten about as neighborhood residents continued on with their bleak lives in the harsh ghetto.

"So, you get in contact with them cats yet?" Jack asked as he slowly turned the corner while peering through the darkness and hoping they spot the other street corner drug dealer that they were looking for.

"Yeah. He's talking about he'll get back to me once he contacts his peoples," Lite responded.

Lite stood equal to Jack in height, but outweighed him by at least forty pounds, with most of the weight being muscle. Lite and his girl were the only ones who made it out of Miami with Jack while the Feds were tight on their asses. Lite suspected that his boss was a little envious of him because Jack's main girl had gotten snatched up in one of the pre-dawn raids.

Disappointed that he didn't find the other guy they had intended to teach a lesson to also, Jack gunned the gas pedal and stated, "Let's head back to the spot and finish up with the other business."

CHAPTER FIVE

Nathaniel Wilson, a.k.a. Ice, stared up towards the off-white hospital ceiling, waiting for his midnight snack. Forty-five minutes later his keen hearing heard flirtatious whispering followed by low giggling coming from behind the door. He knew exactly what was going on, which brought a little devilish grin to his face.

A couple of minutes later the door swung open and a nurse walked in. Her white, soft padded shoes hardly made any sound at all. "Mr. Wilson, I'm here to check your vitals and give you your recommended shot," she said loud enough so the cop outside the door could hear her professional attitude. The nurse walked towards Ice with a huge smile as she handed him a small bag that continued three extra crispy pieces of K.F.C., a large mashed potatoes and a cold Sprite soda. She proceeded to go through the routine of checking Ice's pulse among other things while the patient hungrily gobbled down his illicit meal.

Ice knew he had the nurse Rhonda under wraps when she first came on duty for her midnight shift and flashed him a newspaper article detailing what had jumped off between him and the police. The article portrayed Ice as a major trafficker in narcotics, and paralyzing the movements of honest Queens residents. The writer's rhetorical statements went on to say that with the dedication and relentless efforts of the highly trained New York City Police Department, they were successfully able to bring down this individual who had been a plague on the community, while recovering twenty five thousand dollars in bloody drug money. Ice couldn't hold in his laughter when he first read the bogus article. He knew that the missing seventy five thousand dollars was probably going to pay for the college education of some cop's kid, or to buy a new sailboat for the police to drink their Coors Light beers on.

Ice had peeped the way Rhonda lustfully and excitedly stared at him, so he decided to use his good looks to his full advantage. Being that he was tall, light skinned and had green eyes, females of all ages wanted to get with him. Nurse Rhonda, being no different

"I'm not really trying to fuck with those hoes right now. I'm trying to get my shit in order. But I can always get that nut off with no problem. All you have to do in the hood is roll up a fat blunt and buy a bitch some Chinese food, and they be out of them panties in no time," he responded in a self-assured tone of voice.

Later on, Trina cashed her check and threw the bum in front of A & B Check Cashing Services her loose change. She wanted to get some new wears, but she knew she was limited to what she was working with. So, she decided to head to Macy's at the Green Acres Shopping Mall.

As soon as she walked into the dressing room with a couple of outfits she had picked out, she quickly spotted a small Coach bag on the leather seat cushion. Without hesitation she tucked the medium size bag under her arm and concealed it even further with a waist-high jean jacket.

"Oh, excuse me, Miss. Did you happen to see a brown and tan handbag in there?" a very stylish and well-dressed fortyish white women with baloney thin lips asked just as Trina was about to make her getaway.

"Did you say a brown and tan bag?" Trina innocently asked.

"Yes, yes. Did you see it?" the high maintenance lady quickly asked, hoping that Trina was a Good Samaritan.

"Just as I was coming in I saw a short black girl rushing out with one just like you described," Trina said with her eyes looking up as if she was trying to remember some more important details. "As a matter of fact, she was acting suspicious, like she was up to no good," she added in, playing the part to a tee.

"Oh my God! How can a person be so inconsiderate? They should put all those people in cages!" the white lady stated, her subconscious and blatant racism floating to the surface.

"I think I saw her heading towards the footwear department!" Trina shouted out after the lady, who was hurriedly walking off in search of a security guard.

"Thank you. I appreciate it. I wish the world had more people like you in it," the lady responded, never catching the smirk on the stranger's face as she continued her fast pace.

Trina ditched the clothes, went straight to the bathroom and locked herself in one of the stalls. She sat on the toilet seat as she rifled through the ill-gotten Coach bag. The bag contained a pair of Cabbanna sunglasses, an iPhone 6, some odds and ends, and a matching Coach wallet. She flung open the wallet and counted out eight hundred dollars in crisp fifty and hundred dollar bills. "That's what the fuck I'm talking about!" she said with a smile as she stuffed the money down in her own cheap bag. "Oh shit! It's on now!" she added after finding an assortment of neatly placed credit cards. She had to put the stolen credit cards to work right away before the uppity bitch called them in.

Fifteen minutes later, Trina was in a cab on her way to the store she really wanted to shop at in the first place.

Approximately three hours later, she was walking through the door of her cousin's house that was located on the borderline of Long Island and Queens in a quiet neighborhood that had neatly trimmed lawns, giving it a picturesque effect.

She stripped out of her work clothes and proceeded to take a long hot shower.

Trina hated staying with her cousin, Lilly, who she considered a neat freak. "Why can't you pick your rolled up dirty panties off the bathroom floor? At least take the plate out of the microwave," Lilly often complained. She had to take Lilly's complaining and constant verbal abuse because she had little choice in the matter.

Trina had no idea who was driving the big body Yukon Denali that violently smashed into her partner in crime, Supreme, and shutting their money-making plans down. Moments later, Supreme would later die from his internal injuries.

Trina wasn't taking any unnecessary chances, fearing that whoever killed Supreme might still be after her also. She wasn't about to go back to her apartment, feeling unnaturally paranoid that someone would be there waiting for her. "Fuck that apartment! I was about to get evicted anyway. Those clothes there were starting to get played out too," the frightened woman reasoned with herself when she headed to her cousin Lilly's house.

To make the situation even crazier was that she had no idea where her pimp, Born was or what he planned to do to her when he found out that she had flipped the script on him for Supreme to get the ransom money.

block the savage blow with his free hand as the barrel of his gun found its mark. The first blow shattered the fragile bones in his nose and knocked him instantly unconscious. He fell backwards, pushing the protruding needle deeper into his skull. That fact didn't stop Ice from viciously pistol whipping the bloody man in the face, fracturing an eye socket in the process.

The only reason Ice stopped his vicious rampage was because Rhonda said, "Ice, we got to get the fuck outta here, now!" She quickly ran to the door and peeped out to see if the commotion drew the attention of any hospital staff members. When she saw that everything looked normal, she said, "I'll be back in a minute. Do something with his fat ass." She came back in under thirty seconds carrying a small white plastic bag under her arm.

Ice was still breathing hard and holding the weapon up while listening at the door for any signs that spelled trouble. Every now and then he looked down at the still unconscious cop who was now under the bed.

"Put this on. We don't have much time," Rhonda said, handing Ice the bag almost slipping on the blood.

Minutes later, Ice was wearing light-blue scrubs that the orderlies wore, complete with an official looking name tag.

"What do you need that for? I told you that everything's going to be all right if you do what I say," Rhonda stated after seeing Ice put the gun into his waistband and cover it with the oversized shirt.

"Fuck that shit! If something was to jump off again, I ain't going out like a bitch!" he stated, meaning every word from his heart.

"Don't say anything to anybody. Let me do all the talking if it comes to it," the nurse said before she opened the door.

The now fugitive couple slowly entered the hallway trying to act normal, considering that there was a possible dead police officer twenty feet away. Nurse Rhonda punched in her secret access code that was given to everyone authorized to be on that special floor. Then she followed this with a computerized scan of her thumb print. This procedure opened the elevator doors that led down to the first floor. Once safely inside the elevator, the Bonnie and Clyde couple let out a sigh of relief. It seemed like it took forever for the elevator to reach the ground floor before they quickly exited.

Ice Cold Vengeance

Ice and Nurse Rhonda were half-way to the front sliding doors towards freedom when a thunderous voice rang out, "Excuse me! You two hold it right there for a moment!"

Ice and Rhonda turned around and were face to face with another police officer. All the blood drained from Rhonda's face as she responded, "Yes, officer? What can I do for you?"

"Why are you acting like you don't remember me or something?"

"Oh yeah! You work on the top floor, right? Now I remember you. Working all these hours got me sleepwalking," she answered, trying to lighten the mood.

"I just wondered if Officer Burke was talking shit about me since I'm a half hour late to relieve him," the cop said, now smiling because a lady with such big breasts had remembered him.

"Oh no. I kept him in a good mood tonight. I even brought him some Chinese food from Hop Hings," Nurse Rhonda said, trying to hurry up and end their little conversation.

Before they could turn around and begin walking again, the nosy cop said, "I never seen you around here before, young fellow. Where do you work at?"

Ice tensed up, ready to put a couple of shots into the officer's big fat mouth.

"He's new. He just started working over in the north wing. I'm giving him a lift home since the next bus won't be by for at least twenty five minutes," Rhonda quickly cut in.

"Anyway, I'll see you tomorrow night. Take care," the officer said, throwing in a little flirtatious wink.

They finally made it to Rhonda's little red Honda Civic. As they were leaving the parking lot, Ice noticed a lot of frantic movements going on behind the glass doors of the hospital. He figured that they found Officer Burke's body and started a complete lockdown of that section of the building. "You know we can't go over to your place. That's the first place they're gonna look," he stated.

"I know. I got a friend of mine who's staying out of town for a couple of weeks. I go by there every day to feed her cats and water the plants," Rhonda replied with a smile, like she had a hidden agenda in store for him.

23

When she had finally agreed to help Ice, he had convinced the naïve nurse that she wouldn't get into any trouble. "What do you mean?" she had asked.

"You see, all you have to say is that I forced you to come along and that you feared for your life," he replied. "Hell motherfucking yeah! Just drop a couple of tears and it's a done deal. You don't have a criminal record, plus there's no connection from me to you," Ice stated, speaking in half twisted truths. He knew that the forced kidnapping story only worked with white women when they wanted to flip the script on their boyfriends or husbands. With black women, the police always looked at them as willing participants, or they had something to gain in the fake plot. Not only that, with the circumstances surrounding Ice's escape, even a wet nosed rookie detective could determine that the nurse was in on it from the get-go. Ice knew that the horny bitch was going down sooner or later, but he was going to use her any way he could until she outlived her usefulness.

"We're here," Rhonda said, breaking him out his thoughts. She parked her vehicle in the driveway and motioned for Ice to follow her. They were somewhere on the back streets of Liberty Avenue. The two story brick house was fairly modest on the outside, with a heavy mixture of various plants and flowers dominating a lawn surrounded by large white rocks.

As soon as Ice entered the house an overwhelming odor of cat feces attacked his nose, and a hanging Boston fern plant missed his head by inches. He couldn't take much more so he asked, "Yo, anything to drink up in this piece?"

"I think she might have something in the kitchen cabinet," Rhonda replied as she walked to another part of the house. She came back a few seconds later holding an old dusty looking bottle with brown colored liquor in it.

Ice didn't even bother with the name as he took a long swig, spilling some on his shirt. *"Somebody needs to tear down a couple of walls so a nigga could get some air,"* he thought to himself as he walked up the carpeted steps while holding his nose, with Rhonda close behind him.

"Relax and watch a little TV while I freshen up," Rhonda said with a huge smile.

Ice lay down on a wide bed with a thick flowered comforter, and clicked on the TV. He took another drink as he flipped from channel to channel to see if any news stations were talking about him.

"So, how do I look?" Rhonda asked in an almost a whisper as she emerged from the bathroom. She was wearing an old leopard print panty and bra set with the bra being a size too small.

"Damn! This bitch couldn't wait 'til a nigga gets his bearings first. But at least I'm free," Ice thought as he watched the woman walk towards him.

She climbed in bed with him and started raking her long Lee Press-on fingernails against his hairless chest. It didn't take long for her hands to be wrapped around his stiffening dick.

"The mole with the little hairs coming out of it is a turn-off, but this bitch knows how to get the job done," Ice thought as full lips began wetting his entire organ.

When Rhonda knew that Ice was as ready as he was ever going to get, she stood up on the bed and began slowly sliding her panties off, doing what she thought an exotic dancer might do to her male customer.

"What the fuck! This bitch ain't never trimmed her shit. She act like she never heard of a fucking razor blade!" Ice almost said out loud as he stared at the woman's exaggerated mound of wild looking pubic hairs. The hairs were going in every which way possible, as if they had a life of their own and were trying to escape the confines of the tight, played-out panty design. A powerful miniature lawn mower would have had a hard time trying to get shit in order.

He slipped on a Magnum condom, and Rhonda roughly jumped on his penis. His balls began to hurt from her constant pounding, so he mentally forced himself to cum. His shoulder wound also began to throb, so he decided to call it quits for the rest of the night.

Fifteen minutes later, Rhonda was tapping him for another round. "Damn! I was better off in the fucking hospital bed!" Ice mumbled to himself as the middle-aged woman began expertly sucking him to hardness again.

Rizz get rid of the body, knowing not to ask any questions or he could also end up in a dark ditch somewhere deep in Long Island.

Rizz took another hot shower, then sat on his bed and started rolling up a Philly blunt. He knew he was going against the rules, but he needed something stronger than just some weak ass weed. It seemed that the chronic made him think about his girl even more. "Maybe I should have given her another chance. She probably was fucked up in the head at the time," he said to himself as he crushed some beige crack rocks onto the weed and tightly rolled it up.

Rizz felt a little better after his woolie joint and wanted to hear some loud music to keep his vibe going. He turned on his Blue Ribbon sound system that boasted aerodynamic surround sound speakers, and one of Rick Ross's hit songs boomed throughout the apartment.

Rizz dressed, putting on a pair of fitted twelve hundred dollar Japanese denim jeans, a pair of fresh, out of the box Red Bottom Louis Vuitton sneakers, and a button-down French shirt with a name he couldn't even pronounce. Under the shirt he wore a bulletproof Kevlar vest that fit snuggly against his skinny frame. He still had no idea who shot him in the chest and who emptied an entire clip of hot slugs into his uncle's face, all in the same night. To throw even more bullshit in the mix of things, some new cats were trying to slow up his money flow. *"Yeah, I gotta be on motherfucking point from now on,"* he was thinking.

But for now, the only thing that occupied his mind was running up in some pretty, dumb club bunny who had very little sexual morals.

He went to his very spacious bathroom, reached under the sink and pressed a button. The only way a person could ever locate that specific button is if they had first-hand knowledge that it was there in the first place. A steel plate quickly slid into a slot revealing a hidden heavy-duty floor safe.

Rizz had the safe put in by an independent contractor a couple of days after he found out that his supposed girl was ripping him off on the low. The Italian man who installed it was cool, so Rizz tipped him two hundred extra for doing a professional job. Rizz then had one of his baby faced killers put two in the man's cranium, and said that he could keep whatever the dead Italian had in his pockets. The baby faced killer was all too happy to have the chance to murder a white man, since all he ever killed and maimed were people who looked just liked him. Rizz didn't want to take a chance of anybody knowing that he had the safe… no one!

Rizz took out a heavy rose-colored diamond bracelet that was set in a scratch free platinum band. He then slid on a matching (can't help but hate) pinky ring. He was deciding on whether he should wear the stainless steel blue Rolex Oyster Perpetual watch with a pale pink face, but he changed his mind at the last minute. He then grabbed some cash before heading out the door.

Soon he was in a brand new pecan-colored limited edition Jag that was only four months old, and featured custom made goose down head rests. Even though he was driving a dead woman's car, he didn't seem to mind as he lit up another blunt of the seasoned weed while blasting the CD player.

Rizz activated the car alarm and walked a block before arriving at his destination. It was a little hole in the wall club in Queens called Raven's. He and his boys usually did their partying in the city where they went to outshine other hustlers and scoop up the baddest bitches who were down for whatever.

Raven's always stayed jam-packed because like most local Queens night spots, they let the females in for free before twelve or one o'clock, so the women always flocked there in abundance. The majority of the party girls probably came to Raven's with about thirty or forty dollars. That money would be used to hit up a twenty-four hour diner after partying all night, and for cab fare if they didn't snatch up a guy with a ride.

The local hood rats didn't have to worry about getting their drink on. Their plan was a simple basic one: all they had to do was wear something tight and short, shake their tight asses on the dance floor to get a nigga's dick hard, and the drinks would start to flow freely.

A long line was just starting to form with guys trying to holler at the girls who were being waved in. "Yo, shorty! I'ma see you inside later!"

"Ma, after this spot closes down, you and your friends could come by our after party!" the guys were saying, trying to spit their game to the girls walking past them.

The women skipped right inside, holding their short skirts down as the warm night wind gave some fellows a free peep show revealing brightly colored dental floss thongs.

Rizz wasn't going to wait in line with the other losers, nor did he have to.

There were two bouncers at the front door wearing identical black puffed-up flight jackets to make them seem bigger than they actually were. "Yo, everybody's gonna have to calm the fuck down and stop pushing, or nobody's getting in!" one of the bouncers shouted over the crowd. He wore black leather gloves with the fingers cut out, like he was ready to do some bodily damage to anyone who disobeyed his order.

"Rizz, what's up? How's everything?" the other bouncer asked as soon as Rizz walked around the rope to the front of the line.

"I'm cool," Rizz responded, hardly acknowledging the man while some guys on line started mumbling, "Who the fuck he think he is?"

Raven's was nothing more than a huge dance floor with two long bars on opposite sides of the room.

"Damn! Why the fuck do it always have to be so hot up in here?" Rizz asked himself as a blast of hot, musky body odor hit him. He fought his way to one of the bars and had to push and shove before he finally got a bottle of his favorite drink.

"Hi! How you doing? My name is Tameeka. What's yours?" a pretty, butterfly-faced girl asked after she spotted Rizz buying the expensive cognac and tipping the bartender fifty dollars in the process.

Rizz looked at the girl as best he could in the dim lights. He had to be on point, because under the blinking strobe lights and with some strong drink in your system, a female could look like a young vibrant Beyoncé. Then you would see the same female a week later under normal circumstances, and she would resemble Kimbo Slice in a bad wig. Guys in the hood refer to those specific types of chicks as "strobe light hoes".

Ice Cold Vengeance

He backed up a few inches to peep the girl's style a little better. She was your average ghetto bunny that you would find in any club, with a banging ass body and titties popping out of her skimpy blouse. She had an all right face too so Rizz grabbed her by the hand and said, "I'm cool. So, was up?"

"You wanna dance and probably have some drinks later on?" the bold girl asked as she leaned forward, talking in his ear because of the loud music.

"Damn! This bitch's breath smells like she been chain smoking shit cigarettes!" Rizz thought to himself as he backed up and screwed up his face in a wicked position.

"What's wrong?" the girl asked when she noticed the changed expression.

"Nothing. It's just that you should have dunked your head in a bucket of Listerine before you stepped outta your fucking house," he replied, breaking the seal on the XO Hardy Napoleon cognac and walking off.

The girl looked at him like his statement was something new and totally foreign for her to comprehend what the baller had just implied.

Rizz cooled out, walking around drinking his liquor, not spotting any girl that really impressed him. A few women approached him on some "getting to know you" shit, but he waved them away, knowing that they would probably give him a headache later on. He wanted some pussy from a bad bitch without all the bullshit small talk and lies. He knew exactly where he had to go.

A little while later, Rizz was pulling up to a well-kempt house close by his neighborhood. The doorman quickly ushered in their special client. The doorman quickly had a woman bring Rizz a chilled bottle of the new Gold Label Moët.

"So, where's Jazmine at? I gotta make moves," Rizz said to Heaven, who ran the expensive but well worth it whorehouse.

Heaven was a well-liked Filipino mixed with black transvestite who could satisfy any man or woman's sexual appetite no matter how freakish, as long as the paper was right. Rumor had it that Heaven once sucked a well-known rapper's dick so long that the transvestite's nose bled.

31

"Oh, I'm sorry, Rizz, but she had to take care of some important business. But I have a new girl who would be happy to make you reach for the stars," Heaven stated, trying to please one of his best customers. As he escorted Rizz to a huge bedroom he switched his wide hips in the ankle-length, outrageously expensive gold silk Japanese kimono with custom hand-made printed designs on it.

Rizz got undressed and laid his clothes on an old Victorian style, light blue, plush velvet chair. He then lay down on the bed and lit a cigarette with one of the scented candles that was already burning.

A second later, a short pretty woman with thick lips and an even thicker body walked in, smiling like the only thing that mattered in the world was him and her. The woman, who went by the name Suga Bush, had long black Indian hair that had silvery streaks throughout the hairstyle. Her silky pubic hair was also blessed with the specially made organic dye. To many customers and ex-boyfriends, Suga Bush's pussy juice was so tasty and full of life that a few men jokingly suggested that the lady could make a killing selling her womanly drops in baggies over the internet.

Suga Bush walked over to the young man without saying a word, and took off her glittery halter top revealing a pair of small pierced nipple rings. In the flash of an eye she produced a condom like a magician at a sideshow carnival. Suga Bush was informed by Heaven that the good, high paying client wasn't into the women asking him all kinds of personal questions. Simply put, Rizz just wanted to fuck—none of that getting to know you bullshit. He was all about business, and so was Suga Bush, so they got along just fine having that mutual understanding about one another.

She then popped the prophylactic in her still smiling mouth and went straight for Rizz's crotch. The woman was so graceful in her movements that Rizz didn't even notice her slipping the rubber on him as he grabbed a handful of her natural silky hair.

"Playtime's over!" Rizz thought as he stood up and bent the woman over the side of the bed. He didn't want to waste another minute as he pushed the girl's thong to the side and roughly plunged into her deepest depths. The expensive hooker's pussy was so well-lubricated from the strawberry scented vaginal gel that it made loud

squishy sounds. She tried to hold onto the satin sheets as best as she could while Rizz acted as if he just came home from doing a ten year bid.

Rizz then stuck a thumb into her anus. Then he yanked her backwards by her hair while steadily pounding away at the willing pussy. He soon—almost too soon—made a couple of involuntary spasmodic movements causing his whole body to shake like an out-of-control epileptic. He then a pulled himself out of the girl, snatched the condom off and came heavily on her sweaty back.

"I might have to put this bitch on my permanent payroll," he thought to himself as he fell backwards onto the soft king sized bed, and waited for his body to recharge for round two.

the side of her neck. The X-rated flick must have gotten him crazy hot, because he started talking about how he wanted to taste Trina's pussy juice, even though they only knew each other for less than an hour.

Trina let him rub her breasts while she grabbed at his crouch to see how big his pipe game was. The next thing she knew, the overly-excited man pushed her legs open and started kissing her on the vagina through the silk panties. "Yo! Yo, chill! I'm on the last day of my period," Trina said as she gently tried to push the man's head back up.

Breathing hard, the guy looked up at her and said, "I don't give a fuck! I gotta taste this angel food cake pussy!" He then moved her underwear to the side that had a stained panty shield firmly attached to it. He then dove his head back under her dress and acted as if he tried to catch the dark menstrual blood that the sanitary napkin failed to get.

"This motherfucker's on some other shit, but he sure knows how to work it!" she thought as she opened her legs a little wider. She never knew that she could be so disgusted and excited at the same time.

After ten minutes of tongue pounding, Trina's bladder started to quiver from all the drinks she had at the club. "D, stop now. I gotta take a piss," she said. He didn't respond, so she said a little louder, "I'm serious. I gotta pee for real."

"You know I gotta get my red wings," the man said when he came up for air. He then grabbed both Trina's legs in an unbreakable vise-grip and continued on with his relentless mission.

Trina couldn't hold back any longer and her bladder gave way. Derrick acted as if nothing had transpired, as the slurping sounds increased tenfold. Trina couldn't take much more of the perv, so she began moaning and shaking, faking an orgasm to fool the creep into thinking he did his thing.

"I know you liked that," Derrick said as he finally showed his sweaty face again.

Trina looked at him and gasped. "What the fuck!" She couldn't believe what she was seeing. The man had dark blood matter stuck on the corners of his mouth, and drops of urine glistened on his neatly trimmed beard. While she straightened up her

Prada dress, he grabbed a small hand towel and began wiping up the urine on the back seat. When she saw the man unzipping his pants thinking he was about to fuck, she quickly said, "Oh shit! The babysitter's gonna flip on me. Look how late it is."

"You didn't tell me you had any kids," Derrick responded as he stroked his rock-hard penis with a devilish gleam in his eye.

"Yeah, I got three of 'em," Trina lied as she grabbed her pocketbook.

"Don't worry, I'll give you the extra money so the babysitter won't spazz out," Derrick said, trying to convince the white girl to stay.

"It ain't even about the money. She got to get home to her own kids," Trina said in a concerned voice. "Gimme your number. We could hook up tomorrow. My mother will be watching the kids all day," she expertly added to the extra bullshit lie.

Derrick wrote down his home number, his cell phone number and Face Book information before Trina climbed out of the whip. She acted as if she lived on that block because she didn't want the strange perverted man to know where she really lived.

"Give me a call tomorrow, okay?" Derrick called out as he drove slowly down the block with his eyes still glued to the white girl in his rear view mirror.

As soon as he turned the corner, Trina tossed the piece of paper in the street with his math on it and said, "Fuck that weird creepo nigga! Picture me rolling with his ass so another bitch could say, "Oh, that's the nigga! I pissed in his mouth before."

She finally made it home, hoping that she never ran into the freakazoid ever again.

CHAPTER TEN

Ice woke up and found himself being stared down by three pairs of glowing eyes. "What the fuck!" he said out loud as he reached for a large white ceramic table lamp. He tossed the lamp, missing its mark. It hit the wall with a loud crash and shattered into a thousand pieces.

Two cats scampered away to safety as the third one remained on the dresser, slightly hissing with its back arched up.

"Who the fuck this motherfucker think he is?" Ice asked as he looked at the muscular, overweight orange and white feline who was now baring his sharp white teeth. Ice then threw a thick Bible, which missed his new friend by inches.

The cat jumped down and ran back out the door joining his comrades.

Ice flicked on the TV with the remote, and sure enough the newscaster was on the set talking diligently about him. The newswoman, who had a needle-thin nose and too much makeup to cover her pale skin complexion was saying:

"...Nathaniel Wilson was being treated for a gunshot wound to his shoulder after a gun battle with police. He was being held at the security wing of Hands of Mercy County Hospital under a twenty-four hour watch. He somehow removed his leg restraints and overpowered the unsuspecting officer, and took his service weapon. Veteran detectives believe that his nurse, Rhonda Coleman, age thirty-six, was forcefully taken against her will at gunpoint by Nathaniel Wilson. The investigation is still on going.

This is Heidi Greene reporting."

The scene switched over to a slim doctor wearing a starched white lab coat. He was standing behind a wooden podium surrounded by what looked like high-ranking police officers. The doctor began speaking in a hushed tone as he addressed the media with his worried dark gray eyes:

"James Burke was a well-respected and dedicated police officer who was just doing his job when he was savagely attacked. He suffered a broken nose, fractured cheekbone and a broken jaw in three places. His condition is critical due to the swelling of his frontal lobe. We tried to relieve the pressure to his brain as much as possible, but his prognosis at this time doesn't look too good. Thank you."

Then a tall, fat white man with thick bushy eyebrows stepped up to the podium, while the doctor eased off to the side, looking as if he was going to break down in tears at any moment. The fat white man was a police captain who was dressed in full uniform complete with a chest full of medals. He then stated with pure contempt in his beady eyes:

"Hello, I'm Captain Mahoney from the 110th Precinct. Nathaniel Wilson was first apprehended for the attempted murder of his parole officer, along with a host of other charges. He goes by the street name of Ice, and is known to frequent strip clubs around the Queens area. He is considered armed and extremely dangerous. 1-800-Crime Stoppers is offering a two thousand dollar reward for the arrest and conviction of this individual. You can call the number you see at the bottom of your screen twenty-four hours a day. All calls will be kept confidential."

Then they flashed a picture of Ice that covered the entire television screen.

"Fuck Officer Burke! Fuck the doctor! And fuck everybody else!" Ice yelled out loud as he changed the channel to some rap videos.

"Who you talking to?" Rhonda asked as she walked into the room.

"Huh? Nobody. Where did you put them pain pills at?" Ice asked.

"They're right in the drawer by the bed," she responded, and sat down on the bed and placed shopping bags on it.

Ice downed a couple of morphine tablets, and then began going through some of the bags. The clothes she picked up weren't what he was used to rocking, but it beat what he had been wearing for the last two days. Rhonda also purchased a cheap throw-away cell phone from Boost Mobile. Yeah, she wanted to make sure she had access to the dick 24-7.

Ice took a long shower, thinking about what they said about him on TV. *"At least they didn't mention anything about them bodies I left at the dope house,"* he thought.

He knew that Mr. Spencer, his parole officer would have to answer a lot of questions about why he was in a crack den in the first place. He couldn't possibly tell the authorities that when he was trying to get his freak on with a disease-ridden crack whore, he happened to recognize Ice, one of his newly released parolees. He saw that Ice was stacking that heavy paper and tried to extort him for cash and drugs on a weekly basis. When Ice didn't go along with his bullshit program, Spencer tried to take him in on a trumped up parole violation in the same crack house at that! Then some bodies got dropped with Mr. Spencer barely made it out alive, running for dear life. That's the reason why the police knew nothing about those killings, because Mr. Spencer would have definitely implicated himself with all the questions homicide detectives would have thrown his way.

Ice finished dressing. He was wearing a simple pair of black Levi jeans, a pair of high top Nike winter boots and a sweat hoodie.

He returned to the bedroom smoking a Newport, and automatically spotted Rhonda in bed with the blankets loosely covering her naked breasts. He knew for a fact that she was completely nude and wanted him to bang the pussy out once again. It wasn't that she wanted to fuck day and night that really bothered him; it was the fact that when she came—which was a lot—her vagina produced a strong unpleasant odor, somewhat to that of rotting eggs left out in the hot sun. *"Dumpster juice would have smelled better!"* he had thought the first time around. On one occasion when he was blowing her guts out doggie-style, the smell just seemed to rise and penetrate his nostrils at full force. He had to turn the bitch on her back to finish the job.

"Whatcha all dressed up for? I thought your shoulder was bothering you," she said as she reached out for his arm.

"I'm alright now. I need to go out in the hood to see what's popping," Ice replied taking a smooth drag on his cigarette.

"You know it's gonna be hot out there with all those police looking for you. Why don't you just relax and lay up with me?" Rhonda said, throwing him the sad puppy dog look.

"Nah, I gotta make some moves. Niggas out there got my dough," he responded.

"Okay, then let me go with you. Give me a minute to throw something on real quick," Rhonda hastily said as she started to rise from the comfort of the warm sheets. She wasn't about to let some pretty young thing snatch up her dick that she worked so hard to get.

Nah, I wanna roll alone. Let me get the car keys so I can make it happen," Ice said.

"Hell no! And now you wanna bounce! You probably was on the phone talking to one of your stank ass bitches while I was gone!" Rhonda yelled while putting on her housecoat.

"Check this out, shorty! I don't need your permission to go anywhere. I was just trying to be nice," he responded, trying to deescalate the situation.

"You was trying to be nice? I was the one who helped your skinny pitiful ass get away when you was crying like a bitch and saying the cops was gonna kill you!" she shouted in a spiteful tone of voice.

"First off, who the fuck you think you are comparing me to a bitch? Second, the only reason you really helped me was to have this big dick up in your fucking dusty ass!" Ice shot back, and then started to laugh.

"What, you trying to play me after all I done for you, you ungrateful bastard?" Rhonda squealed as she approached him. The woman's eyes looked like a person who forgot to take their medication.

overcharged. *The eager customers just had to have those specific red-boned women. The Haitian men who had a little money would never go to the "black tar" female streetwalkers, as they called them with disgust.*

After drinking some more of the toxic gin, Jack was led to a private room that consisted of only a bed and a wash basin with a filthy rag hanging on the side. An almost white looking Dominican woman with big floppy breasts and a pancake flat ass stood in the room waiting for him. She was wearing an old-school see-through nightgown that would have caused most men to dig their eyes out with a rusted spoon. Most of Mother Joy's girls were so disease-ridden that their own country kicked them out. That's how they ended up in Haiti where the locals viewed them as "prime meat". Floppy tits wasn't any different.

She ended up giving young Jack three different strains of the syphilis virus from their first encounter.

A month later, Jack began developing obvious symptoms of the venereal disease, syphilis. When the small, pus-filled sores began to burst and leak a thick, yellowish foul smelling liquid, Jack finally went to visit the local witch doctor, whom people guessed her age to be at least a hundred plus years. The hunchbacked, toothless and gnarl handed woman placed him in an eighteenth century bathtub filled with warm water and geranium oil. After a while she sprinkled dry basil leaves and parsley flakes into the water.

After hours of soaking in the now cold water, the witch doctor made a coarse-feeling paste of powered skunk cabbage, dried orris root and the slimy entrails of a male bullfrog. She carefully rubbed the brownish concoction on Jack's entire genital area, even under his scrotum. Before he left, he was told to smear himself every other day for two months, and he would be cured of his infliction.

The symptoms gradually vanished, but what Jack was totally unaware of was that the body-crippling disease was firmly planted in his bloodstream.

******

Jack took a long piss, feeling the familiar stinging sensation followed by a dull pain in his penis and groin area. He'd been feeling that specific pain for close to fifteen years now, so he became accustomed to it, saying to himself, "It's just another part of life."

48

But what he never gave a second thought to or just didn't know was that when syphilis was left untreated (as in Haitian Jack's case), the disease attacks every major organ in the human body. The final stage of the disease is when it finally enters the brain, slowly eating away at the brain matter and making it somewhat resemble old Swiss cheese. During this process, the disease alters the victim's personality and rational thought processes, eventually driving the individual insane.

"Boom! Boom! Boom!"

Just as Jack was putting on his shirt, the pounding on the motel door interrupted his thoughts. He grabbed his shiny black Desert Eagle and looked through the peephole. He never thought that a man couldn't have too many guns. It was his right-hand man, Lite who was staying in the room next door.

Since coming to New York two months ago, they had checked into the Palm Springs Motel. This motel was a cheap and rundown place that let you pay weekly when you needed time to get back on your feet. Everything and anything went down at the Palm Springs Motel, with the night manager getting a piece of everything worthwhile.

"So, Lite, what's cooking on the street?" Jack asked after letting Lite's wide frame into the room.

"Everything's set in two days. Nigga's talking some good shit about the price," Lite replied.

"So you took your girl down or what?" Jack asked.

"She's supposed to meet with the manager tonight. The way he's talking, it shouldn't be a problem," Lite stated.

"That's cool, because we need eyes and ears up in there. And I just got word that the Feds never snatched up my brother-in-law, so he should be getting with us in a minute," Jack added with a little smile on his face.

"Yeah, we need a live wire like him to help get shit off the ground," Lite responded with enthusiasm.

CHAPTER TWELVE

"Damn, this fucking bitch is mad heavy! That's the reason why my balls still hurt, the way she bounced on them all night," Ice said out loud as he dragged Rhonda's lifeless body through the house, leaving a trail of smeared blood on the floors. He was breathing hard by the time he reached the entrance to the basement. He figured that if he hid the body good enough, the police or whoever would think that they were still together.

After drinking a glass of cold water, Ice once again firmly grabbed Rhonda's ankles and proceeded to drag her body down the basement steps. When the corpse's head hit the third step, it bounced up and then back down even harder, causing a thin line of blood and mucus to shoot from the nostrils. A couple of drops of blood landed on Ice's shirt, causing him to curse out loud. No sooner than the words were out of his mouth, the dead woman released a powerful, nose-grabbing fart due to all the body gasses, and acid build-up, from the jarring movements. Then before he knew what was going on, a large lump of shit exited Rhonda's body and rolled down her leg.

"Enough of this bullshit! I don't give a fuck who finds this heavy ass bitch! It's bad enough that those fucking cats stink up the fucking house, but now this bitch gotta go and shit everywhere too! I'm outta here!" Ice shouted as he started to step over the dead body. He then gave the corpse a hard swift kick, not really budging it at all.

As soon as Ice reached the kitchen he spotted the cats staring down at him again. "Come here, kitty! Come on! I got a little treat for you!" he said, talking in a smooth low voice as he slowly approached the animals. Ice snatched up a butcher knife from the wooden block and swung it down at the cat that was nearest to him. The cat howled as he jumped off the microwave, leaving a two-inch piece of its tail behind. Ice then threw the knife at the fat orange and white cat, which missed its mark.

Ice Cold Vengeance

Ice was soon driving the recently deceased Rhonda's little red Honda Civic with his new clothes thrown in the back. He had no idea where he planned to go or what to do, but what he did know was that he needed some liquor to clear his head.

A short time later he pulled up to the local bootleg spot, which was a huge corner house. The owner of the house sold liquor for a slightly higher price when the regular liquor stores were closed. The house also doubled as a gambling spot for the older gentlemen in the neighborhood who had nothing much going on in their lives. Dominos, dice and all night poker games were a common occurrence, as well as drunken brawls when one of the players tried to pass a tall tale as the truth, and not being able to back up his unbelievable story.

Ice reached through a tall, rusted metal fence and pushed a greasy white button. A few seconds later a frail looking woman wearing a faded black Biggie Smalls T-shirt appeared and said, "Okay, okay. Whatcha want? I don't have all day."

"Gimme your best bottle of champagne," Ice responded, trying to hold in his laugh.

"We don't sell no fucking champagne! Where you think you at?" the lady spat back as she rubbed the sleep from her droopy eyes. "Ice, is that you? Get yo' ass in here before someone sees you!" Mrs. Teal said when she recognized the young man standing on the opposite side of the fence.

Mrs. Teal practically helped raise Ice since he was a baby. She and her husband were very close friends with Ice's parents. They played Spades, and basically just enjoyed each other's company.

Mrs. Teal had a daughter close to Ice's age whom she used to leave at his house when she and her husband went out on the town. Ice never really paid the daughter any attention when they got older, mainly because she wore thick glasses, had buckteeth and always kept her head in the books. Every time he would see her studying astronomy, geometry or reading some book, which he found to be a big waste of time, he would comment, "I don't know why you reading that stuff. You still gonna be black."

"Martin Luther King said that with knowledge and education come changes," she would respond.

"That sounds good and shit, but when a racist cop is beating your black ass, you think he's gonna go easy on you because you got some degree? Or when a low life crack head is ready to pound your face into oatmeal for that thin gold chain, you think he's gonna say, 'Nah, I'm gonna chill. She got book smarts, so let me go find another victim'?" Ice would throw back at her while she pretended she didn't hear any of his smart aleck remarks.

Mrs. Teal soon lost her husband to lung cancer, and not long afterwards Ice's father walked out on the family because of the daily verbal abuse his wife heaped on him. After that, everybody just drifted apart, losing contact with one another.

Mrs. Teal led Ice to the living room that was cluttered and piled high with old newspapers and every sort of magazine that no one bothered to read. There were four mini refrigerators filled with various brands of cheap wine in the room.

Ice placed a thick wool sweater on the armrest of a recliner, sat down and asked, "Can I have a drink first?"

"What would you like?" Mrs. Teal asked in a motherly tone.

"Anything except that cheap stuff," Ice answered while adjusting the cops issued nine millimeter gun in his waistband so he could get more comfortable.

Mrs. Teal brought back a bottle of Remy Martin along with two glasses. Ice took his T-shirt and cleaned the inside of the glass, then fixed himself a much needed stiff drink. He thought that Mrs. Teal was going to fix herself a drink also, but after she poured the Remy Martin into her glass, she took her false teeth out of her mouth, placed them into the glass and shook it around gently. "This shit is way better than Efferdent Plus," she explained after noticing the look on his face.

"Well, Ice, the streets keep bringing up your name after what you did to that cop up in the hospital," she went on to say.

"You know me. I ain't trying to go back to jail. Last time, they tried to get me to admit that I had something to do with my ex-girl getting bodied," Ice said before he took a sip of his second glass of Remy.

"I know how the police could push a nigga to wild out, but I can't see you laying your hands on a girl for no reason other than protecting yourself," the woman said, and rubbed her tongue over her pink gums.

"Anyway, you know this Rizz who's supposed to be running shit around here?" Ice asked, wanting to get straight to the point.

"Yeah. Everybody knows that little nigga. He's always running his mouth and acting like he's the King of New York or something," Mrs. Teal answered as she screwed up her face.

"So, what's up with him right now?"

"He's still making major moves even after some of his closest friends got killed. And from what I hear, some new guys wanna take his place, if you know what I mean," Mrs. Teal responded.

"Who are they? Where are they from? They got paper too?" Ice asked, his mind racing a mile a minute.

"Nah, I don't know nothing about who they are, but I'll let you know if I find out anything."

They talked for a while about who else was doing what before Ice said, "Mrs. Teal, I need a place to rest for at least a couple of days so I can get my pockets up and get my mind right." In his heart, he still believed that Rizz owed him whatever money he made from his drug dealing due to the fact that Rizz stole drugs from him in the beginning, jump starting his own vast drug empire. He was planning to get what's owed to him no matter what, and bounce to a different state where nobody even heard of the name Ice.

"Ice, you know I love you like a son, so I want you to be safe no matter what they say about you."

At first he thought that she was going to say no because of the "I love you like a son" speech, until she said, "My daughter doesn't stay too far from here. I'm sure she won't mind if you go over there. You know she's had a crush on you since you two were kids," she said with a smile that showed her gums even more. She then wrote the address down. "If she ain't there, look under the welcome mat for the spare key. Just go inside and make yourself at home," the old lady added.

"Thanks, I appreciate it," Ice said, preparing to leave and hoping that her daughter wasn't the same ugly geek as he remembered her to be. The last thing he needed right now was a bust-down chick wanting to fuck all the time like that goddamn horny nurse.

CHAPTER FOURTEEN

Ice finally made it to the address that Mrs. Teal had given him. He knew that he was riding red-hot in a dead nurse's vehicle. Even though she planned the escape and got dicked down for her efforts, the police would flip shit around against him. The authorities would swear on their mothers' graves that Ice forcefully took the timid nurse at gunpoint and held her captive. When she was no longer needed, he brutally murdered the God fearing woman who was just doing her job. He then dumped her body in the basement like old soda cans. Leave it up to the police, they would make it seem like he was the anti-Christ reincarnate.

"Fuck that shit! If they catch me again this time, they gonna fry my ass!" Ice said out loud as he parked the car in an alley and took off both license plates. He then grabbed the shopping bags from the back seat, walked down to the end of the alley, and placed the license plates deep down at the bottom of a steel garbage can.

******

Ice was just a little off of Hillside Avenue and standing in front of the newly-built apartment building called Edgewood Towers. It was a neat looking brick building that stood four stories tall. He went inside the double doors and started pressing the gray intercom buttons. When someone finally asked, "Who's there?" Ice replied, "UPS." He was then buzzed in.

He took the elevator to the third floor and rang Apartment 3A's bell. When he got no answer after the fourth ring, he looked under the welcome mat and found a silver key.

Once inside, he set his bags by the door and took a look around. The apartment was simply furnished and had a smell of fresh paint and pine oil. He flopped down on a comfortable looking cloth sofa and took his boots off. He then placed his feet on the imitation oak coffee table. "Damn, only five left," he said, taking a morphine tablet out the bottle and popping it into his mouth. He then washed it down with some Remy Martin, leaned back to let the drug take effect, and was soon fast asleep.

"I see you made yourself at home," a female voice said, nudging Ice awake.

"Oh shit! What's up? I haven't seen you for a minute," Ice said, standing up and giving the girl a hug.

"My moms hit me up on the cell and said that you might be here when I get home," Chyna said after breaking their friendly embrace.

"Who's that, Mommy?" a little boy of four asked. He was rocking an Adidas sweat suit and a pair of clean white Nikes.

"Oh, this is Mommy's friend since she was a little girl about your age," Chyna replied, as she bent down to give her son a kiss on the cheek.

Chyna was the unofficial nickname name that her relatives gave her at an early age because of her chinky eyes. She also had a deep dark flawless skin complexion that people compared to a beautiful black China doll.

"Ice, I'm about to make Anthony something to eat. I'll fix you something too if you're hungry, then you can tell me what you been up to after all this time," Chyna said as she flicked on the TV to the Cartoon Channel.

"Hell yeah! I ain't eat all day," he answered while rubbing his stomach. He watched his childhood friend walk towards the kitchen thinking, *"Damn, shorty has definitely filled the fuck out!"*

Chyna was wearing form-fitting Robin jeans with the butterfly back pockets, and a T-shirt that did nothing to conceal the girl's Hershey's Kiss size nipples. He could tell that she had an ass on her, and well-developed thick thighs that would make a grown man cry if wrapped around him during lovemaking. He also liked the way she had her hair done in a Halle Berry hot curl type of style. She was definitely not the same corny bucktooth girl he knew way back when she used to get teased.

While watching the ending of "SpongeBob Square Pants" with Anthony, Chyna came back carrying two plates. She gave her son the small plastic Spiderman plate, and Ice the other one. Ice dug into his scrambled eggs, hot links and home fries like a madman, while Anthony slowly ate his chicken nuggets.

"Oh, Black! Yeah, that's my nigga! Where the fuck he been at?" the voice asked as he started unlocking the door and taking wooden beams off the fortified heavy door.

Ice knew that he wouldn't have a problem getting in, because in every black neighborhood across the city there were always a couple of knuckle heads who went by the nickname "Black" and who ran around getting into all types of wild shit.

The guy swung open the door and said, "Tell your cousin I...."

Before the guy could finish his sentence, Ice caught him with the cop's gun in his jaw.

"Whap!"

The doorman fell to the floor with a heavy thud as Ice slammed the door shut. The guy wasn't fully knocked out. He crawled on his hands and knees and grabbed at his attacker's pants leg. Ice just smiled as he hit his victim on the back of the head, causing a deep ugly gash.

"Just what I needed," Ice said after he searched the unconscious man and found a chrome .38 gun in his waistband. But he cursed when he found only a few dollars in the unconscious man's pockets.

Ice was in a little store that sold white Tee's, DVD movies and rap CD's in a glass display counter.

He crept to the back and heard muffled shouts coming from the back room. He paused for a second, and then slowly opened the door. There were six men so involved in playing the dice game C-low that they didn't even notice the stranger wearing a hoodie standing only a couple of feet away from them.

"Okay, pussies! Turn them pockets out 'fore shit gets real critical up in here!" Ice growled while pointing both weapons at the shocked players. "You heard what the fuck I said!" he continued in a menacing tone of voice as he let off a round, shooting a guy in the foot in the process. The unlucky C-low player fell to the floor grabbing his foot. The other men knew not to fuck around as they quickly emptied their pockets.

Ice looked at the pile of money on the floor. He also spotted a few fat knots of currency that were tied up with thick rubber bands. "Yo, take off the chain and throw it to me," he said to one guy whom he peeped rocking a long gold Cuban link chain that hung down to his stomach.

The man did as he was told and tossed his prized possession to the robber. Ice quickly scooped it up while still watching everybody's moves and looking out for wannabe heroes. *"This shit gotta be at least two hundred pennyweight,"* the stickup kid thought as he felt the weight of the 18-karat gold chain.

"Now, everybody pull your fucking pants down and stand against the wall with your hands up. You, One Foot, put all the dough in that plastic bag," Ice ordered.

The unlucky guy who had gotten shot in the foot grabbed a plastic food bag that was lying around and started stuffing it with the money. Ice knew that the remaining men standing there with their pants down around their ankles wouldn't think about rushing him due to their limited mobility.

Once he made the wounded guy get up against the wall and pull his pants down, he noticed something that he just had to address. "Come on now. It's bad enough that you rocking faggot ass briefs, but you gotta go and have shit stains on them to? What the fuck is wrong with you?" he asked, not really expecting an answer as he chuckled a little while staring at the guy's underwear that looked like he had sat in some coffee.

The guy in question hung his head just a little lower in shame, knowing that the stranger was speaking the truth.

"Nigga, turn your punk ass back around. It's bad enough that niggas die in the hood every day over some pussy. Now you ready to get bodied over peeping at the next nigga's ass!" Ice said, throwing his comment at a guy who had turned his head and looked down at his gambling partner's butt out of sheer curiosity.

"As a matter of fact, all you faggots get the fuck in the bathroom, now!" Ice shouted, waving his weapons around.

All the men duck-walked to the small, piss-smelling bathroom that was meant for only one person at a time. Once they were inside, Ice kicked the door shut and propped a chair up against the doorknob. He knew that the chair would never keep them in there but for a few minutes. But that was all the time he needed. He stepped over the doorman who was still knocked out, and headed out into the night air.

DeJon

After driving approximately twenty blocks, he pulled over to check his stash. There were four cell phones, some bullshit rolling papers and a few condoms. Way in the bottom of all the money was a half-filled Ziploc bag filled with potent smelling weed. He took a good whiff and then began counting stacks after stacks of money. He grinned a satisfying smile before peeling off.

CHAPTER FIFTEEN

It was another boring work week at the group home for Trina. She stuffed yet another, what she thought was useless paycheck into her pocketbook. Having the young guys drool over her while she gave them little freak shows no longer amused her. What she craved was an exciting street nigga that was making moves, and who could supply her with an endless amount of drugs.

Cooped up with a bunch of bad ass, snot nosed kids and having her lame coworkers constantly telling corny stories just wasn't doing it for her. She felt that she would be better off working in an insane asylum where the heavily medicated patients walked around like zombies. At least at a mental institution you knew every day would be a surprise with the crazies flipping out every now and then.

The only person she thought was all right was Cory, who from what she heard was no longer a resident. He was mature for his age and seemed like he had it in him to make major power moves if hooked up with the right people, which is the real reason she was attracted to him.

Trina waved a couple of fake goodbyes, adding an even faker, "I'll see you all Monday." She then rushed to get the hell away from her coworkers as quickly as possible.

A short while later she was driving away from a rental car dealership in a smooth, silver-colored Nissan Altima 3.5 RL that had crisscross stitching across the leather interior. She was on her way to pick up her cousin from Port Authority, who was arriving from Little Rock, Arkansas where Trina was raised.

"Miss, you can't park here. You're going to have to move," a stern faced police officer said as he poked his head inside the passenger side of the car, showing off his late-century handlebar mustache.

"Come on, give me a break. If I park in a parking lot a couple blocks away, my sick grandmother's gonna have to walk all the way back," Trina replied as she got out of the car and stood inches away from the cop so he could get a good whiff of her new Burberry Brit perfume.

"I don't care if you have to pick up the goddamn Pope! You still gotta move!" he rudely spat back, not caring that Trina was practically throwing her breasts in his face.

"Why you gotta come off like that? You act like I'm the one who's got you babysitting losers all day," Trina shot back, referring to the homeless people begging for change, and other folks down on their luck offering to carry bags for a few dollars.

"Excuse me, what did you just say?" the officer asked, his face turning beet red.

"Laura! Laura, it's me! I'm over here!" a female voice squeaked.

Trina rushed over to her cousin and quickly grabbed the smaller bag of the two. "Come, on let's roll. That cop is being a real asshole," Trina said as she pushed the trunk button on the key chain, causing the truck to pop open.

Meanwhile, the police officer had his ticket pad out and was saying something as Trina jumped behind the wheel. "Miss, I'm not done issuing you your ticket!" he yelled as the Altima started pulling away from the curb.

"What you need is a little pussy in your life!" Trina called out while driving away and merging in with the busy Manhattan traffic.

"I see you're still the same old Laura," the twenty something woman said.

"Up here in New York everybody calls me 'Trina', okay?" Trina said in a forceful manner. On the way back to Queens, she stole glances at her younger cousin, Jenise, who was visiting the Rotten Apple for the first time.

Jenise had a light-copper skin tone complexion, being that she was a Mulatto. Word has it that Trina's aunt was married and creeping around with somebody on the low. Nobody pretty much cared until the baby came out brown with shiny, curly black hair. There was a deadly silence among family members with nobody saying a thing, but they were all thinking what they knew to be an undisputable fact.

Ice Cold Vengeance

Soon, nosy folks in the town started whispering behind the husband's back whenever he showed his face around town, adding to his already shameful situation, to put it lightly. The husband was a well-liked popular car mechanic who had a lot of redneck friends whom he got shit-faced drunk with every weekend.

About a year later, Jenise's mother acted like she didn't give a fuck and started openly being seen going into cheap hotels with her black lover, who happened to be the father of her child. A few months later the black boyfriend was run over by a train and killed. The official police report stated that it was a clean-cut case of suicide, even though he was beaten and had his skull caved in. The insurance company denied his immediate family's claim, saying that the twenty thousand dollar policy clearly stated that it doesn't pay out on suicide deaths. But everybody in town knew exactly what had jumped off. Some of the husband's backwoods hillbilly friends had sought what they deemed an injustice done to their good buddy and drinking partner.

The incident died down eventually, with him loving Jenise just as his own, while his wife secretly hated him every waking moment of her life.

Jenise had on a short, tight, no-frills jean skirt that hugged her slender hips, and wore a pair of cheap Payless high-heeled wedged sandals. Her body was slimmer and tighter than Trina's. She also had bigger and firmer breasts that no sane man would ever deny. Her biological father had blessed her with full African lips, and model-type high cheekbones that Trina has always been envious of.

Trina knew her cousin to be a scatterbrain chick who sometimes took a while to fully catch on to the obvious. Already Trina was scheming on how that particular fact was going to benefit her somehow.

After the cousins chitchatted about what was going on back home, Trina asked, "So, do you smoke or drink?"

"Hell yeah! You got some weed on you?" Jenise answered, ready to get her party on in the big city.

"Nah, I could get some later. But we could get something to drink right now," Trina stated as they were entering Queens.

A little while later Trina pulled up to liquor store around the way and bought a couple of bottles. Once the women were comfortably settled in the house and Jenise shown her room, Trina said, "This is how we do it up in Queens." She poured some Grey Goose vodka mixed with some Amaretto Sour into a glass, and then splashed in some ice cold Remy Red to complete the deal.

"This is some good shit, whatever it is," Jenise said, and took another sip.

"We call it 'Gang Bang'. Shit flows down your throat just as easily as cum!" Trina responded, laughing at her own joke.

"Later on I'll show you some of our drinks back home," her cousin said as she started to enjoy herself a little more.

After a while the drinks started taking affect, causing Trina to become horny. Less than a month ago her pimp, Born had her working eighteen hours a day out of his luxury whorehouse, turning sometimes fifteen tricks a night. Even though she fucked and sucked countless men in the past, she still wanted a stiff hot cock up in her right now. "I gotta make a quick run," she stated while getting up and reaching for her jacket.

"That's cool. So, when's my sister supposed to be coming home?" Jenise asked while mixing herself another glass of the gang bang.

"She went to the movies with some guy, so it's no telling when she'll be back," Trina responded.

******

Trina was back in the rental car, smoking a Newport and thinking what she could get into, and before she realized what she was doing, she was in South Side driving by Cory's house. She had gotten his address from his file, and now she was parked in front of the rundown, weather-beaten house. She walked up to the front door having no idea what she was going to say to whoever answered.

A neighbor eyed Trina suspiciously, thinking that when a white person came to the ghetto, they came for one of three things: money, drugs or trouble.

Trina looked back at the fat woman with an expression saying, "Mind your own fucking business!"

The lady stared back while munching on a thick, dry ham sandwich with her eyes saying, "This is my property! I can look at whomever I want and for how long I want!"

Trina knocked on Cory's door because where the doorbell should have been was a square hole with small multi-colored wires sticking out.

The door swung open and Cory stood there in a white tee, long basketball shorts and slippers. "Miss Davenport, what you doing here?" he asked, looking past her to see if she came with the police or anybody else.

"Oh, everything's all right. I was just driving by and thought I'd drop by to see how you were doing," Trina said with a reassuring bright smile.

"I'm cool. Nothing's going on," he stated, still not trusting the situation fully.

"I've seen the way you carried yourself in that place, and I would like to say you're nothing like the other boys," Trina said, trying to keep the conversation flowing,

"I just do me," Cory responded in a flat tone of voice.

"Listen, I don't want your neighbors or friends to think that you're in some kind of trouble talking to me. You wanna go inside?" Trina asked, hoping that he didn't have some freak chick inside, and that he would say yes.

"Yeah, we could kick it for a while. My pops is knocked the fuck out," he replied.

The inside of the house didn't look much better than the outside. The first thing Trina noticed was a man sleeping on an old flowered couch, snoring loudly as if he was trying to extend his nostrils even further. His clothes looked as if he had worked all day in some dust covered factory, and then went straight to sleep.

"Don't worry about him. That's my pops. He always comes back from wherever and passes out. That's his favorite spot," Cory explained, easing the slight tension.

"Sometimes I feel the same way," Trina replied, smiling as she sat down on a matching loveseat that had two thick phone books replacing a missing leg.

Cory pulled up a folded metal chair just as Trina was taking off her jacket, showing a Halliburton T-shirt that had the words, "I

69

Heard Her Breasts Were Bigger," printed across the front in bold letters. "You want something to drink? I think my pops got a few more beers left around," he said, knowing that the older woman was already drinking heavily by the smell of alcohol on her breath.

"I'll take whatever," the woman answered.

Cory left the room and then returned with two short cans of Old English. He cracked one and gave the other one to Trina.

"Oh, let's go to my room before he starts talking some wild shit," Cory said as his father started moaning and twisting like he was coming out of his drunken stupor.

Trina followed Cory up the steps that had worn carpet covering them from constant use up to his room. The room was an average one with posters of LeBron James, Kobe Bryant, and other basketball stars taped on the wall. His desk was littered with rap CD's and car magazines.

"You can sit right here," Cory stated, moving about four boxes of brand new, never worn sneakers off of a black leather computer chair.

Cory already knew what time it was with Trina from how she always cut her eyes at him when he did his pushups with his shirt off. He also noticed that she had shut the door after she entered his room, so he wasn't about to waste useless time talking. He suspected that she was just a horny white girl from the suburbs who needed some black dick. What could they ever possibly have in common? "I know this is what you really came here for," he said, taking out his semi-hard dick.

Trina sat in the chair as Cory stood in front of her stroking his organ. She was nowhere near shocked by how he just flipped out his penis so suddenly. She once saw a crack head bitch giving a drug dealer a sloppy blowjob by the twenty four hour store window at three in the morning, while customers waited in line for whatever they needed.

Trina reached out, grabbed the swinging cock, and took it into her mouth without the slightest bit of hesitation. What threw her off was how big his penis was. It seemed to be at least a good ten inches. The white girl tried her her best to take it all in. She twisted his dick one way with her left hand and twisted in the opposite direction with her right hand.

70

Ice Cold Vengeance

Cory grabbed her hair, enjoying the feeling while Trina reached down and lifted up her shirt, letting him know they were his for the taking. Cory took the hint. He bent down and grabbed a handful of milky white titties.

After ten minutes of Trina's magical tongue and lips putting in work, Trina felt his dick veins pulsating at a rapid rate. She knew that the young man was about to explode. Cory didn't disappoint the woman as hot semen covered her tonsils and the roof of her mouth. Trina held on for dear life, daring not to miss a single sticky drop. When she was positively sure she swallowed everything, she stood up and started to unbutton her jeans.

"What are you doing?" Cory asked as he took a dirty T-shirt to wipe himself clean.

"We're not finished, are we?" Trina asked in a little girl's voice.

"I don't know about you, but I'm straight," Cory replied while pulling up his basketball shorts.

"This is the first time a motherfucker ever turned down my cunt," Trina thought. She didn't know whether to be offended or turned on even more. She knew that she had overstayed her welcome as Cory led her back down the stairs. She didn't know where it came from, but she asked for his number right before she left his residence.

The liquor and beer made Trina a little hungry, so she decided to stop by a Crown Fried Chicken restaurant for a snack. She hoped to be in and out quickly, when she spotted a very familiar shaped body standing in front of the eating establishment. She slowly approached, and once her headlights hit the man's face, she involuntarily called out in a shocked voice, "Oh shit! It's fucking Born!" Trina didn't know whether to run or act like nothing had ever happened, when both of their eyes locked.

71

CHAPTER SIXTEEN

"**I**'m telling you, these motherfuckers ain't playing. I say we make an example out of them quick before other niggas starting getting ideas," Universal said with urgency in his voice.

"You think I'm worried about some clown ass niggas that nobody ever even heard of before? Niggas can't touch me in these streets," Rizz replied before he took a strong drag of his woolie blunt. He started smoking the sprinkled weed on a regular basis like he was smoking Newport shorts. As far as he was concerned, he was the head honcho and could do what the fuck he wanted no matter what anybody thought. "Come on, shorty. This is some good shit," he said as he turned around in his seat and gave the girl sitting in the back a powerful shotgun blast of crack smoke.

The girl giggled as the drug took its effect. She then began massaging Rizz's neck and shoulders.

The three people were sitting in Rizz's brand new cranberry-colored Hummer H6 Limited Edition Series that had the chrome colored grille that was trimmed in twenty four-karat gold. The Hummer was imported straight from Germany which sat on 26-inch Messiah rims wrapped in Pirelli Scorpion tires.

"Yo Rizz, I think we should kick it in private. You don't know who the fuck she knows," Universal said as he looked directly at the girl, not caring if she became offended or not.

"Come on, man. You know me better than that. Shorty's cool. What's your name again?" Rizz asked the girl, as he took a swig of a 40 ounce malt liquor to help get rid of the dry sawdust taste in his mouth.

Universal knew very well that Rizz was starting to act more and more erratic day by day, and doing things on impulse. It seemed that his only function in life was to fuck bitches, get high and talk shit like he was the Sheik of Arabia. It was a disastrous combination no matter how you looked at it. He was spending money like water, and not raking it in like the crew used to.

Ice Cold Vengeance

"At least the crazy fuck gave me the Jag just because somebody put a scratch on the hood. I also wish he decided he don't like the Hummer no more to," Universal thought to himself as he stared at the custom suede embroidery with the white piping around Rizz's name inside the Hummer's interior. He had heard that the sick fuck paid an extra ten G's to have a rush job done like he was P. Diddy or somebody. Universal wasn't really sweating the Jag because he had his own Range Rover Sport and an aqua-blue Maserati that he only drove on special occasions.

"Yo, playboy, you need to relax and chill for a minute. I got this on lock," Rizz stated after noticing his second in command deep in thought.

"I'm about to go check the spots out to see how things are moving," Universal said as he prepared to get out.

"That shit can wait. Come hit up the strip club with me a little later on. I heard they shipped in some new pussy so ill that niggas would wanna make one of them hoes wifey," Rizz stated, causing the girl to frown up her face. Rizz laughed even harder, knowing that no matter what he did or said, shorty wouldn't say a goddamn word. Even if he took a dump in this chicken head's mouth, she would gladly accept it and still chill with him. He was the man on the streets of Queens, and for now she was riding with the top nigga.

"Nah, I'll get with you another time. I'll just make sure shit keeps flowing. Peace!" Universal responded and jumped out. As he climbed into his new present that was parked in front of the Hummer, he saw out of the corner of his eye the hood rat chick quickly getting into the front seat. She was happy as hell that she could be seen better by the neighborhood residents.

******

The same time Universal was heading to one of their crack spots, so was Haitian Jack and his partner, Lite. Jack parked his old BMW with the souped- up engine down the street. Both he and Lite were wearing shabby looking clothes. Jack carried a fancy shopping bag that had "Na Hoku's Custom Furs" expertly stenciled on both sides. The men went straight to the back door of the dope house and knocked twice.

"Whatcha want?" a rough sounding voice yelled from behind the heavy barred door.

"I want six twenty dollar rocks, but I don't have any money right now," Jack answered.

"Then get the fuck away from here, and quit wasting my time 'fore I put my foot in your ass!" the voice angrily barked back.

"I got something else you might want," Jack said with a little desperation in his voice as he held up the bag and took out a brand new men's black mink jacket.

"Get that shit outta here! It ain't real!" the guy said as he looked through the peephole to check out the two crack heads who were trying to get over on him.

"I wouldn't do you like that. Come on and feel it so you know what I'm talking about," Jack whined.

"Okay, slide a piece of it in here," the guy said as he opened a slot that was big enough for money, dope and other small items to fit through.

Jack pushed a sleeve through the slot, and a couple of seconds later he heard two voices arguing:

"Nah, I'm copping this shit for real!"

"Fuck outta here! He stepped to me first! Plus, I let you bag that diamond ring the other night," another man shouted, his voice full of base.

Jack heard heavy wooden bars being lifted before the door slightly cracked open.

"I'll give you three big rocks for it," the guy said, already wishing it was wintertime so he could roll up to a night spot in style, and knowing that every female would sweat him to the fullest. *"What bitch could resist a nigga in a brand new mink?"* his mind quickly raced with the thought.

"You said we was gonna get at least six rocks. That's three apiece," Lite quickly added, getting in the mix of things.

"Who the fuck is he?" the guy asked, opening the door wider.

"Oh, his girl helped steal it, so he thinks he deserves half," Jack said while stepping a bit closer and holding the jacket up.

"Fuck it! I'll give you niggas two apiece," the guy said as he reached in his stash for the product.

Jack quickly threw the mink coat over the guy's head and pulled out his gun just as fast.

The guy's partner was no slouch. He had already snatched his ratchet out of his waistband and was ready to gun down the supposed robbers. But Lite already had his sawed-off double-barrel shotgun pointed in his direction and pulled the trigger. The blast caught the man dead center in the chest, causing him to fly backward into some boxes. Lite ran over and stepped on the man's gun hand while his other foot was standing on his bloodied, wounded chest cavity. "Just breathe deeply and it'll all be over in a second," Lite said to him, smiling as if he was a doctor assisting in a hospital bed suicide.

The shooting victim's eyes were wide with fear. He never thought in a million years that his last seconds on this earth would be in a dirty, roach infested crack house.

"Get the fuck up and sit over there!" Jack ordered the other man while Lite closed the door. "Now, I'm gonna keep this as simple as it's gonna get. I want all the dope and money right now," he said in a calm but deadly voice.

The guy didn't even think twice about holding out. He told the killers where everything was exactly. The man silently prayed about ten Hail Mary's that he wouldn't end up like his dope slinging buddy who was stretched the fuck out.

Jack came back momentarily while Lite held his shotgun in the guy's trembling mouth. The only thing that kept his teeth from chattering was the warm barrel that was between them.

"Okay, I want you to tell that bitch ass nigga, Rizz his days are up. As for you, I don't ever want to see you around here again," Jack stated.

"Oh, thank God! Thank you, Jesus!" the guy said, putting his face in his hands and finding religion all of a sudden.

"Don't thank the fucker yet," Jack replied before he emptied half a clip into the guy's kneecaps, sending shredded bone fragments and bloody flesh flying everywhere. The man then passed out from pain and shock.

The two men then walked out carrying garbage bags filled with money and drugs.

After he took care of that snake bitch ass nigga Rizz, Ice planned to finish off what he started with his parole officer, Mr. Spencer. *"That motherfucker is the reason I'm on the run in the first place. That lame ass cracker tried to extort me for a weekly payoff because he saw me up in the trap house. Then he had the nerve to try and violate my parole when I wasn't with the program,"* Ice had thought, wishing for the thousandth time he had murdered the man that night.

Ice had been thinking about shit too much, so he decided to relax a little since his shoulder was doing much better. *"What better way to unwind than to see some sweaty bitch's ass swinging from a seven-foot pole?"* he thought with a wicked grin.

Wearing a light red and black camouflage suit and a pair of ACG Black Elite boots, he climbed into the Infiniti. Chyna gave the okay for him to floss in the whip the majority of the time, so to show his appreciation he planned on buying her some banging ass rims. Plus, he didn't want to be seen riding around in some factory made shit.

"What the fuck happened here?" Ice asked out loud when he pulled up in front of his old strip club hangout, Jezebel's and saw a big white sign that read, "Closed Due To Ongoing Investigation". Directly underneath the lettering was an NYPD insignia. He pulled off, remembering where he had seen another strip club around the way, but never had a chance to check it out.

Ice was soon walking through the crowded Foxxy Sista with a large Thug Passion drink in his hand. Ice's long, heavy Cuban link chain swung back and forth, but he wished he had on an ill, big ass cookie monster piece to go with it. Being cautious and always watching everybody, Ice took a quick look around before taking a seat close by the stage. The DJ had the place jumping, playing "Na Na" by Trey Songz.

A dark skinned lady with Arabic writing down the outside of her thigh was swinging upside down on a pole, and came down with her butt hitting the stage floor with a loud *"Whump!"* Her ass cheeks began wiggling to the beat of the music as the crowd of men enjoyed the show.

"That hoe's ass is almost as big and round as that bitch, Buffie the Body. I don't know; they might be related," Ice said with a playful smile as he leaned in closer to the stage. He had ten singles in his hand to stuff into her pale-blue G-string. The thong was so deeply imbedded in her thick ass cheeks that the only way you would ever know that she had anything on was the tiny bit of material covering her groin area.

Ice sat by the stage with the money in his hand and let the dancer know he was feeling her act. She took off her bikini panties right before she strutted over to her waiting customer. When she got to Ice, the healthy stripper turned her back to him, grabbed both of her ankles and began shaking her ass in his smiling face. Ice threw the singles on her sweat-drenched back, and then grabbed both meaty cheeks, leaving his fingerprints.

Then it happened. The foul smelling odor drifted up to his nose, causing his brain to say *"What the fuck!"* He backed away as the woman turned around to face him. He was not taking any chances that her breath might be kicking as well.

Another guy caught the look on his face, so Ice said, "Them bitches should know to wash their ass on a regular. With an ass that big all kinds of bacteria gets trapped up between the cracks." Ice put his drink down, swearing that the stripper had sprinkled ass dust in his Thug Passion. He then walked off to find out what else he could get into at the club.

Ice made his way towards the back where the club had a couple of pool tables. But before he got there he saw a stripper dancing totally nude in front of an empty chair, looking like a damn fool. Upon closer inspection at the out of the ordinary situation, he saw that she wasn't a fool at all, but a real go-getter. Directly in front of the dancer was a pile of tens and twenties at her feet. Ice knew exactly what was going down because he had seen it a couple of times before. A baller had thrown a pile of money down for some lap dances, and was off somewhere else fucking around with some other bitches, and letting everybody know he had it like that. Ice wished he knew who the guy was so he could throw a big ass gun up in his face to see how much of a player he really was.

He made it to the back room, and just like he expected there were guys everywhere with their eight quarters on the pool table ledges to let others know that they had next. A few guys were getting grinding wall dances, hoping to bust a nut before the women busted their pockets.

After a while Ice got bored and went back towards the stage to see what female was performing now.

"...And put your hands together and dig into them pockets for Miss Latin!" the DJ yelled into the microphone as he turned up the music.

A stunning Latina woman who looked like she just crossed the border came out on stage in full force. She wore a naughty devil costume, and a pair of bright-red booty shorts that had a long tail with a forked tip attached. Miss Latin also had a pair of cute little horns on top of her head as her long black hair flicked back and forth.

The crowd, including Ice, couldn't wait until she took off her shorts, and when she finally did, the hollering drowned out the music. Her ass wasn't as big as most of the black dancers', but nobody was complaining. One of Miss Latin's stripper friends had to come on stage twice with a silver champagne bucket to gather up all the money. Before she left the stage, she let the wild crowd get a good peep at her tattoo. She had a picture of a tiger crouching down by her ass crack, drinking out of a puddle of spring water maybe three inches away from her anus.

Ice ordered himself another drink and waited for Miss Latin to hit the floor. He wanted to see what she was really about. About twenty minutes later she came out looking just as good, rocking a simple but form fitting dress with a split up the side showing a mouthwatering thigh. If he had to say something, he would say that her only flaw was that her feet were a little too big. Even so, who would care?

A couple of guys tried to grab her arm to let her know they wanted a lap dance, but she went straight to Ice and asked, "You wanna dance?"

Ice had given her "the look" when she first hit the stage that clearly said, *"Fuck these other bird ass niggas! Come check me first."* "Hold up. Let me get you a drink first. Whatcha sipping on?" he asked her.

"I'll have a Hypnotic Remix," she responded.

A very short while later while the woman was sipping on her drink, Ice asked, "Yo you definitely did your thing. Where you from?"

"Thanks. I'm from around the way. What about you? Are you mixed or what, with them pretty green eyes?" she curiously asked.

"Nah, I'm full black. And don't let the looks fool you," Ice said with a sneaky grin.

"So, you want that dance now?" Miss Latin asked, ready to stack that paper again.

"I just wanted to hear your voice. Anyway, I gotta go. Where you gonna be at later?" he asked, not wanting to be like the other customers coming off in a desperate manner by feeling all up on her like they just did a ten year stretch.

"I'll be here," she answered, and snatched up the twenty that he left on the table. Moments later the stripper was grinding some guy wearing thick, fogged-up glasses who looked as if he was about to propose marriage any minute.

"Yeah, I'm gonna fuck shorty something proper, and she's gonna be giving *me* that dough!" Ice said to himself as he headed for the door.

Just as he made it to the sidewalk, he spotted a Hummer with a guy leaning out of the driver's side window talking to a couple of men. *That's that faggot nigga, Rizz! Now I know what he's pushing,* Ice said to himself as Rizz peeled off, blasting a Meek Mills song.

CHAPTER EIGHTEEN

"Nights like this, I wish raindrops would fall. Nights like this, I wish rains drops would fall..."

Trina heard someone singing as she approached Crown Fried Chicken. It was Born all right, singing the lyrics to the classic movie "The Five Heart Beats" as he stood in front of the fast food store acting very strange.

"Hey Born, what's up? I been looking for you," Trina said, getting a good look at the man who was wearing a hooded sweatshirt with a football jersey thrown over it. Even though his clothes weren't dirty, he looked tacky as hell from her vantage point. Born always stepped outside like he was walking on the red carpet of a Hollywood movie premier, so this came as a complete shock to Trina.

"Trina, is that you? Get the fuck outta here! Come give me a hug!" the man said as he spread out his arms.

Trina gave him a hug while her eyes held a surprised look. Something wasn't quite right with her ex- pimp, with the corny ass clothes, the singing, and not to mention the fact that he never gave her a hug in his life. "Yeah, it's me. What you been up to?" she asked, breaking the embrace while wondering what he knew or didn't know about how everything jumped off when she tried to flip the script on him for her fuck partner, Supreme.

Soon they were peeling off in the Altima as Born started munching on Trina's chicken dinner without asking her.

"After that shit that went down at Jezebel's the police rushed me, and the next thing I know I'm up in the hospital, see?" Born explained. He then pulled his sweatshirt hood down and leaned to the side. He had a circular scar on the side of his head like he had been operated on by a crude Mexican surgeon. He then tapped on his skull to let the woman know he had a metal plate in his head.

"Damn! The police sure tore into his ass!" Trina thought, now knowing why he was a little off.

"So what happened with your case?" she asked.

"I really don't know, except something about the witness didn't show up or something, and then my brother bailed me out," he answered.

"So what's up with your brother? Is he still stacking that paper or what?" Trina asked. She knew that Born had made crazy bread off of the ladies, but with the way he's dressed and acting, she seriously doubted that the man could even get a five dollar crack whore to work for him. Born's brother is the one that put him onto the skin game in the first place.

"That nigga's still making it happen. He opened up a new house that ain't no joke. That's why I was out here. I just had a bad bitch on lock ready to put in work before you showed up," Born stated as he threw a chicken bone out the window.

"Born must be living in a fantasy world if he thinks a bitch is gonna sling some pussy for him looking like that, and with a goddamn frying pan stuck up in his head," Trina thought. She had wanted to meet Born's brother for the longest, but the opportunity never arose with Born keeping a tight leash on her like a runaway slave. She heard through the streets that he was a silent partner in a couple of the hottest clubs in New York, giving him the opportunity to snatch up even more women for the whorehouses.

Trina had no intentions of going back to work lying on her back with her legs cocked up in the air while some loser asked if he was good or not. She wanted to call the shots for a change, running the house or maybe owning it if she laid her plans down just right. "Show me where the new spot is at?" she asked.

"So, my little snow bunny wants to get down with old Born again, ain't that right?" the man asked with a little hopeful gleam in his eyes.

"You know we're always gonna be down together," Trina replied, placing her hand on his thigh while thinking that Born a damn fool.

They finally pulled up to a nice looking clean white house that was located in a mixed section of town. As Trina and Born started walking towards the front door, two Mexican men came walking out laughing and patting each other on the back. Trina liked dealing with drunken Mexican men. Most of the time they would cum from

"That's sad to hear, but I've heard one too many hard luck stories from past tenants who thought that was all they needed say to pay the rent," she stated as she walked quickly through the house, giving the man a brief tour.

"I understand where you're coming from, Miss. I'd feel the same way if I worked hard all my life for something, and then had someone come and try to get over on me. To show you my sincerity, I'll pay you four months in advance right now, if that's cool with you," Jack stated, opening up his Brazilian made crocodile brief case.

The lady didn't see a ruthless, murderous, soon-to-be drug lord in front of her. All she saw was a decent human being who knew how she felt about rent issues. "The rent is twenty one hundred a month, plus a security deposit," she said with her beady eyes fixed on the money like she worked at the Treasury Department.

"That's no problem," Jack replied as he began counting the money on the kitchen counter. "Here's a little something extra to buy yourself something nice, or have a nice lobster dinner with a friend," he added, and peeled off three crisp hundred dollar bills when the woman asked for some form of ID.

When Jack left the Bengay smelling woman, he was feeling good knowing that his plans for New York were beginning to materialize the way he envisioned them from the jump.

CHAPTER TWENTY

"**I** knew it! The way I pounded on that cop, I knew his faggot ass was gonna bite it!" Ice said out loud. He was sitting in Chyna's apartment reading the *Daily News* article about the police officer at Hands of Mercy Hospital. The article stated that Officer James Burke had passed away from the injuries he sustained at the hands of Nathaniel Wilson a.k.a. Ice during his daring escape from police custody. It went on to state that a nurse, Rhonda Coleman was first thought to be taken hostage during the escape, but now authorities believe that she may have been a willing participant.

The article also stated that the fugitive couple may have fled to New Haven, Connecticut where Ms. Coleman is believed to have family ties. "The only good thing about the article is that they think I'm in another state, and that the horny bitch is still alive with me somewhere."

But the one thing that worried Ice was that he had no idea when the nurse's friend was due back in town. When she comes back to her house, she's sure to find the dead body in the basement and call the cops. Even though he regarded all cops as idiots, it wouldn't take a rocket scientist to put two and two together.

What was working toward Ice's favor though was that the article was way in the back of the newspaper by the horse races. He just laughed out loud because he knew that the white folks in charge considered the dead police officer just another black man whom they gave permission to carry a gun, and whose luck had finally run out. So it was that, and the fact that the front page now held the top story about five men of Pakistani descent who were caught with bomb making materials in a fancy Manhattan apartment building.

"Ding-dong! Ding-dong!"

The doorbell rang, causing Ice to jump up and grab his gun. He quickly crept to the front door and looked through the peephole. There standing on the other side was a guy about twenty-something looking like he was in hurry. "Yeah, wuz up?" Ice asked, being cautious.

89

"I'm here to see Chyna," the man answered.

For some reason Ice swung the door open after putting the weapon in the front pocket of his pants, and keeping his finger on the trigger.

Both men quickly checked each other out before the stranger said, "Is she home or what?"

"Nah, she ain't here. Who should I say came by?" Ice asked as closely watched the guy who was wearing a Breitling watch that was flooded with canary-colored diamonds. He also noticed that the guy was rocking a pair of expensive Evisu Revisited jeans with crocodile skin zip-up pockets. Ice's first thought was to catch wreck on this bird ass nigga, but somehow he decided against it... for now.

"She knows who I am," the guy responded before he turned around and headed for the staircase instead of using the elevator.

"That must be the dude who be hitting Chyna off with all that loot," Ice said to himself. He then made a mental note to himself to find out more about the guy before deciding how to make a move if he decided to do so.

Ice was feeling kind of bored so he decided to ride around to see what was popping in the hood. He wanted to go to the strip club to see Miss Latin again, but he didn't want to seem like a stalker, or worse, a trick ass customer whose only way to get a bad female to pay any attention to him was by stuffing money in her G-string.

Pushing the Infiniti exclusively now, he felt like the car was his, so he headed to the twenty-four hour car wash for a hot wax. After eight o' clock the customers sat in their vehicles while the car went through the automatic wash and wax system.

The Ecuadorians working at the car wash were preparing to put some Turtle Wax Platinum Tire Shine on the tires, so Ice decided to get out and wipe away the excess water drops with a clean white rag. But before he ever got the chance to get out, someone knocked on his window. When he rolled down the tinted window, a guy said, "Yo, man, could I wipe down your car for a couple of dollars?"

Ice was about to tell the bum to get the fuck outta here, but he recognized the shabbily dressed person immediately. It was Rob from Southside. They used to run together robbing niggas, smoking weed, and running trains on bitches in cheap motels.

Ice Cold Vengeance

Ice very vividly remembered when Rob had just come home from prison and didn't even have a decent pair of jeans to wear, so he gave him some money to tighten up his pathetic wardrobe. Later on that same night Ice took his boy to the strip club and they ended up sipping champagne in the VIP room with a couple of top-notch dancers. Rob was his boy back then, so it wasn't a big deal for him to show mad love to one of his peoples who was down and out.

Later on Ice himself had wound up in jail and ended up getting raped by a prison homo thug who called himself "Mother Dear". Being that Ice was a so-called pretty boy with light skin and green eyes, most inmates suspected that he might have been a willing participant in the so-called rape allegation.

When the warden pressured Ice to sign a sworn statement against Mother Dear, he refused because he didn't want to be labeled a snitch as well. The warden tried to get even by making Ice bunk mates with a well-known homosexual, and soon everybody in the prison was calling him "Ice Cream" behind his back, and some in front of his face.

Later on after the incident Ice ran into his right-hand man, Rob in the prison yard. Rob acted like he didn't even know him and went as far as to say boldly to a group of guys from Queens, *"That's fucked up how niggas like that be giving Queens a bad rap."* From that moment on, Ice hated Rob with a passion that words couldn't even begin to describe.

"Yo, Rob, what's up? What the fuck you doing out here hustling for chump change in the cold?" Ice asked with a slight smirk on his face.

"Oh shit! Ice, is that you? Damn, this is a phat ass whip! I see you still that nigga," Rob replied with a shit-eating grin.

Now that Ice was sure that his so-called ride or die friend knew exactly who he was, he was going to put two hot ass slugs into the nigga's nappy ass head, but instead he asked, "So, whatcha doing out here? Is times that hard? You ain't on that shit, are you?" It felt good to rub more salt into the wound of his ex-homie's predicament.

"Before I came home from jail my moms had died, so I had nowhere to go and no dough to get back on my feet," Rob answered, hoping Ice would invite him inside the car for a little heat.

Ice then got out of the Infiniti so Rob could fully see the long heavy Cuban link chain that swung low towards his stomach and said, "Well anyway, I might have a job for you. Where you resting your head at?" he asked, totally ignoring the fact that his one-time friend stated that his mother had passed away.

"I'm in that new men's shelter on Rockaway Boulevard," Rob responded, feeling more ashamed by the minute. "Let me get your number so I can keep in touch with you," the man practically begged.

"Nah, man, I don't have one right now. Where you be hanging out at? I'll contact you," Ice replied.

"I'm always here. You think that you could throw me something so I could get something to eat?" Rob asked in a low voice.

"I don't have it right now, but be here in a couple of days and I'll see what I could do," Ice replied, pulling out a roll of money and handing the guy who just finished shining up the tires a twenty dollar tip, letting Rob know that he didn't care if he died of starvation or not.

"Ice, you know what happened in jail. I wasn't trying to dis you or nothing. It's just that niggas were saying some wicked shit about you. I never believed it 'cause I know how you get down. I just thought you didn't want to be bothered with anybody at the time," Rob said, praying that Ice believed his bullshit lie.

"I feel you, but that's in the past. Let's just get this money again," Ice said before driving off. He had to hold his anger in check before he murdered the man on the spot. Even though there were a lot of witnesses around the carwash, he didn't care. He was being hunted for killing a police officer, so what difference would it make if he murdered some bum ass nigga slumming for change? No, he had something better in mind for snake ass Rob.

CHAPTER TWENTY-ONE

"Where the fuck this bitch got the shit hid at?" Trina spat out in a whisper. She was in her cousin Lilly's room, searching diligently for the stash she kept hidden. Trina made sure she put everything back in its original position so as not to arouse suspicion. "Yeah, jackpot!" she said with a self-assured smile on her face. She pulled two small stacks of money out of a sneaker box that was on a top shelf in the closet and covered with a stack of magazines. She placed everything back like it was before, and silently crept out of the room.

Trina had just stolen her cousin Lilly's money that she was saving for a down payment on a new house. "I'm tired of paying this high ass rent and never getting anywhere. I'm going to have my own place real soon. Just wait and see," Lilly would often say.

Trina wasn't nowhere near stupid when it came to reading between the lines of her cousin's hood dreams. She told herself that she would replace the cash, but a voice deep down told her that was just another lie. *"Fuck her! You snooze, you lose! Lilly knew what she was getting herself into when she invited me to live with her,"* Trina reasoned to herself. She had more important things to buy with the money than having it sit up in some moth infested closet.

"Everything all right? We still leaving or what?" Jenise shouted from downstairs.

"Yeah, gimme a minute. I'm just grabbing my jacket," Trina responded. She quickly counted out seven thousand dollars and tucked most of it in the inside of her Blue Label Dolce & Gabbana jacket. She didn't want to take a chance of putting that much cold hard cash in her bag because anything could happen. She could fuck around and get high and leave it somewhere, or some dude in the hood might think she was an easy victim because she was white and try to snatch her bag.

"I just moved to Manhattan from Jersey to start training on a new job," Ice said while looking at his watch as if to say that he wanted to get home as quickly as possible so he could be ready for work in the morning.

Both Ice and the still suspicious older gentleman chitchatted through the locked screen door before a voice yelled, "Willie, who you talking to for so long?"

"It's a young man who's waiting for a tow truck!" he shouted back.

"Why you got him out there in this chilly night air? Don't be rude, invite him in," the woman shouted back in a friendly voice.

"You seem like you're all right," the old man said while giving Ice the once over again as he unlocked the screen door.

That's just what Ice had counted on; the old, unconscious slave mentality that a lot of older folks lived by. Just because Ice was light skinned with green eyes he was to be trusted a little more than the average black person. If he was African dark with thick lips, they would have called the police from the jump, thinking he had to be up to no good.

"Have a seat. Can I get you anything?" the man asked once Ice was inside.

"No thank you," Ice politely replied.

Just like clockwork, a knock came at the front door. "Somebody called a tow truck from this address?" Rob asked after the old man answered it.

"Oh yeah, he's right in here. Come on in," the man said, knowing that Rob had to be a tow truck driver by his old street shirt and greasy stained up work jeans.

"Who's at the door now?" the wife asked as she walked into the living room.

Before another word could be said, Ice pulled out his gun and said, "Now, everybody keep quiet and get over there!"

"What's this about?" Willie asked, holding onto his shocked wife.

"You been in the hood long enough to know what time it is," Ice said before giving his accomplice a signal.

Ice Cold Vengeance

"I have a jewelry box upstairs in the bedroom, and some money in the top drawer. Just don't hurt us," the woman said through already teary eyes.

"Just do as I say so we could get outta here real fast," Ice said, still pointing his weapon at the couple. He was carefully watching the husband who was glaring at him through murderous eyes. "I bet you won't open the door to no more strangers," he stated with a chuckle after catching the look.

Rob left the room and came back with some clothesline rope and a couple of chairs.

"Hurry up and tie these old fuckers up!" Ice ordered.

Once the trembling senior citizens were firmly tied to the chairs, Ice told Rob that he could keep whatever drugs and cash he found in the house.

"We don't have any drugs in here," Willie said, now believing that the robbers were drug addicts.

"All that sounds good and shit, but I'm sure that you know that your grandson, Rizz controls most of the dope that flows through this here part of town," Ice stated sincerely while looking at a framed picture of a much younger Rizz on the wall above the piano.

Ice then started thinking: *That's one thing about drug dealing niggas from the hood. No matter how much wealth they acquire, they always seem to leave their closest relatives in the ghetto around ever present predators or people who want to get rich quick. The dealers seem to have the notion that no one would dare try and violate their vulnerable kin because of their wild street reputation. But reputations don't mean dick when someone does decide to violate, and their family members end up six feet deep."*

"All I found was a few hundred dollars and some old cheap gold rings and chains," Rob said, coming back down the steps.

On the way over to Rizz's grandparent's house Ice had gassed Rob up by saying that reliable sources had told him that Rizz often stashed large amounts of drugs and money over at his grandparent's house, which caused Rob's mouth to water out of pure greed.

"Where's the motherfucking money at?" Rob shouted angrily as he pulled out a butcher knife and walked over to the wide-eyed couple.

"We don't have anything to do with no money or drugs. Just take what you have and go," Willie stated, wishing that he had his .45 pistol that he carried in Vietnam right now.

"Gag both of them and search the kitchen," Ice said, still convincing the desperate Rob that there had to be large amounts of currency somewhere in the house.

While Ice was puffing on his second Newport, Rob came back into the living room and said, "Nothing. Not a motherfucking red cent." Rob had torn up the newly remodeled kitchen searching for a stash that never was.

"Watch them. I think I know a place where shit might be hidden," Ice said, walking towards the kitchen. He came back a short while later wearing a pair of plastic dish washing gloves and carrying a heavy hammer that he concealed behind his leg. "This is for fronting on me, you bitch ass nigga!" he growled.

Rob turned quickly around and asked, "What?" before the steel hammer crashed into his eyebrow bone shattering it into fragmented pieces. Rob screamed and grabbed at his damaged face as the heavy, dangerous tool struck again on the top of his head. Ice swung the weapon once again, finding the back of Rob's fragile skull and ending the traitor's life for good. With a twisted smile, he stood there for a moment looking down at his ex-homie while holding onto the hammer that had hair, blood and bits of gray brain matter grotesquely stuck on the end of it.

The old couple just stared at Ice like he was a sick madman, not knowing what to expect next.

Ice then kicked his one time running partner in the face and said, "Yeah, nigga, karma is a motherfucker. What comes around goes around."

He then spit on the still warm corpse and turned his attention to the couple who once trusted him. "Everything that went down here, you can thank your grandson, Rizz for," he said before walking over to the old woman and untying her. In one quick motion, he ripped open the old woman's flowered housecoat sending buttons flying in every direction. Her husband started struggling feverishly against his bonds, knowing what was about to happen from being around so long.

Ice Cold Vengeance

Willie remembered when he was a young soldier fighting the war in Vietnam never believing that he would make it to next week. He and his fellow Marine buddies were on the fast track, smoking dope and drinking red slush (homemade liquor from Cam Ranh Bay). They felt that they could do just about anything to the country's sandal wearing soldiers and its native inhabitants without the slightest bit of repercussions. After all, everybody in the unit witnessed at one time or another one of their friends getting blown to hell by the crudely made booby traps set by the Vietcong.

Willie and his die-hard Marine buddies brutally raped women and innocent young farm girls, most of the time in front of helpless family members while laughing and knowing that their war crimes will never be found out in this war torn madhouse of a country. The inhumane tortures and rapes went on so often that the American servicemen often repeated a well-known slogan: *"Whatever goes on in the field stays in the field."*

Willie would have never suspected in a million years that the same psychological torture that he perpetuated on his victims would be eventually turned on him in the same ironic way years later, with his loving wife now being the victim. Many years after he retired from the military he had read a passage in a book that said: *"We can run from our sins, but sooner or later they all catch up with us when we least expect it."* The word *"Karma"* exploded in old man Willie's brain.

"Bitch, what the fuck you think you trying to do?" Ice yelled as he gave the woman a good slap when she tried to claw at his face. She fell backwards in a groggy, painful haze as Ice ripped away her thin nightgown.

In no way did this old woman with the wrinkled up saggy tits turn Ice on in the slightest way, but his uncontested hatred for Rizz made the blood flow to his organ at a rapid pace that even surprised him.

Just as the woman was coming to, Ice ripped off her white control-top panties, revealing nappy gray pubic hair. He started unzipping his jeans as her husband began struggling even more against the ropes while staring at the horror that was being forced on his wife.

As Willie fell backwards in his chair, Ice plunged deeply into the old woman. It felt like his dick was being rubbed against sandpaper. He didn't worry about wearing a condom because he knew he wasn't going to cum in the old bag, leaving unmistakable DNA up in her. He just wanted to hurt the feeble woman a few times while her husband watched.

While the rapist pumped unemotionally, the woman kept repeating, "Sweet Jesus! Sweet Jesus!" over and over again as if she was in some kind of hypnotic trance. Ice didn't know if what she was blurting out was a good thing or a bad thing.

Just as Ice was getting up Willie ceased moving, so Ice figured that the old man knew that there was nothing he could possibly do to stop the brutal assault. "At least your bitch didn't have cobwebs on the pussy," Ice said out loud to the husband as he stood up and began straightening out his clothes.

The old woman just stared up at the ceiling as if she was in total shock, not even bothering to cover up her semi-nude body.

Ice then walked over to Rob's corpse and plucked the butcher knife from his fingers. He then casually walked over to the half nude woman and stabbed her in the chest like he was simply carving up a Thanksgiving turkey.

He then went over to the husband to finish his devious work, and that's when he noticed the husband's haft opened glassy eyed stare. Old man Willie was already dead. "The fucker must have had a heart attack when he saw his wife getting banged out," Ice said out loud. Even though the man was dead now, that didn't stop the murderer from carrying out the rest of his insane plan. He sliced Willie a few times against his forearms before stabbing him twice in the stomach.

Ice then untied the old man and placed the hammer tightly in his hands. He dragged the dead body over by Rob and looked at the scene to make sure he didn't leave anything out. Ice figured that the so-called educated crime scene detectives would guess that the whole drama played out like this:

Rob broke into the house looking for valuables, and tied the old couple up. Being that he was high on speed and crack, the hardcore drug addict decided to rape and kill the wife. Somehow, the husband broke free and a fierce struggle ensued because Rob the crack head had underestimated Willie. He was caught off guard by the hammer that Willie somehow happened to have nearby. Rob tried to fight back with the butcher knife, slashing at the man's arms before fatally stabbing him, and then succumbed to his own injuries.

Ice knew that with today's ever growing technologies dealing with forensics and computer generated replays of crimes scenes, they could easily find a thousand holes in this setup. But the three victims were black people living in the ghetto, so New York City wasn't going to spend hundreds of dollars trying to make sure that's exactly how everything played itself out. No, that money could be spent on something worthwhile, like making a judge's chambers more comfortable.

"Oh yeah, I almost forgot," Ice said out loud as he took the butcher knife that was dripping with blood and placed it in Rob's hand.

Ice then calmly walked away from the bloodbath that he created in this quiet neighborhood.

The stripper was well proportioned in every sense of the word, standing a couple inches shorter than her co-worker. Her 32-inch waist and 45-inch ass could easily have held a pitcher of water steadily on her overly developed backside. She was that jet African black that made her almond shaped eyes and long, shiny eyelashes even more prominent. A good two hundred years ago, she could have been a Nigerian princess, with her children playing with precious gems in the royal chambers.

"What's your name, shorty?" Rizz asked, pulling her bikini top to the side to have her breasts fall into his hands.

"My name is Nutmeg," she responded in a sexy, bedroom voice. She then got up and started slowly dancing for her customer whom she knew to be caked up by the way he carried himself, and by the dazzling jewelry he wore.

Meanwhile, Nature was in the dark section of the room with his pants already open and trying to run up in the other stripper who was more than willing if the money was long enough.

"Which one of you is Rizz?" a woman asked as she walked into the room with her high heels making soft sounds on the carpeted floor.

"I am. Who wants to know?" Rizz asked as he stared at the very attractive lady.

"Silk said that you're a special customer, and that you need a special bitch like me," the Latina woman said, her eyes cutting into Nutmeg.

Even though Nutmeg was an official dime piece in her own right, Rizz could never turn down a bad, light skinned girl; and a Latina one at that, with long, jet-black hair. All thoughts of going to the whorehouse went straight out of his mind, knowing he was going to fuck some high quality pussy tonight.

"I got this. You can go back to doing whatever you were doing," Nutmeg spat out, feeling a little jealous that the new girl was getting all the attention now. Up until now, Nutmeg was considered the pick of the litter in a ten-mile radius of the dancing circuit.

"Come on now. It's obvious who he chose. He hasn't even peeped at your black ass once I stepped on the set," the woman replied, speaking with a slight Spanish accent.

"Half white bitch! We gonna see how much he wants you once I mark up that face!" Nutmeg shot back, knowing that her rival was a hundred percent right. She had to admit that Miss Latin definitely had top star potential. Even though Nutmeg was strictly dickly, she would have gladly eaten Miss Latin's snatch and tossed the salad like she was at a breakfast buffet. But right now, it was all about the Benjamin's.

"Nah, y'all cool out. We don't have to start bugging the fuck out up in here. Let me talk to shorty for a minute and I'll holler at you a little later on," Rizz said, directing his comment to the fuming Nutmeg who had already started gathering up her outfit.

"You'll probably get crabs in your clothes fucking with that hoe!" the Latina stripper said loud enough for Nutmeg to hear.

"I like your style. What you all about?" Rizz asked after taking a look over at Nature, who was now getting a blowjob while he drank from the champagne bottle. The couple acted as if they were in their own private world instead of a crowded establishment.

"I'm about having fun and recognizing real niggas when I see them," she answered, stroking Rizz's already inflated ego.

"I feel you. So, turn around so I could peep that ass," Rizz said, not wasting any time.

Miss Latin did as she was told and started wiggling to the beat of "Gold Digger" by Kanye West.

Rizz untied the bow in the back of her dance outfit, causing the top to drop to the floor.

Minutes later when the DJ threw on a fresh song, the bottom part of the woman's dance outfit was slipped out of. The exotic dancer then bent over and spread her long legs, giving the lusting Rizz a bird's eye view of her feminine assets.

Rizz couldn't get over how fine the stripper looked with her glow-in-the-dark fingernail polish that happened to match the color of her eyes. *"Damn! This bitch should be on the cover of Top Ten magazine!"* he was thinking. He just couldn't help it, and without warning, he double-dipped, running his tongue from her vagina to her pink asshole. *"Damn! Shorty tastes better than fresh-squeezed orange juice!"* Rizz thought, still feeling lightheaded from all the drinking he'd been doing all night.

The woman let Rizz get in two good licks before she turned around and said, "Not here, playboy. I like to take my time."

"How much you talking about?" Rizz asked, pulling out straight hundreds, knowing that everything was based on cheeder; especially up in some damn strip club.

"I don't rock like that. If I like a nigga, that's all there is to it," Miss Latin said as she looked straight into his eyes, all the while throwing the drunken Rizz some old school bubblegum game.

"Well, I wanna chill with you right now, and I don't want to wait 'til you get off, so I'll just hit you off with whatever you could have made," Rizz stated. He was used to paying for the pussy.

"Oh, then that's different. Give me a minute to change," she replied, giving him a light peck on the cheek.

Nature was busy rubbing his chick's feet and kissing her on the neck when the Latina dancer came back wearing her street clothes. Not wanting to waste any more time, the horny Rizz said, "Nature, get your ass up and come on."

"You don't want to chill for a little while longer?" Nature asked as he ran his hand up the stripper's smooth thigh not wanting to move from his comfortable position.

"Nah, nigga. Let's roll out," Rizz said before taking the last swig of the champagne bottle.

Nature whispered something to the laughing girl and then said, "She can't leave with us 'cause her baby's father is coming through to pick her up."

"Well, you can stay here. I'm out. Come on, let's roll," Rizz stated and smacked the Latina woman on her ass.

After the two made it outside, Rizz gave each of the bouncers a big-faced Franklin C-note before he and his new jump-off pulled off in his cranberry-colored Hummer.

"This is some nice shit. What do you do?" Miss Latin innocently asked, checking everything out.

"It ain't hard to tell. I run these motherfucking streets," Rizz answered. He was feeling good that he snatched up the baddest bitch out of Foxxy Sista.

******

Ice Cold Vengeance

"Oh shit! There goes that nigga, Rizz! He must not know what happened to his peoples yet," Ice said after he saw Rizz hugged up and laughing with a pretty Latino looking woman and acting like he didn't have a care in the world. The woman turned her head and Ice said, "Miss Latin's fucking around with his ass!"

Ice then followed the couple around the block to see where they were headed to. He drove maybe four blocks before he saw a police car with its lights flashing, pulling Rizz's Hummer over. "You're a lucky motherfucker!" Ice said to himself as he drove past them.

******

"Sir, did you know that you ran that stop sign back there?" the officer said while shining his flashlight into the Hummer's interior.

"I didn't see it. I was too busy concentrating on getting to where I was going, if you know what I mean," Rizz responded, caring more about the piece of ass he was about to smash than the drugs and the gun he had on him.

The cop ran his steel-gray eyes over Miss Latin's body. Miss Latin had on a tiny top that barely covered her breasts. "Okay, I'm going to let you off with a warning. Just get off the streets before you kill somebody," the officer firmly stated. He then smiled to himself while reminiscing about when he was twenty-five years younger and somebody actually cared about him.

Rizz slowly pulled off, still thinking about sopping up Miss Latin's across-the-border pussy juice. He never noticed that a car was closely following them.

CHAPTER TWENTY-FOUR

Haitian Jack was greedily wolfing down his late night dinner consisting of yucca, chunks of cabbage, and a few pieces of stewed *manioc* meat when the phone call came. "That's cool. We'll be there right away. Yeah, I'll be waiting to see what car you get in," Jack had said before pressing end on his cell phone. "Lite, let's roll! Your girl finally hit pay dirt!" he excitedly said.

Minutes later, both men were driving off in the new BMW, armed to the teeth and anxious to get to where they were going.

"There she go right there," Lite said, his eyes peering through the darkness. His girlfriend Carmen, better known to her lustful customers as "Miss Latin", was slowly getting into a shiny, cranberry-colored Hummer.

******

"I'm glad that fucking cop kept it moving. I'm definitely not in the mood for any more of their bullshit tonight," Rizz replied.

"What's wrong, baby?" Miss Latin asked.

"I got some bullshit drama with some dirty fucking Haitians. They should ship all their ashy asses back on the boat in body bags!" he replied, getting himself hyped up.

"Is it that serious?' Miss Latin innocently asked.

"Come on! Look at me! I run this town. Can't nobody come close to a nigga like me. Anyway forget all that shit. I know an ill hotel where they got a four person sunken in floor Jacuzzi," Rizz stated, flipping his mind back to fucking again.

"I like that, but stop by the store first so I could pick up something," she said, giving him brightest smile.

Rizz smiled to himself, thinking that she wanted to get some condoms or buy a strawberry flavored douche like so many other girls did when he bagged them on a late night creep.

After they stopped in front of the store and Miss Latin got out and walked off towards the twenty-four hour bodega window, Rizz yelled out, "Make sure you get a Dutch, and get some extra-large condoms too!"

"What did you say you wanted again?" the woman sweetly asked after she turned back around.

"A Dutch cigar! Fuck it, get two!"

"I can't hear you!" Miss Latin shouted, drawing all of Rizz's attention towards her.

Rizz leaned towards the passenger window and repeated what he said. When he sat back up, hard metal met his soft nose.

"Whap!"

He didn't even realize that he was being snatched out of his luxury SUV and thrown into the back seat of another car as painful, white stars floated across his vision.

"Hurry up and get your ass in that nigga's whip!" Lite shouted to his girl.

Miss Latin quickly jumped behind the wheel and peeled off in Rizz's Hummer.

Rizz started to mumble something when another hard blow to the side of the head ended that.

"Slow down before you get us pulled over. You know how the cops like to fuck with niggas this time of night," Haitian Jack growled as he steadily watched the unconscious Rizz.

"I think he has a gun on him. I feel something in his waistband," Lite stated. He then snatched out a nickel-plated .45 and what little drugs Rizz had left on him.

Rizz was just starting to come to when the car pulled up in the darkened driveway of the house that Jack was renting. Miss Latin had already driven Rizz's Hummer into the garage and secured it. Moments later, the group hustled their still dazed prisoner through the back door with Rizz dripping blood throughout the partially decorated house. The four people ended up in the basement, where there were all sorts of tools thrown about. The owner had stopped fixing the basement up as a separate apartment because it ended up costing more than she had anticipated.

"Strip this nigga to make sure he doesn't have anything else on him," Jack ordered while keeping his weapon pointed at Rizz just in case he tried to make any sudden moves.

"Oh, look at the big shot rocking a vest! You think just because you got this shit on we wouldn't be able to touch you? But I like your style anyway. I'll take it though. It might come in handy someday," Jack said with a laugh as Lite threw him the bulletproof Kevlar vest.

Lite had placed Rizz's diamond bracelet and ring in his pocket, and laid the heavy chain and money on a nearby workbench.

Rizz solemnly knew that his hungry thirst for new pussy had caused him to be caught sleeping in the worst way. "What you want, some dough? I got plenty. We can work shit out," he said, standing in his boxer shorts now and trying to control the helpless situation. Right now he didn't care who they were, because everybody in every slum across America respected and wanted only one thing... *Money!*

"Listen, boy! Shut the fuck up! You're gonna be doing enough talking soon enough!" Jack spat out while staring intensely at the young man whom he had dreams of meeting face to face one day.

"Lite, go get that big piece of lumber leaning against the wall. Carmen, go get that roll of copper wire," Jack said in a sneaky voice, like only he knew what was about to happen.

"Come on, man. We don't have to go through all this. I can take you to more than three million dollars right now," Rizz pleaded when Jack told him to lay down on the wide piece of raw wood.

Jack just hit him in the mouth with the butt of his own gun, splitting his lip like a sun exposed mango.

Lite and Carmen had Rizz firmly tied up on the board with the strong copper wire as Jack stood watching with a devilish grin on his face. Once Rizz had his hands secured above his head and his legs spread apart, Jack produced a small orange box cutter.

"I told you I have money at my place. It's in a safe under the bathroom sink. Somebody can stay here with me, and the rest of you can check it out if you think I'm lying," Rizz said, speaking rapidly through swollen lips and spraying his bare chest with thick blood drops as Jack began cutting away his underwear.

"I thought you said you needed extra-large rubbers. You got to be kidding!" Carmen said, and laughed so hard that it brought tears to her eyes. She couldn't help staring at Rizz's tiny shriveled up penis. "And can you believe this nigga kept saying how he was gonna beat my guts out and make me leave my man?" she mockingly added, giving Lite a wet kiss on the lips.

Ice Cold Vengeance

Rizz cut his eyes at the grimy woman, thinking that he would give everything he owned in this world just to be in a room with her alone for five solid minutes.

Meanwhile, Haitian Jack had gone over to a corner and retrieved an old wooden hammer and a couple of six-inch heavy duty steel nails.

Lite had no idea what was going through his crazy friend's mind so he said, "Should I find something to cover his mouth?"

"Nah, I want to hear this nigga scream like a bitch," Jack said as he bent down and took hold of one of Rizz's testicles.

"Please, God! No! Give me a chance to take you to the money! Please, I'm begging you!" Rizz shouted out, still thinking it was just about the money.

Jack took a sturdy nail and hammered it into the man's testicle in less than three seconds.

Rizz let out an inhuman scream, thinking that when guys had beef in the ghetto they settled it with guns like gangsters, not like madmen in a Hollywood horror movie. He passed out in less than a minute with blackish bile dribbling from the corner of his mouth.

"Lite, go upstairs and get me a filled up bucket of ice water," Jack ordered.

Carmen just stared at the scene. She was horrified and thinking that no man deserved what Rizz had just gotten. There was something definitely wrong with Jack.

Lite came back with a plastic pail and handed it to the still grinning Jack. Rizz was still moaning in his unconscious state when Jack splashed him with the cold water, shocking his system awake. Almost instantly Rizz started screaming and begging for his torturer to pull out the nail. Jack took the nail out the man's scrotum only because he didn't want Rizz to pass out again too soon.

"Okay, Mr. Untouchable, what do you want to tell me?" Jack asked as he bent down close to his victim's mouth.

Rizz was breathing hard, as if he had just run a one hundred meter race. He told Haitian Jack about every one of his stash houses, where his money was exactly, and anything else he could think of just to stop the unbearable torturous pain.

"This it just to make sure you told me everything," Jack said sickly as he reached for another sturdy nail.

Rizz started screaming again even before the nail tore into his only good nut. His entire body went into unnatural convulsions as he screamed himself into unconscious once again.

Carmen grabbed her man's hand. She desperately wanted to tell Jack to just put a bullet in the young man's head and end his suffering. But she kept quiet, fearing how the unpredictable Jack would react.

Jack threw the last of the water on Rizz and then plugged the other nail into the other damaged testicle.

Rizz then vomited up his last meal, and other unknown substances.

CHAPTER TWENTY-FIVE

"Yo Universal, you heard what happened to your man, Rizz?" an inmate asked, being way too late with the news.

Universal had been on Rikers Island close to four days now, and all he'd been hearing on the news channel was how the police found Rizz's body.

Somebody had dumped his mutilated corpse right smack in the middle of the projects where he had a crew of ride or die soldiers slinging dope for him. His head was battered in so much that it resembled a squashed melon with chunky Ragu spaghetti sauce spread all over it. The long-time residents had seen that and much worse before, but what they weren't prepared for was what they saw early that morning. Rizz was totally nude, and there was a gaping bloody hole where his genitals used to be. The hole was stuffed with a fistful of tampons which caused the nervous residents to wonder what kind of sick psycho monster was walking the streets amongst them.

Universal ignored the guy and went straight to the phone. "You almost finished?" he asked a guy who was arguing with somebody over the phone:

"Bitch, don't try to lie to me! My scrap told me he seen you riding around with some nigga in my whip! What? I ain't trying to hear the bullshit! When I get out I'm gonna stomp a mud hole in your ass! Hello? Hello?" the inmate yelled into the phone, not believing he just got clicked on.

"Hey, playboy, I guess your phone call over," Universal stated. He took the receiver out of the guy's hand and made his call.

The guy just stood there wondering how his wifey could flip the script on him so quickly in only two months of his being locked up.

"You got that loot yet...? That's peace... I want you and my baby's momma to come up here and bail me out... No, you gotta be a certain age... You remember the address, right...? Okay, I gotta make other moves," Universal said before hanging up.

He then tried to contact Nature unsuccessfully. He had heard that Nature was the last person seen hanging out with Rizz. *"Could Nature be somehow involved with Rizz's memory getting dissed like that? Nah. Scary ass Nature's probably somewhere shaking like a pair of Las Vegas dice,"* he thought to himself.

Universal wasn't gonna front. He was kind of worried about these off the chain Haitians running around murdering everything in sight. And now that Rizz was dead, he was the next man to step up to the plate and run things. There was a lot of money at stake. *"But am I ready to have an all-out war with some crazy ass Haitians who seemed to pop out of nowhere?"* he quietly thought to himself.

The streets were barking that if the big man could be taken out so easily, then what about the rest of the crew? Universal had to admit that if they found out where Rizz's people lived, they probably know where he and his family lived also.

Universal sat on his bed thinking all day on what his next move should be, when the correction officer yelled for him to pack up. He then went through all the hours of standard procedure when getting bailed out from the Island for security reasons:

"What's your full name? Date of birth and address? How much is your bail? Who's bailing you out? What's your ID number?"

The same questions went on at every checkpoint. He was then given a large manila envelope with his property, and then he waited for the bus to take him across the bridge.

******

"What's up, nigga? You sure took your time getting out," a guy said, giving Universal some dap.

"Where's my baby's momma at?" Universal asked.

"She said she couldn't wait any longer and bounced with the V. But I got this cab driver friend," the other man replied.

Soon both men were in the crack head's vehicle and driving away.

"I wanna lay low at your crib, 'til I figure this thing out," Universal said to his younger but loyal friend.

Later on both guys were in a house, smoking weed and talking.

Ice Cold Vengeance

"So, what's everybody saying about Rizz?" Universal asked.

"People are just saying that whoever bodied Rizz ain't no joke. Do you know who did it?" the guy asked.

"It's some Haitians from outta town that we been having problems with. I don't know how many niggas they got rolling with them or who they down with," Universal answered, and then puffed hard on the blunt, still deep in thought.

"Well, whatever you decide to do, I'm with you," the guy said, meaning every word.

****** *

Back at Chyna's apartment, Ice sat with his feet up on the coffee table drinking his second 40-oz. Old English. "They really put it on that nigga, Rizz," he said out loud as he sat watching a boxing match on HBO.

Word got around in a matter of hours on how Rizz's killers had obviously wanted to make a statement by going to such an extent. They say that Rizz had to have been tortured, and when someone's being tortured to such a degree, he had to give up something. Ice knew that the something must have been the cash and drugs that belonged to him. He suspected that the stripper, Miss Latin might have had something to do with what happened to Rizz, and he planned to find out exactly what she knew. The police were sure to try and connect what happened to Rizz's grandparents with what happened to the recently deceased Rizz, leaving him in the clear.

Ice didn't know what to make of his childhood friend Chyna. She started prancing around the apartment practically butt naked, making him hard with the slightest contact. But what activated his curiosity ten-fold was that she always rocked expensive gear like Prada and Valentino calf-length leather boots. He saw her more than once jumping out of ill expensive cars, but he didn't mention it.

He still wanted to know who the dude was that dropped by the apartment the other day. Thinking about the strange guy made him feel a twinge of jealousy, even though he never had sex with her.

Kowalski banged on the door with the radio and then said, "They're probably peeking out behind the shades."

The majority of residents living in the ghetto would never answer the door when they see policemen on their doorsteps. They always brought warrants and bad news with them. In most incidents they say they just want to talk, and the foolish people believing this sham end up being their number-one prime suspect. In the slums the long-term oppressed residents never open their door for two types of people: the police or salesmen.

******

Approximately twenty minutes later while cruising through the neighborhood, Matthews spotted someone. "Pull over in front of that hardware store. There's one of my boys," he said to his partner.

"I see you're still trying to break into cars," Matthews said, catching a man off guard who had a slim jim in his hand that was used to break into vehicles.

"I don't get down like that anymore. I borrowed this car from my aunt and lost the keys somewhere. I was trying to hurry up and unlock the door so I could pick her up from work," the man said, knowing very well that the detectives wouldn't fall for this pitiful lie. He then leaned up against the dented up Oldsmobile Cutlass Supreme waiting for the detective's next move.

Matthews and his partner slowly climbed out their car. "I should bust your ass for attempted car theft, destruction of private property, and whatever else I decide to think of. But I'm going to give you a chance to make shit right. What's going on?" the detective asked.

"What you talking about?" the tall, rail-thin man asked.

"Don't play dumb with me or I'll jack your fucking ass right now! Who wanted Rizz taken out?" Matthews shouted while his partner stood behind the snitch.

"That's fucked up how they did that boy. His folks were good Christians—"

Before he could rattle on some more, Kowalski cut him off and said, "Just answer the fucking question!"

Ice Cold Vengeance

"I don't know who did that foul shit, but I heard that Rizz and his boys been having some beef with some Haitians," the man stated as he looked around to make sure no one saw who he was conversing with.

"What're their names, and where do they hang out at?" Matthews asked.

"I don't know. It's like they just popped out of nowhere. But my peoples told me they got some banging smack," the dope fiend responded.

"Give me a call when you hear anything else," Matthews stated and gave the man his card with a folded twenty-dollar bill underneath it.

The man took the card and slithered away with only one thought on his mind: *I hope the dope man got some good shit right now.*

"It ain't hard to tell what happened; a turf war. And our little friend Rizz just got the bad end of the stick. We find the Haitians, and this case is one for the books," Kowalski said, pulling away from the curb.

While Kowalski was busy talking about how he had pulled over a beautiful woman and slowly searched her, Matthews was deep in thought. He had a strange feeling that Ice was somewhere close by. He knew just who to talk to find out where the murdering asshole might be holed up at.

CHAPTER TWENTY-SEVEN

"No, it wasn't like that. He was just letting me know the police were sitting up the street watching the block," a woman in her early thirties pleaded, stating her case.

"Bitch, whatcha think; I got a flower pot for a head or something? You don't think I haven't been watching your stank ass for the last couple of days?" Cherrish responded as he viciously brought a couple of steel clothes hangers that were twisted together down on the girl's bare back.

"Ahhhhh! Please! I swear the only other time he ever spoke to me was when he said something about how hot my outfit looked on me!" the woman who went by the street name Kiwi yelled out as hard metal met soft, venerable flesh.

Cherrish had already planned how he had intended to punish Kiwi, so he had rubbed the clothes hangers with raw garlic and then soaked them in olive oil for a few days.

"Swisssssh!"

The homemade "pimp regulator" flew through the air and found its mark once again on its victim's already bruised shoulders.

"I should kill your motherfucking ass! But instead, I'm gonna dismiss you like the trash you are," Cherrish flatly stated. He then threw the weapon on the bed, grabbed his imported gold silk shirt off the chair and wiped down his sweaty chest after the light workout—if you could call it that.

Kiwi looked up at Cherrish, not believing what she was hearing. It was one thing for a whore to leave her pimp for any number of reasons, but it was a totally different ballgame when the pimp threw one of his girls out of his stable. In a situation like that, the particular female would be considered a suspected savage and an unmanageable whore in the underworld skin trade. Well-established pimps and young pimps moving up the ranks would be wary of such a questionable girl.

Ice Cold Vengeance

Kiwi knew very that well she deserved the brutal fifteen minute lashing for the unauthorized conversation with another known pimp. Every girl knew from day one that the number one rule was never, under any circumstances talk with another pimp for any reason. One guy from Chi-Town went as far as to slice his girl's tongue down the middle for such a violation. "If your ass was covered in flames and a pimp was standing a few feet away sipping on ice water, bitch, I rather you burn your motherfucking titties off then to talk to him," Cherrish would say to the newly acquired girls.

"Baby, don't do me like this. I'll make it up to you. Just give me one more chance," Kiwi begged, already forgetting the intense pain in her blood stained back.

"What could a five dollar, project, cum face bitch ever do for a nigga like me, huh?" Cherrish spat back as he lit up a cigarette.

"No, I wasn't saying that I ever could. Remember how you said I could have a few days off to visit my grandmother who's dying? Well, I could call my sister and tell her that something came up. Then I could try and get that girl you been after for a while," Kiwi quickly replied while crawling towards her man on her hands and knees. She then began rubbing his leg up and down in an affectionate manner.

It was true. Cherrish had been trying to bag some stuck up waitress for over a month now, with very little progress. *"You seem like a nice person, but right now I'm not interested in dating anyone at this moment in my life. I have just enough time for my studies, work and my son,"* she would say, turning him down like he was just another nigga trying to pick her up. Cherrish wanted the waitress because she had this quiet, reserved, sweet persona about herself that the paying customers would just eat up. The banging body didn't hurt either.

"Okay, you got exactly one week to get shorty up in this apartment, and then I'll decide what to do with you," he said as he flicked the ashes from his cigarette on top of the still nude woman's head.

"Don't worry. I'll get that bitch up in here even if I have to drag her by her fucking weave!" Kiwi responded, happy that she was being given a second chance by one of the most sought after pimps in Queens.

To everybody's surprise, Jack began hacking away at Rizz's genitals, leaving a sickening bloody wound. The tortured victim was already dead when Jack placed the man's privates on a piece of plastic he found lying around. He then went outside and threw the ripped out flesh over the fence to the dog next door. The Doberman pinscher sniffed at the strange meat and pushed it around with its long black nose before finally gobbling down its unsuspecting, tasty late night snack.

******

"And another thing. He got all this money now, and all he gave you was a hundred thousand and a few pieces of jewelry he didn't want. What's up with that?" Lite's girlfriend asked, still talking in hushed tones.

"He said we gotta flip the rest of the dough, and then keep flipping it so we could make bigger and legitimate moves. You know we can't be getting all this bread without the government starting to ask certain questions. That's how we took that fall before," Lite responded, not really believing the game himself that he was trying to throw at his girl.

Even in Miami Jack controlled most of the money, with the rest of the crew riding around with ill whips and flossing with platinum jewelry. They gave the appearance of having major paper, but when shit got thick most of them couldn't even afford private attorneys, much less money to bail themselves out of jail.

Along with Haitian Jack, Lite and his woman were one of the few people that the Feds failed to snatch up during their city-wide, joint effort pre-dawn raids. The way shit was going down in New York right now with Rizz's money and all the dope, Lite found himself back in the same position as before.

"Y'all two finish counting that loot yet?" Jack asked as he took a swig of Barbancourt 5-Star Haitian rum.

Jack had sent for a couple of young guys from the old neighborhood who looked up to him. Their job was to help run the drug business from the motel that was flowing more steadily now that Rizz was out the picture. They were all in Jack's hotel room playing Caribbean stud poker while Lite and Carmen counted the money from the past couple days' drug proceeds. The room was filled with Hydro smoke as the young men puffed away on their blunts and gambled.

"Come on, let's wrap this game up. I'm tired of whipping up on y'alls' little asses. Let's finish packing up the product," Jack said as he grabbed a pile of money from the middle of the table.

Haitian Jack wanted to make sure that when his little wild soldiers came up from Miami to New York that they enjoyed themselves before putting in that work. When the young guys touched down on the "Rotten Apple", he already had something set up for them in their motel room. Two thick identical twin sisters known throughout the neighborhood as the "Onion Twins" were already in the room. They were lying comfortably on the bed, and smoking some potent weed while dressed only in their panties and bra. Even though the sisters were certified dope fiends, they were still pretty and had asses that would make most grown men cry. The Onion Twins did things to those boys that would make the ancient whores of Babylon blush.

But now it was back to business. Soon both of the Miami guys were in the room next door serving fiend after fiend and raking in that dough. They had bundles of crack rocks, cocaine packages, and that powerful scag (heroin).

"Ain't it about that time to hit the club?" Jack asked as he put the stacks of money already in rubber bands into a brown shopping bag.

"Come on, girl. Let's make tracks. I got shit to do myself," Lite said, watching Carmen roll her eyes up at Jack who missed the millisecond movement.

Forty-five minutes later, Lite and his woman were cruising towards the strip club in their brand new triple silver Lexus LX 570 SUV.

"Why the fuck I gotta still be dancing when we got all this money?" Carmen angrily asked. She wished that she could have taken back the "we" because in all actuality, Jack was the one who had all the loot, and they had spent more than half of their money on the new ride, and the rest on some new clothes.

"You work at the perfect spot to hear what's going on. Plus, we don't know what Rizz's right-hand man might be up to. He might be trying to take that nigga's place and get rid of us in the

CHAPTER TWENTY-NINE

"What's up? You're not working at the group home anymore? I can't keep covering for you," Trina's cousin said, visibly upset.

"To be honest with you, I can't survive on the chump change they were throwing at me," Trina responded while putting lipstick on in the bathroom mirror.

"So, are you quitting or what?" Lilly asked.

"Duh! What do you think?" came the sarcastic remark.

"Well when you first came to live here, you promised me that you would stay on the straight and narrow, that's why I looked out for you," Lilly responded.

"I appreciate it, but I'm not gonna be kissing your ass every time you mention that you helped me out. Plus, I just couldn't take another day with those lames at the job," Trina spat back, growing annoyed with the boring exchange.

"Okay, do what you want. Just don't get my little sister mixed up with your street bullshit," Lilly roughly said while walking back towards her room.

"Oh don't worry. I'll make sure she stays as pure as an angel!" Trina yelled and rolled her eyes as she walked down the steps.

"What was all that about?" Jenise asked her.

"Oh, nothing. Only that your sister wants everybody to be just as broke as she is," Trina said.

"Fuck that shit! I didn't come to New York to walk around with only lint in my pockets. I wanna get paid just like you," the girl replied, remembering how Trina was pulling out wads of cash and buying her anything she wanted.

Soon both cousins were in the car and on their way to meet with Born's brother Cherrish. Trina still didn't know how she was going to play out her hand, but she was determined to end up with a Royal Flush.

A little while later the women were walking up to the whorehouse. A state of the art surveillance camera followed their every move.

"This is Trina. I'm supposed to meet Cherrish tonight," she said after a voice asked, "Who you here to see?" from a glossy black intercom box by the front door.

"Oh, hi Trina. I see you brought us a friend," Heaven, the mixed transvestite who ran the business said while looking both women up and down.

"This is just my peoples. So, how you been?" Trina asked, trying to get more familiar with the lady-boy. *"You can never tell when someone might come in handy,"* she would always say. She took a good look at the thin, exotic looking Heaven who was wearing another long, hand painted silk kimono that was open slightly. He had on a La Perla push-up lace bra that barely covered his small, chemically induced breasts.

"He's waiting for you down the hall and up the steps. Follow me," Heaven stated as he waved to a couple of customers who were waiting for the specific girl they ordered.

The trio walked up the stairs on the plush, imported red carpet that led to the luxury rooms that were reserved only for VIP guests or the high paying tricks.

"He's in there. Just go right in," Heaven stated before he rushed off to tend to a client who was dropping by any moment.

The first thing Trina noticed was a large Bradford solid mahogany pool table with leather drop pockets sitting in the middle of the floor. The man they were there to meet was sitting in a dark brown leather swivel chair behind a desk, and looking intensely at an Apple laptop.

"Come on in ladies. Take your coats off and have a seat. Can I get you anything?" Cherrish asked as he expertly scanned both women's bodies while they took their jackets off.

Jenise had on a Saran wrap, super tight winter sky-blue satin Memoir one-piece body suit that outlined the picture perfect shape of her puffy vagina lips. The Garnier high-shine lip-gloss went perfectly with her fresh out-of-town sweet looking face.

Trina rocked a simple short skirt, a white blouse with the wide Russian collar, and a pair of black leather Matti Rousa boots.

"We'll have whatever you recommend," Trina said, taking a seat.

"Here you two pretty women go. Let me guess. You're Trina, right?" their host said, giving each of them a glass of dark cognac.

"Yeah, how did you know?" Trina said playing along.

"I have a sense about these things," Cherrish said as he sat down on the desk in front of the girls.

Trina quickly scoped out Cherrish's style. He looked nothing like his brother, being that he was high-yellow with his long hair in a neat ponytail. Even though he had on a slightly baggy button-down shirt, she could tell that he worked out on a regular basis. If she had to say anything bad about him, it would be the scar that he had stretching from his earlobe down to his neck. But she thought it gave the man a more dangerous air about himself, which was a plus in her book. The white diamond and 18-karat solid gold rose-colored Calibre de Cartier watch adorned one of the man's wrist. The other wrist held a customized matching Cartier love bracelet that wasn't missed by Trina's always scheming eyes.

"So what's your name?" Cherrish asked Jenise.

"I'm Jenise. Is this your place? I like it," she said as she looked around his office that had Nino Madia custom made furniture throughout the room.

"It's all right. It keeps the rain off my head," the man replied, showing even white teeth before he took a sip of his own drink. "So Trina, what is it that you wanted to see me about?" he asked, looking at Trina because he knew that she was the one of the two women making all the decisions.

"I don't know what Born told you, but I'm about that paper," she flatly stated.

"You know Born's not saying much these days after his run-in with the cops. You're about paper, I'm about paper. So, what are you prepared to bring to the table?" Cherrish asked, liking what he saw in front of him.

"I feel you, but can I holler at you in private?" Trina said, cutting her eyes sideways at Jenise as if to say she didn't want her to hear what she had to say.

Cherrish has been around some of the foulest people— men and especially women—to know that Trina was up to no good when it came to her girlfriend. "Yeah, no problem. Hey Jenise, you can watch anything you want. This will only take a minute," he said as

134

he pressed a button on a fancy looking remote control, causing a panel to slide open revealing a wide screen plasma TV.

Thanks," Jenise replied, taking the device from his manicured fingertips.

A couple seconds later a rap video flooded the screen with some Atlanta rap artists performing at a pool party. They were surrounded by big booty females all trying to throw their asses at the camera thinking that the only thing they needed was a fatty to become a star.

Trina and Cherrish walked out in the hallway where a young woman was just saying to a well-satisfied customer that she would see him again in a couple of days. "Hi, Cherrish. I didn't know you were here tonight," the woman said, tip-toeing over to him and giving him a little kiss on the cheek. She then gave Trina the hood once over.

"Baby girl, you know how I do. Anyway, get back to the room and straighten it up a little bit. I'll be by in a while to kick it with you." He gave her a playful slap on her butt. Once the girl was back in her room he said in a devilish voice, "Whisper is one of my best girls. She licks everything from elbows to assholes. Her specialty is the Anal Rain Dance." The pimp smirked to himself knowing that he had something for everybody up in his spot.

"Well anyway, that's my cousin in the room. She just hit New York, and we wanna make that paper no matter what it takes," Trina explained.

"Okay, I feel you. She definitely has super star potential, but what's that got to do with you?" Cherrish asked, still trying to find out Trina's angle.

"Think of me as a broker. I seal the deals and get a percentage. I'm working on a couple more bad chicks right now to throw up in here," she smoothly replied, acting as if she had it like that.

Cherrish was about to say, "Bitch! When I have to depend on a pale-skinned white slut to help replenish my stable, it's time to call it quits!" But he kept his anger in check and said, "Okay, maybe we could work something out for now. I got this client who's dropping by in a little while. He's been asking for a fresh new face, and your girl here definitely fits the bill. If your cousin throws her legs

around a newborn baby's neck if they thought it would fatten their pockets. *"That's street life for you!"* he thought as he sank the 8-ball in the corner pocket.

A short time later Jenise was sitting in one of the deluxe rooms, steadily drinking her cognac.

"Oh, they didn't lie. You are a new one. How old are you, sweetheart?" a middle-aged white man asked when he walked into the room, grinning like he had just hit the jackpot.

"I'm twenty one," she answered.

"Well, ain't you gonna invite me to sit down?" he asked, walking over and sitting down on the bed anyway.

"Some fucking businessman!" Jenise thought as she checked out his cheap brown suit that was so wrinkled it looked like he just finished waking up from sleeping on a park bench.

"So, what's your name, darling?" the trick asked, putting his arm around the tensed up girl.

Throwing out the first name that came to her mind because she didn't want the creep to know her real name, she responded, "Umm, Jazmine."

"Oh, I see you have an accent. A country girl. I know you probably had your share of rolls in the hay," the man said, and laughed out loud spraying Jenise with sour spit.

Jenise gulped down the last of her strong drink and started getting undressed. She wanted to get the act over with as quickly as possible.

The man with a twisted sense of reality took this as a sign that the pretty young woman found him irresistible. He quickly began taking off his wash-and-wear suit, all the while never taking the stupid grin off his red face.

In less than a minute the excited man was humping away on Jenise. She had her eyes wide open staring at the mirrored ceiling trying to think of anything else but this loser who smelled like Old Spice deodorant and musky sweat.

"I know you like this. It feels good doesn't it? Talk back to me," the man was busy saying between gasps of air.

Jenise just ignored the man who now began to run his tongue up and down her neck, bringing a cold shiver down her spine. As he roughly groped her breasts, she just kept thinking what kind of car she was going to buy in less than a month, with the help of her favorite cousin.

Without warning, the man with Jack Daniels breath tried to kiss her on the lips as he gave one good loud grunt like a pig that was being stuck for a Sunday dinner. "Oh God, that was good!" he said, not bothering to take his heavy weight off the girl.

Jenise pushed him to the side, grabbed her clothes and went straight to the bathroom. When she came back out the bathroom fully dressed the man was putting his tie in his pocket. "I wanna see you again, and maybe…" He was steadily running his mouth while the only thought on Jenise's mind was getting another stiff drink, or maybe another hit of coke.

******

Meanwhile, Cherrish watched the entire episode through a monitor that was connected to a hidden camera in the room. "I got to admit, shorty got a banging body. Almost flawless," he said to himself, taking a drag of his cigarette. Now that he knows how Trina operates, she could actually be of some use to him. She was no joke in the looks department, and he planned on having her ass tooted in the air in no time also.

CHAPTER THIRTY

"Damn, look at you! How many drinks I gotta buy you to be alone with you butt ass naked?" a short, stocky man asked as he stepped in front of Miss Latin.

"If you would'a stepped to me like a real man ought to instead of like an asshole, you might have gotten some play," she barked, towering over the rude customer in her high heels.

"Oh, you think just because you got niggas throwing dollars at you all night, you can talk to anybody anyway you want? Fuck that! I ain't the one!" the man shot back, feeling as if he was being insulted by nothing more than a hooker who happens to be working as a stripper for now.

"If you got problems at home, I suggest you take shit up with your woman... or man by the looks of you. You really don't know who you fucking with," Miss Latin coldly replied, turning her back on the man like he was a bothersome insect.

"Don't you turn your fucking back on me!" the outraged customer shouted as he attempted to grab the woman's arm.

"Come on, playboy. You don't wanna get kicked out for no bullshit," Ice said, watching the much shorter man for any signs of aggression that he might try and throw his way.

Ice had seen too many times in the ghetto when a couple was having a physical or verbal altercation, somebody wanted to intervene, not knowing all the details. Most of the time if it was a somewhat pretty girl being screamed at or slapped around, a guy would quickly come to her defense. That specific guy wouldn't come to the woman's aid because they had so-called high moral standards; they did it because they hoped the woman in distress would be grateful for the help and give him a piece of thank you pussy later on. Sometimes the knight in shining armor routine worked, and other times the rescuer would get stabbed in the stomach and end up with a shit bag for the rest of his life. When he was asked how he ended up with a colostomy bag, he would have no choice but to say that he got it over trying to snatch up somebody else's girl.

Ice Cold Vengeance

Ice had to be careful, because the last thing an angry man wanted to hear was advice from another guy when having a heated verbal exchange with a female. He really wouldn't give a fuck if the man stomped the bitch's throat to jelly, because he was all about business. And business, which meant money, came before anything else.

"Why you all up in mines when I'm about to check this hoe?" the customer said, trying to stare the much taller man down.

Ice had two choices: Either he set it off on the man who was obviously suffering from a Napoleon complex and draw attention to himself inside of a crowded club; or he could throw out some game to keep things quiet and simple. "I'm not trying to be in your business, I'm just trying to handle mine. I gave shorty some dough to suck me off earlier on, and I just wanna get mine before she gets all upset and shit," he whispered in the man's ear.

"Okay, do you. Just let the bitch know next time she better watch her mouth," the irate customer said before walking off.

"What did you say to him?" Miss Latin asked, her curiosity getting the best of her when she walked over to Ice a minute later.

"I told him that I knew you for a while, and that you were just trying to stack paper like the next bitch without all the drama. If you had drama, then he had beef with me," Ice told her, gassing the story up in his favor.

"He's still an asshole. Oh, I remember you," she stated after getting a good look at Ice's face in the light.

"I think you gave me a dance or we talked; something like that," Ice said, playing it off like he vaguely remembered her.

Most beautiful women were used to lusting men remembering them, and when he wasn't sure if he knew her, it threw her off a little.

"So why would you wanna step up and be on some peaceful shit?" she asked, trying to figure the stranger out.

"If you knew me, you would know that I'm nowhere near some loving, stop the violence movement. My sister dances too. She has three kids and a fucked up baby's daddy who don't do shit. Sometimes she would go to work stressed the fuck out, and the last thing she wants is to get into it with other chicks or niggas who don't know how to act. I just thought you might have needed a break

141

too," he told her while looking into her eyes like he meant every word. But he was laughing on the inside at how quickly he came up with the bogus story.

Miss Latin felt everything that Ice had kicked to her. She didn't want to be in a dark strip club dealing with S.I.M.P.S. who thought they were balling with their weekly paychecks in their pockets. She was still upset with Lite for letting Haitian Jack direct whether she should be stripping or not. She wasn't in Foxxy Sista for more than half an hour, and already some cornball lame gave her a migraine headache with his bullshit. "You right. I wasn't ready for no shit tonight. Anyway, you want a lap dance? We could go into the VIP section and I'll only charge you the regular price. I really don't want to be around crowds right now," she replied, and walked away so Ice could follow her.

Ice and Miss Latin ended up in the dark VIP room that was lit with a soft, dark blue light bulb, giving a soothing effect. There were two other couples in the room. The men swore on God's word that they were getting their mack on.

The gentleman closest to Ice had on a crème-colored blazer with a pair of matching slacks, and a pair of shiny Solomon Brothers, Now-n-Later colored gators. One of his hands was tightly clutching a bottle of warm Moët champagne, while the other one was fondling the stripper's breasts.

The dark skinned stripper was sitting on the man's lap facing him while grinding to Chris Brown "These hoes ain't loyal" song" She turned her head towards Ice and Miss Latin when they entered the room. Ice automatically felt the air in the room stiffen up when both women's eyes locked on each other. The woman sitting on the guy's lap whispered something in his ear, and they both looked at Miss Latin and broke out in a hearty laugh.

"What was all that about?" Ice curiously asked.

"She's a nobody. She's just some jealous bitch who's always watching my pockets. What she should be doing is worrying about that shit on her lip that she claims is a cold sore. She calls herself Nutmeg, probably because of all the nuts she takes in her mouth," Miss Latin said loudly, hoping the woman in question heard her.

"Fuck her! She looks likes she swallows babies," Ice added, siding with the woman to get on her good side.

Females working in strip clubs, as well as in other establishments where women worked always had some petty beef going on amongst themselves. Sometimes the drama had something to do with another woman hating on someone for as little as the outfit they might have had on that particular day.

"I forgot to get something to drink. You want anything?" Ice asked.

"I feel like some vodka."

Ice left the room and came back with a bottle of Grey Goose Vodka, two glasses filled with a few ice cubes, and a small plastic bottle of cranberry juice.

"So, you ready for that dance or what?" Miss Latin asked Ice after downing her drink.

"Maybe a little later on. Let's talk for a minute," Ice replied, trying to act like a friend.

They talked about regular things such as, "How did you start dancing? Where are you from?" to which Miss Latin gave vague answers.

"You seem like you have a lot on your mind. What's up?" Ice finally asked, looking a chink in her armor.

"Well, my man is letting another nigga tell him what to do, which is causing problems between us," the woman replied, speaking from the heart.

"That's fucked up. He acts like you don't have a mind of your own or something. It's obvious that you're very intelligent," he said while looking intensely into her eyes once again.

"I am, but he don't want to listen to me. He only listens to his boy, and that's some real bullshit!" the stripper stated, her voice taking on a colder tone.

They talked some more about her problems before Ice said, "Would he mind if I take you out after work one night? For a quick bite, that's all," he added.

Miss Latin stared at him for a minute, thinking, *"He's real nice, not to mention cute as hell. Plus, I could tell he don't take no bullshit from anyone."* "He don't have to know. All we're going to be doing is getting a late night snack," she said, trying to convince herself that was all that was going to go down.

"Okay, I can work with that. How about I come check you out on Saturday?" Ice asked.

"That's cool. Well, it was nice talking to you. Let me get back to work," the dancer said as she got up preparing to leave.

He watched her walk to the door, with her firm ass bouncing up and down. She turned around and gave him a gleaming smile before finally leaving.

Ice was back in the Infiniti and smoking a Newport. He was feeling tipsy after knocking out the bottle of frosted Goose with Miss Latin. He made it back to the apartment still thinking about how good the woman looked in her glittery silver bikini outfit with the sheer sarong wrapped around her thin waist. The ill tattoo down her lower back made him want to fuck even more, but business came first.

The apartment was quiet, but he knew that Chyna was home because her jacket was thrown across the arm of the sofa. He got undressed and walked to her bedroom in his boxer shorts to see if she was indeed home.

Chyna was sleeping with the covers pulled down around her waist, revealing one of the thin nighties she often pranced around in. Without even knowing what he was doing, Ice slowly and quietly crawled into the bed with his childhood friend. Just looking at her sleeping so peacefully and smelling like a fresh bar of pink Dove soap caused him to become the man of steel. He snuggled up against the sleeping girl and put his arms around her.

"Ice, is that you? What are you doing?" Chyna asked groggily when she woke up and looked over at her longtime friend.

"I didn't feel like being on the couch tonight," he responded.

"Okay, whatever," she said, and turned back over.

Seconds later he began slowly rubbing his hand up and down her thigh while pressing himself up against her warm body even more. When he discovered that she wasn't wearing any panties, his dick almost busted out of its skin. The throbbing head of his penis lightly touched the entrance of the girl's vagina.

Then Chyna hoarsely whispered, "Ice, no. We're friends. I think you should go back to the living room."

"Come on, Chyna. You don't walk around in them short skirts for nothing," he responded as he glided himself into the girl's deepest depths.

She unconvincingly tried to scoot forward, but he grabbed her hips and pulled her back towards his swollen-beyond-capacity penis. Once he started kissing on her neck, Chyna lost it and began throwing the ass back at him like he owned it.

Ice pumped the pussy so good that it began making slurping, sloshy sounds. He didn't want to fuck up the moment by flipping her over and putting her in all kinds of gymnastic positions that the women often went crazy for. "I'm about to cum!" he whispered, not wanting to bust off in his good friend.

"No! No! Stay in me! I'm about to cum again!" Chyna quickly responded as she reached behind her and grabbed Ice's thigh in an attempt to keep him from pulling out.

Ice couldn't hold back any longer as he shot stream after stream of semen into the waiting pussy that absorbed every drop.

For the first time in Ice's life he held on to a girl after cumming instead of making up an excuse to leave, or just bouncing without saying anything at all. They slept together, enjoying each other's company in total silence.

CHAPTER THIRTY-ONE

"Damn! The old lady was raped and then stabbed to death," Detective Matthews stated in a sickening voice. He and his partner were sitting in a booth at a small but busy café in Queens, going through the medical examiner's reports. "Mr. Robert Jenkins didn't have sexual intercourse with her on the day they were killed as somebody wanted us to believe. So now we know that there had to be at least one other person in Rizz's grandparents' house the night they were murdered," Matthews added before taking a sip of his strong black coffee.

"So what did the M.E. say about the grandson?" Kowalski asked and lit up a Marlboro cigarette and ignoring the many No Smoking Allowed signs that were posted throughout the eating establishment.

"Nothing really, except that his bloodstream was polluted with crack cocaine and all kinds of intoxicants before he was tortured to death. They list the cause of death due to massive blood loss and shock," Matthews flatly stated.

"That's no fucking surprise. Ouch!" Kowalski responded, grabbing his own crotch. It would be a long time before the bloody image of Rizz was to even slightly fade from his memory.

"At least we do know that the last place Rizz was seen alive was at that strip club, Foxxy Sista on 109th Avenue. I put the word in the streets to the snitches that there's something in it for them if they cough up information on who Rizz was hanging out with on the night he was murdered," Matthews stated, as he gulped down the last of his bitter coffee.

"I know that spot. I busted some crusty-ass black bitches who used to dance outta there, if you could call it that," Kowalski replied with a hearty laugh and forgetting once again that his partner was African American also.

Before another word could be spoken between the two detectives, Kowalski's police radio went off. "Okay thanks. I appreciate it. And tell the little lady I said hi." To his partner he said,

"Come on. They just found out Rizz's last place of residency," he stated while mashing his cigarette on his half-eaten bagel before getting up.

Soon both men were pulling up to Rizz's luxury apartment building. They quickly located the apartment manager who turned out to be an elderly Jewish man with taped up glasses holding the frames together.

"You two sure you're policemen?" the manager asked while looking at Matthews suspiciously.

Matthews knew the man really meant him only because all he saw was the black skin and not the professional air of authority he carried about himself.

"To protect and serve!" Matthews said, pulling his suit jacket to the side and showing his detective's shield and holstered firearm.

"You wanna see mine too?" Kowalski jokingly asked.

The old man just ignored him and asked," What do y'all want?"

They told him that they needed to get into apartment 5C that a Mrs. Vicky Bromwell had a lease to. The detectives followed the man back into his cluttered office, and he went through some grayish metal filing cabinets. "Here it is; Mrs. Vicky Bromwell. I liked her. She paid rent for a full year in advance," the manager stated, not bothering to say that he received an extra five thousand dollars for his troubles.

"We know that Rizz couldn't get an apartment in a building like this without a little help. He's probably got a friend or relative with good credit," Kowalski said to his partner.

The three men took the elevator to the fifth floor and were soon at the late Rizz's apartment door.

"Open it," Matthews ordered the manager who held on to a special laser coded key that opened all the apartment doors in the building. As soon as the key touched the lock, it opened slightly. Both detectives drew their weapons, and Kowalski pushed the door open wider.

"Who's gonna pay for this mess and clean it up?" the manager shouted after he saw the apartment looking as if a Category-3 hurricane had hit it.

"Shut the fuck up and stand back!" Matthews said in a stern voice, putting the man in his place.

"Kitchen, clear; dining room, clear; bedroom, clear... etc.," both officers said to each other as they methodically searched each room to make sure that no one was hiding in the apartment.

"We know these weren't any ordinary burglars. You see some of this high tech shit they left untouched?" the white cop, Kowalski said while picking up a sterling silver and platinum-trimmed computerized champagne bucket.

"Yeah, they definitely didn't want this crap. They were after bigger things," Matthews replied. Both men knew that bigger things meant cash and dope.

After hours of searching the apartment and not finding anything useful, Kowalski said," You think we should have the guys come down and dust for prints?"

"Hell no! This guy probably had everybody up in here showing off. By the time we chase down and question every person that had prints up in here, the captain would have already had us directing traffic somewhere in Harlem," Matthews said, speaking the truth.

"You're right. Let's go. We'll radio to have some uniforms secure the place," Kowalski stated as he fingered the small expensive digital camera in his pocket that he found in the dead man's bedroom.

CHAPTER THIRTY-TWO

"Nah, motherfucker. You gots to wash up first. I don't know what that white shit around your dick is," Kiwi firmly stated as she intensely stared at the man's genitals in disgust.

Kiwi was standing in the middle of a room in a cheap, rundown but convenient hotel located in a nondescript part of Queens. She was wearing only a pair of skimpy baby-blue satin panties.

The man who ran the seedy, three story dusty hotel charged rooms by the hour. He received a small cut from the local street walkers when they came in with a horney customer. All he ever got was a dried up five dollar bill from each hooker who brought their tricks up for a quick sex session. Five dollars wasn't a big deal to the women, but on the busy weekends the small change eventually added up to something worthwhile. Taylor, as the many girls who frequented the spot called him, swelled his pockets even more by selling glow-in-the-dark condoms, half pints of cheap liquor, and all kinds of deviant sex toys, if that was your thing. Basically, he could come up with anything or anybody at a moment's notice if the money was right. He once even sold an inflatable Tiger Woods sex doll to a freakish Long Island soccer mom. Everything went down at the hotel.

"Oh, that's nothing. It's just a little dick cheese. I told you I just finish coming off a double shift," the man explained while grabbing the starchy corner of his bus uniform shirt and attempting to wipe away the foul smelling, whitish bacteria that had obviously accumulated over a long period of time.

"I don't give a fuck what you call that nasty looking shit or how long you been working! If you want this here pussy, you gots to come correct!" Kiwi spat back as she twisted her nose up in pure disgust. She then walked to the bathroom and returned momentarily with a soapy washcloth. She rudely threw the cloth to the unhygienic bus driver and watched him closely to make sure he completed his task. "Come on, I don't have all night. Let me do it," the woman said as she walked over and snatched the washcloth from the man's hand. She then bent down and grabbed the smiling man's limp, three-inch penis. She pulled his foreskin all the way back and began expertly wiping the foul smelling organ down.

Seconds later the man was fully aroused. His now stiffened erect penis was at its maximum of five inches.

Kiwi was so into trying to clean up the diseased looking dick while holding her breath that she didn't notice the trick's eyes rolling to the back of his head as his breathing became more and more intense.

"You straight now, big boy. Let's—"

But before Kiwi could finish her sentence, the bus driver shuddered and ejaculated his pent up load like he didn't have a care in the world. Hot sticky semen caught the surprised woman flush in the face, causing a large dew sized drop to splatter in her eye. "What the hell!" Kiwi yelled as she jumped up and wiped her face with the back of her hand. She then ran into the bathroom and splashed handfuls of cold water on her face. Kiwi knew that she couldn't be mad because that was part of the game. When dealing with horny total strangers, anything was expected. She then walked back into the room and began getting dressed.

"Whatcha getting dressed for? We ain't done yet," the man said as he sat naked on the edge of the bed while stroking his penis into hardness again.

"It's a wrap, nigga, unless you want to go at it again for another hundred," the business-minded woman coldly stated as she slid her pale-pink J-Lo miniskirt up around her slender waist.

"Hell no! I'm not paying you another goddamn penny. I didn't hit you off so that you could jerk me off and then bounce," the man spat out, growing visibly upset.

"Like I said before, when you bust that nut, it's over. It's not my fault that you couldn't hold your own and skeeted so early," Kiwi threw out.

The cold hard truth hit the man like sharpened daggers. "All I have is sixty left. Can we do something with that?" he asked, his voice now taking on a softer tone.

Kiwi thought that she could quickly get the man off with a mouth shot, then decided against it when she spotted a couple of oversized lint balls dangling from the man's hairy nut sack. "Nah, playboy. I gotta holler at another client right now. I'll catch you another time," she replied with an air of professionalism as she put on her shoes and grabbed her purse.

Kiwi was soon back on the block, with her five-foot eight, slender but well-stacked frame trying to get that dollar for her man, Cherrish. She knew that no matter how much money she brought back he would still be mad at her for the stunt she pulled a week ago. The only way she could ease the pressure of his relentless wrath was to turn out that waitress over at the club for him. Kiwi was still thinking of the best way she could go about it as she climbed into a shiny black Ford Explorer for another "date."

CHAPTER THIRTY-THREE

Haitian Jack, Lite, Carmen, and two of the new young boys from Miami were having a late night meeting at the house that Jack had rented. The house was starting to shape up since Jack had given Lite's woman a stack of cash and told her to go shopping for some new furniture. She hated taking any type of orders from the man whom she so despised, but the house did need some new shit.

"Why we gotta live here with him? We got some money. Let's get our own place so we could have some privacy sometimes," Carmen complained while brushing her long, jet-black hair in a gold lighted oval mirror. The mirror was part of an expensive bedroom set they had just purchased.

"Now's not the right time," was all that Lite had to say, trying to change the sticky subject.

"Pussy!" Carmen whispered so low that even she couldn't hear her remark.

Lite knew how she felt, because he wanted a place of their own too. But he didn't want Jack thinking that he was going against him after all he had done for him.

******

"If you was on your game, you wouldn't be going through this type of shit," Jack stated when meeting Lite for the first time.

Lite was standing around various pieces of cheap furniture that was put out by the marshals after he had gotten evicted. He was staying in the projects and slinging fat dime bags of Hydro and crack on the side. He thought he was doing all right for himself pushing a brand new platinum colored Honda Accord with peanut butter interior and chromed-out rims. He also had a sizable chunk of cash stashed away for a rainy day. He always made sure he stayed dipped up in the wears department and wore eye-catching jewelry to complete the baller effect.

152

Ice Cold Vengeance

Miami's special narcotics unit had raided Lite's apartment early one morning, taking him down to the county jail in his boxer shorts and house slippers. He repeatedly called his place for his girl to come bail him out, but to no avail. Lite finally said, "Fuck it!" and begged his mom to put her house up for the bail bondsman. When he did finally touch the streets again, all his jewelry, money, and even his clothes were gone, along with his girl.

To make the situation even more fucked up was that he got evicted 72 hours later due to a clause in his lease that clearly stated: "Any tenant selling or possessing any narcotics, or engaging in any type of illegal activities will be evicted within 72 hours."

"It's all good, but what it got to do with you?" Lite asked, watching Jack sitting behind a fire engine red 500 SL convertible Benz and smirking behind a pair of burgundy-tinted Louis Vuitton shades.

"Nothing... and maybe a lot. You wanna get on some real shit, then give me a shout out," Haitian Jack replied, and handed the man his number. He then peeled off while drinking a bottle of frosty Cristal champagne in the middle of the hot afternoon.

Just like Haitian Jack knew he would, Lite called him two days later. In even less time than that, Lite was pumping crack out of a dope house that Jack had on lock down. The crib was rundown and leaning to the side, but it beat stressing everybody else to let you chill at their place for a while. Lite said, "Fuck bitches for now!" and he just steadily stacked that paper like it was going out of circulation or something.

Jack always preached loyalty and dedication above everything else. He saw that Lite had both by throwing him a little test. Jack had hit Lite off with some product purposely throwing in a couple extra ounces of the cooked up cocaine. Lite had knocked the work out; plus the added dope and gave Jack back every dollar.

After a while Jack put his new protégé in charge of two crack houses which eventually put Lite back on his feet. Lite was shining once again, and more than ever before.

To this day he wasn't really sure if his main girl was the one who ratted him out to the Special Narcotics Unit just to have him knocked out the picture. But one thing he was sure of, was that she was the one who stole all his shit. And to add insult to injury the sheisty bitch was seen riding around in his Accord with some dude while he was on lock down.

Lite had seen that same episode play itself out countless times around the way. A female would meet some guy who made her cum so many times with his extraordinary pipe game, or just ate the pussy so damn good that she'd flip on her most loyal long-time friend just to keep him around. Yeah, a good piece of dick will have most women's heads spinning like in the "Exorcist". Or maybe his so-called girl just saw the perfect opportunity for her to get paid when Lite got arrested. In the hood, grimy ass females often got down like that, thinking that they'll never ever see the guy again. But sometimes that line of reasoning could prove to be a fatal miscalculation because they never realize that it is indeed a small world.

******

"So, what's up with them niggas on the block? They coming correct or what?" Jack asked his street soldiers.

"Fuck them shook ass New York niggas! They scared to death. They banging our shit out like they was giving it away or something," one of the guys with a thick mix of Florida and Haitian accent replied.

"Them dudes even said, 'Fuck Rizz! He was soft anyway'," the other youth threw out while passing his friend a rolled up blunt.

"Y'all stay on them dudes. This is just the beginning. Soon I'll have this town on lock for real," Haitian Jack stated, pumping his chest out while fingering Rizz's dinner plate size diamond-encrusted medallion that he took the night Rizz was murdered.

After Rizz's unfortunate and mind altering demise, Jack had sent word through the street grapevine to Rizz's get-money hood soldiers that he hasn't any beef with any of them. If they still wanted to make money it was cool, only this time around they would be only pushing Haitian Jack's product. Jack made it clear that the offer was non-negotiable, because they'd end up in worse shape than Rizz.

Almost all of them said yes with the street reasoning: "Okay, our boss, Rizz is now lying cold on a fucking zinc slab in the morgue. We'll pour some drinks out to his memory, but we still gotta eat and take care of home." The low guys on Rizz's totem pole weren't about to go to war with some crazy out-of-towners. They just wanted to keep their pockets fat, stay dipped up, and fuck bitches. Yeah, loyalty was often forgotten like yesterday's breaking news story.

"Hey, Lite, you heard anything about that bitch, Universal?" Jack asked, making sure he had all the bases covered.

"Nah, nobody heard anything. He might not even be in town anymore after hearing about what happened to his man. He's probably thinking that he was next," Lite replied with no trace of emotion.

Later on, Lite was in the Lex truck with the smooth, kitten-soft leather interior, talking to his woman. "Fuck the club tonight. Let's me and you do something tonight," he said while rubbing Carmen's leg. They were just riding around, talking about their future plans.

"I think I should work tonight," she replied.

"Whatcha talking about? Just the other day you was kicking on how much you hate dancing. Now all of a sudden you have a change of heart. What, you fucking with somebody up in there?" he asked suspiciously.

"Come on, Lite. Don't even come at me like that. You know these corny ass New York cats can't even come close to you. I'm starting to hear people talking about that nigga, Rizz. You know how them bitches are always running off at the lip. I just don't want nothing to happen to my baby," she said in a girlish voice and then gave her man a passionate kiss.

"Yeah, okay. But I'll be by to pick you up when shit closes down!"

"That's cool. And I'll try and find out if Universal is still around. Don't forget to come by and scoop me up," Carmen said while grabbing her bag and jumping out the luxury SUV after Lite pulled up in front of Foxxy Sista.

No more than ten minutes later inside of the strip club, Carmen a.k.a. Miss Latin spotted Ice over by the bar. He was leaning over the counter talking to the waitress.

"Yeah, we could swing something, but you seem like the type of guy who's always busy running around with a lot of different women," the waitress said, trying not to say the wrong thing and run Ice off.

"But a cute female like you, I'll find the time," Ice was saying as the waitress handed him a free mixed drink.

"Gimme your number, 'cause I only work here two nights a week," the waitress said, feeling good that someone looking like Ice was interested in her. She just knew she looked irresistible with her new reddish-pink Strawberry Shortcake, long horse weave.

Miss Latin walked over to Ice, tapped him on the shoulder and said, "Hey, meet me outside in about five minutes." Once she saw that he knew who she was, she pushed her way through the crowd and headed out the front door.

"I gotta go make some moves. I'll catch you another time," Ice said, dismissing the waitress who already had her cell phone out ready for the number.

Ice made it outside and quickly scanned both sides of the street. He knew that the foul ass stripper most likely had something to do with Rizz getting bodied, which he didn't mind, but he really wanted to get the job done himself. He didn't know what Miss Latin had planned, so he stayed on point for whatever.

"Ice, I'm over here! Come on!" he heard a female voice yell.

He walked over to the woman who was standing up the block in front of an old storefront church. "I thought you said you wanted to hang out when you got off," he said as he looked around for any cars that might be creeping.

"I didn't feel like being up in there tonight. I told you to meet me outside 'cause I didn't want them nosy ass bitches at work to start talking shit," she explained. She really didn't care what her co-workers thought. She wanted to kick it with Ice tonight after work, until her man got on some other shit, talking about swinging by to pick her up when she finished dancing.

"I feel you," Ice responded, satisfied with her answer.

They were soon peeling off in Ice's Infiniti listening to Nicki Minaj latest hot single.

Ice looked at the woman sitting next to him. She was wearing a simple pair of tight blue jeans, a pair of crisp white K-Swish sneakers, and a form-fitting baby-blue Von Dutch sweater that showed off her diamond belly ring. He knew that she was used to getting real money because she didn't mention how much she liked the car like other chicken heads often did when first getting in nice ride. "So, whatcha wanna do?" he asked, lighting up a Newport.

"Whatever you feel like," she answered while changing the track on the CD.

"I know this spot I think you'll like," Ice said.

They ended up in a spot that was located in Hempstead Long Island. It was a fairly decent pool hall. The crowd was equally mixed with Latino, white and black people just enjoying their Saturday night out. Ice ordered a pool table, and was soon racking up the balls for a game of 8-Ball.

A short time later, a short, smiling, freckled faced white girl came over to their table and took their order.

Ice and Miss Latin ate from a food platter that had held jumbo shrimp, spicy hot wings with blue cheese dressing, along with some cheese jalapeño sticks. They also sipped on some frosty Heinekens. They played pool, ate, and talked like they were long lost high school friends.

"Miss Latin, you wanna go play some air hockey?" Ice asked, placing the pool stick back in the rack on the wall.

"I don't want to hear that Miss Latin shit tonight. Call me Carmen, okay?" she said in a good-natured tone of voice.

They played air hockey, some videos games, and ordered stronger drinks the second go around.

Carmen was having such a good time being with Ice that she forgot about the time. "I got to be back to Foxxy Sista," she said as she finished the last of her drink.

"What, your man got your on lock or something?" Ice asked, wanting to get on the subject of the guy she was fucking with.

"Well, you know how niggas be tripping once you give them a little taste. They think they have a pink slip to the pussy or something," she said, throwing the obvious hint at Ice full force.

Sticking to his game plan, Ice brushed off the subliminal sexual comment, fucking with the woman's mind even more.

******

There were three men walking behind Ice and Carmen in the parking lot who had just come out the pool hall.

"How the fuck did a skinny motherfucker like that bag a bad bitch like her?" a guy asked his friend.

"I'd sell my soul to get a piece of that ass," the friend responded, slapping the first guy on the back.

Ice heard their remarks, but decided to chill this time.

"Hey! Hey you! Is that your sister or what?" one of the guys yelled out to Ice.

"What, you wanna say something to me?" Ice asked, turning around.

"A girl that fine can't be your woman," the guy replied with a snicker.

"What's it to you?" Ice asked, his temper getting hotter by the second.

"Hey, shorty, why don't you give my man your number?" the other guy said, acting like Ice was invisible.

Before another word could be spoken, Ice whipped out his gun and hit the closest guy to him.

"Whap!"

The cold hard steel struck the man's temple, and he fell and rolled halfway under a parked car.

Pointing his weapon sideways, Ice said to the guy who was talking the most shit, "Don't move, pussy! Now, what were you were saying?"

"I was just playing! Please! Just let us go!" the guy begged while shaking like a lost kitten in a blizzard.

"Okay, tough guy. So now you wanna go home, is that it?" Ice asked after grabbing the scared out of his mind guy by the shirt.

His other friend had already taken off, running wildly and zigzagging back and forth, thinking that he was about to get a bullet in the back. He didn't care that he left his two life-long friends behind.

"I'm sorry! Please, give me another chance!" the man said with tears the size of watermelon seeds building up in his eyes.

"Damn, nigga! You sure are coward ass motherfucker. I'ma let you go," Ice said, still pointing the gun at his frightened victim.

"Thank you! Thank you!"

"But first, you gonna apologize to this woman right here," Ice said. He was beginning to have some fun now.

Ice Cold Vengeance

"I'm sorry!" the guy pleaded with his tears flowing freely now.

"Fuck that! Get on your motherfucking knees and say it like you mean it, or your mother's gonna have a closed casket funeral!" Ice spat out, deadly serious in his threat as he held the gun up to the man's forehead. He was already wanted for the death of a New York City police officer—not to mention having a few other bodies under his belt—so what difference would it make if he sent another loser to hell?

The man weakly got on his hands and knees and started whimpering like a pitiful, sick puppy that's been brutalized too many times.

Carmen just stood there smiling and motionless. She was enjoying the show that was for her benefit.

"Okay, now get the fuck outta here! You make me sick to my stomach!" Ice said, kicking the guy in the face with a heavy Beef and Broccoli Timberland boot.

"Aaah!" the man screamed out in pain as he clutched his shattered nose bone and ran off wailing like a deranged old woman.

Once they were back in the car, Ice calmly lit up a cigarette like nothing ever even happened.

Carmen just stared at him, feeling his gangster swag. The way he rocked his black Yankee fitted cap to the side, along with his overconfident attitude the entire night, made the Latina firecracker moist between the legs. The woman wanted him so badly that she could barely control herself as she bit down on her bottom lip thinking about how good the man's dick would feel right about now. But time was of the essence, and she didn't want to start something they couldn't finish. *"When the time comes, I'ma show this New York nigga on how us Miami bitches make the sheets gushy,"* the dancer thought as she lit up her own Newport.

"So, when you wanna hook up again?" she asked while gazing over at Ice as they neared the strip club. The next time she saw him, she was going to have him put her in more positions than the ancient Indian sex book "Kama Sutra".

"Here's my number, and we'll talk about it," Ice responded in a "whatever" manner.

She took his number and climbed out the Infiniti a block away from Foxxy Sista.

Ice then slowly drove by the club as the woman ran inside. He knew that she would be playing if off like she's been there the entire night, as women who creep often do. He also knew that he had her mind, and now all he had to do was throw some dick up in that fat ass to find out where Rizz's loot was stashed at.

CHAPTER THIRTY-FOUR

"I know you took my fucking money! How could you? You know I was saving up to buy a house!" Lilly screamed while standing in the doorway of Trina's room.

"I said, I don't know nothing about no missing money," Trina replied in a low voice as she flipped through a hair magazine.

"So how the fuck can you afford all this new shit after you quit the job you begged me to get for you? Huh? Answer that!" the angry woman shouted while walking closer to her back stabbing cousin.

"I'm making moves. I don't need your little stash that you probably been saving for ten years," Trina responded with her head still down, looking at the pictures.

"I helped you out when you had no other place to go, and now you're here talking this slick shit to me! If I don't have my seven thousand dollars on my dresser by the weekend, I'm calling the police and you're getting the fuck outta my house!" she clearly stated.

"I don't need you accusing me of something I didn't do. What you need to do is interrogate that lame ass nigga you always taking out. From the looks of him, he might be on the ya-yo," Trina shot back as she stood up and snatched her jacket off the bed.

Just before Trina drove off, Lilly yelled, "And the rental car company called and said that if you don't bring their car back or pay for another week, they're reporting it stolen!"

Trina just stuck up her middle finger and skidded off into the night. "I don't have to take that shit from that square ass, uptight bitch. Maybe next time she'll put her shit in the fucking bank," she said, talking to herself. She wanted Jenise to roll with her, but the girl was knocked out from putting in work at Cherrish's whorehouse. Once her little cousin had fucked her first trick, it was all downhill after that.

******

"Jenise, I don't mean to get on some other shit with you, but I need to ask you for a very important favor. Two of Cherrish's best

161

girls got involved in some other shit and got their asses locked up in Vegas. Cherrish is trying to get their dumb asses out, but it doesn't look good right now," Trina said as they sat in the car a couple of days later after Jenise had fucked her first trick.

"What's that got to do with me?" Jenise asked, wondering what was coming next.

"Cherrish has some important big wigs coming through who always carry mad credit cards with them. One even got the unlimited Black Card I heard. We just need you to keep them busy while we do our thing," Trina explained to her.

"Why can't some other bitch keep them busy? Why me?" Jenise asked, her mind already made up that she wasn't waiting in another bedroom for some horny, hot breath stranger who would be trying to grope her all night.

"To be honest with you, them other females can't even come close to you. You remember how when we first stepped on the set? Those guys' eyes lit up like Christmas lights when you walked by. Cherrish told me that they all wanted to know who you were and how much would it cost to spend a little time with you," Trina said, speaking really fast. "When Cherrish told them you didn't get down like that and you were here as his guest, one customer said he'd spend a thousand dollars on you right now," she continued, sprinkling as much sugar on the bullshit as humanly possible.

"Word? A thousand dollars just to chill with me?" Jenise asked, her dimwitted eyes opening wide.

"That's nothing. I know niggas who'll pay you twice that much for a quickie," Trina said, knowing that she had her cousin's full attention now.

"How long will I have to do it for?" Jenise innocently asked.

Trina grinned and said, "Not long. You know I got your back."

******

Trina drove up to the weed spot, but she changed her mind, thinking that she needed something much stronger after arguing with Lilly.

She parked on a dark side street after copping her drugs and sniffed up two bags of nose candy. She was feeling good as an inner warmth began taking over her whole body. Yeah, she was a regular snow blower now.

Right now she wanted a strong, heavy dick to help put out the fire, but she didn't want to be bothered with the bar scene. She envisioned Cherrish fucking her over his expensive pool table while he yanked her hair, but she knew that the pimp would give her more than just a nut. He'd most likely try and give her a room just like Jenise's.

Trina found herself pulling up to Cory's house and parking in front just like the last time. As the horny white girl walked up the walkway she noticed a brand new pecan-colored Jaguar sitting on twenty inch chrome Glacier rims that gleamed in the moonlight. *"Don't tell me he got a bitch with a little paper up in there,"* she thought to herself. But she knocked on the door anyway. After the third knock she heard a rusted chain being lifted off its latch.

"Yeah, who are you? Whatcha want?" a man in his early fifties asked while looking Trina up and down like she was from some alien world.

"Hi. I'm here to see Cory. Is he home?" Trina asked in her best, "I'm just a friend".

"I'm his father. What the fuck did he do now? Whatever he got himself into this time, you can fucking keep him. He's in the kitchen," the man coldly stated as he took a long swig out of a half-empty bottle of cheap Wild Irish Rose wine that can only be found in black neighborhoods.

Trina walked into the living room as Cory's father called out, "Cory, get your ass out here! Somebody here to see you!"

Trina spotted a dime-store picture of Jesus on the wall, hanging by a nail. Jesus was a white man with long, blond flowing hair, and had a pair of sad blue eyes looking towards the heavens for forgiveness of men's sins. His pale white hands were clasped together in prayer. She had been in many homes both black and white and saw all kinds of pictures of Jesus Christ. The one thing that stuck in her mind the most was that in every black family home, they either had a picture of Jesus as a white man or as a black man with nappy hair. But in every white home, including hers, you would, without a doubt, always see a Caucasian Jesus. It would be a miracle if a white family was to have a portrait of a black Jesus on their wall for all to see.

"Trina! What's up? Come on in the back," the young man said when he saw the woman.

Trina walked behind him and was momentarily startled when she was another guy leaning against the rusted stove, smoking a cigarette.

"This is my man, Universal," Cory said before grabbing a seat and looking through a stack of music CD's.

"This your girl, Cory? I hope she got a sister," Universal said with a wide smile as he openly admired the white girl's voluptuous body.

"I don't have a sister, but I got some cute friends who like to party," Trina quickly responded, knowing that the guy was feeling her. She knew he had money by his flashy jewelry that sparkled every time the light hit it at certain angle. *"Damn! I know I know this dude from somewhere,"* she thought, trying to place the face while peeping his diamond platinum chain with a heavy piece of the virgin Madonna attached to it.

After about twenty minutes of talking and listening to some mixed CD's that Cory had made, Universal said, "Yo, Cory we gotta roll out. You know what we gotta do."

As soon as the man made that statement, it clicked in Trina's mind where she knew him from. He was the guy from Club Raven's who had all the local hood rats sweating him like he was a celebrity or something, including Trina. "I gotta make a few runs myself," she lied, disappointed that they were leaving so soon. At first she wanted the guy to leave so she and Cory could be alone again, but now she wanted to talk to his friend a little more to find out exactly what he was into.

******

"So who was that white girl?" Universal asked Cory while they were speeding down the street.

"Just some lady who works at the group home where I used to be at," Cory answered.

"I know you hit that. Can a nigga live to?" Universal asked, wanting to lay some heavy dick to the thick white girl.

"Whatever. So, you spoke to your peoples or what?" Cory asked, getting down to business and not really impressed with Trina's antics.

"Yeah. I spoke to my cousin already. He said he got some shit cooking up that's gonna have all of us living lovely," Universal replied, giving his boy a pound.

"That's what I'm talking about! We can't let niggas take food outta our mouths," Cory said, eagerly wanting to get into the mix of things with Universal so that he could start raking in the real money. He didn't really care that Rizz got murdered or who did it, as long as he got his foot in the door of what was once the illest crew in Queens.

CHAPTER THIRTY-FIVE

Kiwi walked into Liquid Neon nightclub wearing a ultra-black short dress with scalloped shoulder straps, and a pair of red leather wrap-around high heel shoes. She had her hair done in a stylish French twist as she tried to maneuver her way through the thick hot musty crowd.

"Shorty, what's up? Can I buy you a drink or something?" a guy with a drenched, sweaty neck asked when he stepped in front of the fast moving Kiwi.

"I don't have the time right now. Maybe some other night," she replied, automatically sizing the man up to see if he was a trick in the making.

Being the money making whore that she was, Kiwi quickly thought on how long it would take for her to get him twisted and have the mark spend his hard earned cash on her. She and the other girls working the streets knew there was money to be snatched up in the clubs in Queens, but most of the time it turned out to be a time consuming gamble. You could meet a guy who offers you a drink, or dance while you innocently play the, "I don't go home with strangers" routine, while at the same time acting like your pussy is on fire and he's the only one who extinguish it.

The men in around-the-way clubs could sometimes be hard to read with so many wanna be ballers acting like they were stacking major chips. They would wear their best clothes, some expensive cologne and floss with a variety array of eye catching jewelry that wasn't even fully paid for yet. The hooker might spend most of the night with that one particular guy trying to make up for a slow night, only to find out later that his whole act was one big front.

On more than one occasion Kiwi had peeped a few guys walking around the dance floor all night, fronting with the same hot bottle of Cristal and knowing that they spent their last dollar but still hoping to attract a quick fuck.

Ice Cold Vengeance

Then, you had the lower class cornball niggas who had just enough money to enter the club and maybe buy a drink or two for the entire night.

So, basically it took too much time to establish who was who when time was a luxury. A majority of the girls out to get that quick paper stuck to the streets because they knew exactly what to expect when they were approached by the trick looking for some no questions asked pussy.

"Okay, then bless me with your number and maybe we could kick it another time," the persistent guy stated, grabbing Kiwi by the arm when she attempted to go around him.

"I told you, I'm in a motherfucking hurry. If you can't accept that, I suggest you put an H on your chest and handle it!" Kiwi spat out as she shook his hand loose.

"Bitch, you ain't a dime piece, you just a nickel outta the projects!" he shouted over the loud club music as he watched Kiwi walk away. *"Damn! I should have cooled out and stepped to shorty a little later on. I know I could have fucked her once I got a couple of drinks up in her,"* The guy thought to himself as he hungrily looked at the woman's meaty thighs that the split in the short skirt failed to conceal.

Club Liquid Neon used to be an old warehouse built in the sixties. It had been expensively renovated to be one of the hottest spots in the city. There were three spacious levels of dance floors catering to whatever type of music suited your taste that night. You had your choice of Hip-Hop, R & B, Reggae and contemporary Latin music. To get to each floor you had to go up a wide winding staircase that had early Davacee Italian marble steps that led to a different floor. There were plush leather lounge sofas with lighted candles on the tables in front of them. If you wanted to be close to the dance floor, you could sit at one of the many round, highly glossed mahogany tables to enjoy your drinks on.

Kiwi made it to the second floor and scanned the crowded room. She was searching for the girl that Cherrish seemed so intent on having join his team. She had to laugh to herself. If Cherrish ever heard her say that he was sweating a potential whore, there would be hell to pay. As punishment for that remark, Cherrish would, without a doubt, probably shave Kiwi's head completely bald and make her work the block in the daytime to humiliate her even further.

Kiwi went over and sat down on one of the leather couches. She crossed her legs, showing off her large butterfly tattoo on her well-formed thigh. She knew that she would never spot the girl in the sea of party goers. It also would be a waste of time asking any of the other women if they knew her, because there were so many employees that came and went unnoticed.

"How you doing, Miss? Why you all by yourself in the corner looking so sad? What, did you and your man get into it or something?" a guy asked as he took an uninvited seat next to Kiwi.

She turned to face the man who was clean-cut, somewhere in his mid-twenties, and had a medium build. She thought he was all right, but a lame by his corny, unimaginative approach. "I'm just chilling. And for the record, I don't have a man," she said with a smile.

The guy's face lit up at Kiwi's response. He thought that it was obvious that the attractive woman was feeling him. "My name is Shameek. What's yours?" he asked, sliding a little closer to the woman and getting a whiff of her feminine odor.

"I'm Kiwi. Nice to meet you," she responded, looking past him. She was still trying to find the girl she came here to see. She roughly cleared her throat, which caused the man to ask what's wrong.

"My mouth a little dry from walking up all those steps," she answered.

"Don't worry, I got you. What you drinking?" the anxious man quickly asked.

"Let me get a Long Island Ice Tea in a highball glass." Kiwi wouldn't normally let a guy—much less a stranger—go off by himself and bring back a drink, giving him the opportunity to pop a Molly in her glass for some easy, unrestrained pussy in the bathroom, or in a darkened corner. She had been in the ruthless streets long enough to know that was just how some guys got down in dirty. She'd had drugged a drink or two in her day.

Shameek rushed back at a record breaking time with a drink in each hand. He secretly prayed that beautiful woman hadn't left with some other guy while he was at the busy bar. He breathed a sigh of relief when he spotted Kiwi still sitting there, smoking a cigarette while waiting for his return.

The man talked on endlessly. He mindlessly chitchatted about his job, and how every bitch up in the club acted like a stuck up whore; nothing like the refined Kiwi... or so he thought.

Kiwi merely just answered no or yes questions while wishing she could have gassed this nigga for a bottle of Remy Martin.

On her third Newport she finally spotted the girl she'd been looking for. She was bringing drinks to a group of men and women at their table. Kiwi quickly threw her half-smoked cigarette into an empty glass and began walking toward the female she had been waiting over a boring hour for.

"What happened? Where you going? I'll get another drink for you if you want," the disappointed man called out as he watched Kiwi's shapely form disappear through the crowd. Shameek never in his life had a conversation with a woman of Kiwi's caliber. He had planned to show her off to his co-workers at his sanitation job so the guys would get off his back for dating fat, ugly chicks.

Kiwi watched the girl's movements as she approached the waitress. She was thinking, *"This bitch ain't all that. I'll have this bitch laid up in Cherrish's place in no time. I'll probably get her to eat my pussy too!"*

CHAPTER THIRTY-SIX

"Hi! How you doing? You remember me?" Kiwi asked as she stood by the bar in the club.

The woman studied Kiwi's face for a moment and then said, "Didn't you come up in here once or twice with that light skinned guy who keeps trying to push up on me? What is he, your cousin or something?" she asked while waiting for another order of drinks.

"Yeah, something like that," Kiwi responded. This time she took a really good look at the woman. The waitress had that rare, blemish-free dark skin that any skin care company would gladly pay her to be their official spokesperson. She had on a pair of stylish Prada frames, but you could still see her chinky eyes. The waitress gave off the aura that she would be down with her man for whatever. Now Kiwi fully understood why Cherrish wanted this girl so badly. "Anyway, my peoples call me Kiwi," she said while waving away a guy who was trying to start a conversation with her.

"Well, Kiwi, what can I do for you?" the waitress curiously asked.

"My cousin's been feeling you for a minute, and he thought that maybe you had the wrong impression about him or something," Kiwi stated, trying to sound as real as possible.

"What, you his agent or something?" she replied with a little humor, and then said, "I'm just playing. He seems like cool person, but like I told him before, all I have enough time for is studying and working here at this spot. Plus, I heard from a couple of girls that he's supposed to be some kind of pimp." She then took her tray full of drinks and walked off.

About twenty minutes later the waitress came back to the bar as Kiwi was sipping on another drink. "I'm sorry, but it's crazy hectic up in here. Is there anything else I can do for you?" she asked, placing another order with the bartender.

Ice Cold Vengeance

"All that pimp shit, that's just jealous ass niggas talking sideways 'cause they're not secure about their game or themselves," Kiwi explained in her most sincere voice. "I don't really care if he's a pimp or not. I'm not really interested. I gotta go. It was nice meeting you," the attractive waitress said. As she walked off leaving Kiwi just standing there, she received a few lustful stares from the patrons.

Kiwi went back outside of the club and made a phone call. "It's me, Kiwi. No, I don't have time for that right now. Remember that favor you owe me? Well, it's time to come correct. Fuck everything else! I'll be in front of Liquid Neon. I'll explain everything when you get here," she said, and ended her phone call and waited for the excitement to begin.

******

It was 4:30 a.m., and Kiwi sat across from Club Liquid Neon in an old, long-nosed Cadillac with tinted windows, just waiting.

The other two occupants in the car were growing restless. One of them asked, "Where's the bitch at? You sure she didn't leave?"

Kiwi just ignored the question and kept her eyes focused on the front door. The club officially closed at 4, but a few last minute stragglers were slowly exiting, not really wanting to go home. There she go," she stated to no one in particular with a little excitement in her voice as the pointed to two women walking down the block, laughing.

"Which one?" the short, stocky guy asked, puffing on a Kools cigarette that was already down to the butt.

"The dark skin one wearing the glasses. Hurry up before they leave," Kiwi said, still keeping her eyes glued on the pair.

The shady looking men quickly got out the car and headed towards the unsuspecting women.

"It's no problem. I can drop you off," one girl said.

"Are you sure? I don't—"

Before she could finish her statement, a rough voice barked, "Don't you bitches move or I'll put one in you!"

171

The tall, slim man had jammed an old .22 revolver gun with a taped up handle into one of the women's ribs. The shorter man grabbed the other girl in a dope fiend chokehold and slowly increased the pressure.

"Whatcha want?" the other woman asked while backing up against the brick wall.

"What the fuck you think I want?" the taller man with bad acne scars spat out as he ripped off the girl's small, diamond heart-shaped pendant.

Meanwhile, the other woman had slumped to the pavement after the oxygen to her brain had been cut off from the choke hold.

"Here! Take my purse!" the girl said through tearful eyes as she held her Arturo Chang bag out for robber to take.

The shorter thief stepped over his fallen victim and snatched the bag from her hand.

"That's not all we want either," the taller man said with his eyes and voice taking on a whole new meaning.

Before the girl could utter another word, she found herself in the same chokehold her friend had succumbed to seconds earlier.

The short guy started slowly dragging her towards the dark parking lot as his partner stuck his hand under her shirt, finding a firm breast.

Just as the would-be attacker ripped away the struggling girl's French lace underwear, a car jumped the sidewalk with its high beams on and the horn blaring. Kiwi jumped out of the car yelling and swinging a blue steel baseball bat. "What the fuck you crack heads think you gonna do with her?" she screamed, catching one of the men in the arm with the bat.

The attacker then let go of the crying woman, grabbed his bruised arm and backed away from the out of control Kiwi.

"Get the fuck outta here before I smash your fucking heads like a rotten eggshell!" Kiwi shouted, swinging the weapon again at the taller man causing him to slip and fall into his partner in crime. "Come on, get in!" she shouted at the woman who was too stunned to even react.

When the terrified girl saw the two would be rapists regain their balance, she practically dove into the waiting vehicle.

Ice Cold Vengeance

As Kiwi was speeding off the woman said, "No! We got to go back! My friend is still back there!"

"Don't worry. I saw a couple of bouncers running up. They'll make sure she's all right," Kiwi said.

"They were gonna rape me! Them niggas tried to rape me!" the shocked waitress breathlessly said over and over again.

"Luckily I saw what was going down. Don't sweat it. You all right now," Kiwi replied sympathetically as she rubbed the girl's back. Inside she was laughing her head off because her devious little plan had went down just like clockwork.

After fifteen minutes of driving the girl asked, "Where are you going? I want to go home and forget about everything."

"Hell no! You can't go back to your spot. Them dope fiends got your address and your house keys. What do you think their first move's gonna be? They gonna try to snatch up a TV or DVD player as soon as possible," the fast talking Kiwi stated while driving closer to her place.

"So what we gonna do?" the confused girl asked.

"I say we chill at my place tonight and then we change your locks in the morning," Kiwi replied, pulling up in front of a brick house in Queens Village, better known as "Shady Ville" because the neighborhood residents had the infamous reputation of always trying to get over on each other.

Once the two women were safely inside the comfortable looking neat house, Kiwi asked "So, what's your name again?"

"I'm Chyna," she responded, still trying to come to grips of what almost happened to her.

"Well, Chyna, I think a long hot shower will do you good," Kiwi said, and handed the still trembling woman two fluffy towels and a brand new set of Victoria's Secret satin pajamas that still had the sales tag attached to the garment.

"I appreciate everything you did for me, but why are you helping me since I've been so rude to you tonight?" Chyna asked after coming out the steam-filled bathroom with one of the towels wrapped around her head.

"I'd help even my worst enemy in a situation like that. I was sexually assaulted before by my stepfather, so I know how it could fuck up a female's mind. I didn't think you was rude; I respect a strong-willed woman who speaks her mind," Kiwi, who was now wearing a short red terrycloth robe, answered, speaking 98% of the truth. "But fuck all this depressing talk! You want a drink to help you relax a little?" she asked.

"Yeah, I'll take some Henny if you got some," Chyna replied as she looked at the different movies that were on demand. Yeah, she definitely needed something strong in her system right about now.

Minutes later both women were sitting on the bed, sipping on Hennessy Black with a splash of vanilla Coke and watching a Jamie Foxx movie. Unknown to the now trusting Chyna, Kiwi had slipped her a pink special-K tablet, known in the hood as the "get over drug" for guys who wanted quick pussy without all the hassle of spitting game all night long.

It didn't take long for Chyna to be laid out on the bed; her body totally immobile.

Kiwi knew it was her duty to call Cherrish right away, but she felt that she deserved some kind of release. Looking at Chyna and smelling her fresh-scented body, she just couldn't help herself. She never considered herself a lesbian, but a woman this fine doesn't come along too often. She carefully and delicately took off the pajamas set as if she was painting a Michelangelo masterpiece. She sucked and caressed the woman's full dark breasts, savoring every inch and causing Chyna to slightly moan. Kiwi then traced her tongue down the girl's stomach and stopped to passionately kiss her belly button.

"Nah, I gonna front. This pussy smells too good." Kiwi thought as she went straight for Chyna's hot box, licking and sucking with the ferociousness that a hungry alley cat might have over a bowl of warm milk.

Chyna's legs involuntary spread a little farther apart as her sticky, musky pussy juices started to flow more freely. Her clitoris soon popped out of its hiding place as Kiwi's moist lips did their job while her thumb messaged and prodded the girls quivering velvet-soft asshole. Kiwi always came prepared. She poured some coconut seed massage oil on her fingers and slipped them inside Chyna's virgin bung hole. She momentarily took a break while Chyna's face revealed that she had cum enough times and didn't want to pass out from dehydration. Kiwi gave the woman enough time to recuperate before she placed Chyna in a different position and attacked her fire hot box from every direction.

The next morning as Kiwi lay next to the smiling and very much satisfied Chyna, she thought of a way that she could have this beautiful heart-stopping woman for herself. But for now she was going to play along with Cherrish to see how everything fell into place.

CHAPTER THIRTY-SEVEN

"So, how the hell did you ever got hooked with Cherrish in the first place?" Trina asked while sipping on a glass of Lucky Knights liquor which consisted of strong cognac with a splash of vodka in it.

"I was tricking with this big ass biker type of guy, you know, the ones with all the crossbones and dagger tattoos. Well anyway, when he found out that I had the same thing between my legs as he did, and 'my friend' happened to be bigger than his, I guess he lost his goddamn mind," Heaven said, gulping down his own drink.

Trina and Heaven were in the VIP lounge at the whorehouse, just kicking it. Trina, being the person that she was, was steadily scheming and trying to pry information out of the talkative Heaven. Trina was hoping to flip an angle in her favor on Cherrish's skin operation. "Word?" she said, pretending fake concern.

"Before I knew it, the biker snatched out some kind of heavy steel chain and started whupping my ass. I had to admit that he would have killed me if Cherrish didn't step up. I really don't know what happened after that 'cause I was kinda fucked up in the game. But later on I found out through the streets that the so-called biker bad-boy couldn't eat solid food for three weeks after Cherrish finished with his punk ass," Heaven continued, and then tossed a peppered sparrow's egg into his mouth.

"I didn't know he could get gully like that," Trina stated, trying to keep the conversation flowing.

"He had a couple of his girls take me to one of his old spots he had before. He looked out for me, and I've had his back ever since," Heaven stated, meaning every word.

Trina, having been around every sort of person imaginable, both black and white, knew that everyone, no matter what they told themselves in the mirror, would set up their own mother if properly gassed up. Heaven was on the "Cherrish, I owe you my life" tip. That's how the most successful pimps kept most of their women working the longest. They always appear in the picture when the girl was the most venerable, either physically or mentally. It could consist of a place to stay for a while until they got their mind right, a good hot meal, or just a friend to talk with over their family problems. It was up to the pimp to find that niche, which wasn't hard to do.

In most situations you could find out what a girl's going through after the first couple of minutes of talking. People, no matter what their gender, have the tendency of letting things off their chest. Most times it's with complete strangers because they know they won't be judged as quickly as their friends would when spilling their most intimate secrets.

In Heaven's case, Cherrish was his savior from the brutal biker's attack. It will be just a matter of time and patience when Trina would find out on how she could get into Heaven's head for her own benefit.

******

At the same time while Trina was having her little get together with the transvestite, Cherrish was smoothly talking to his newest girl in his most charming voice. "I like your style. When first meeting you I could tell that you're a very intelligent young lady who has that special way when dealing with people," the pimp stated.

"That's true, but why I gotta keep spreading my legs for every guy that walks through the door?" Jenise asked while yawning. She was dead tired after a busy night of throwing the ass in the air for the overly-eager customers.

"I told you, I'm short on women and you're just doing this temporary until they get back."

"When do you think they'll be getting out?" the gullible woman asked.

"Any day now. Any day. You see, somebody with your looks and smarts don't need to be dealing with drunk motherfuckers every night. You have too much going on for yourself to be getting down like that," Cherrish said with fake sincerity.

"Whatcha mean?" Trina's cousin innocently asked.

"Well, I didn't want to say anything until I set everything in motion, but I want you to run this house for me while I work on some other things," Cherrish said with a bright smile.

"What about Heaven? Don't she—I mean *he* runs things right now?"

"That queer freak motherfucker's been fucking up lately. I need someone like you who's on top of their game. So, what's up?" he asked, acting like he couldn't survive without her.

"Hell yeah! I can do whatever," Jenise said, full of enthusiasm and already imagining how everybody was going to be looking at her in a different way and giving her props she never had before.

Cherrish's tactic was always to make promises that he never intended to keep, and stringing the women along by giving them false hope. "Oh, in a couple of days I should have everything set in motion. Let's me and you go out and relax a little. You definitely deserve it for helping me out of my jam," the man said as he got up.

Cherrish left the smiling, on top off the world country girl on the bed. He left the room thinking that he would have Jenise on her back making money for him forever if it was left up to him. Yeah, she had a natural talent when it came to sucking the clients off. In a few months she had the potential to be more skillful then the porno star "Lethal Lips" who could tell exactly down to the last second how long it would take for a man to blow his heavy load.

Cherrish talked on his giant Galax S Plus Smartphone while heading back to his office. He punched in the code locking the door and pulled out some heroin that he kept in a hidden secret compartment under his desk. So far nobody suspected at he was a down-low dope fiend who spent thousands and thousands on the powerful drug every week. He tried his best to keep his addiction a secret, because people, especially the women, tend to look at you in a different light if they knew you were using. He had to keep the psychological edge on everything associated with the game.

Once the drug was racing through his system he drifted off to the past as he often did when he was high and feeling good.

******

"When is Dad coming back?" little Luis, now known as Cherrish would repeatedly ask his mother.

178

Ice Cold Vengeance

"You just keep quiet and eat you food. Let me worry about your father," his mother would respond as she placed her worn out feet in a steel bucket filled with warm water and Epsom salts.

The same scene would play itself again almost every night, with Mrs. Ramos arriving home to their tiny apartment above the fish market from her sixteen hour a day job at the clothing factory. The workers who toiled at the job every day compared it somewhat to a modern slave labor camp. The workers, who were all women, were allowed only three bathroom breaks each shift. If you took more than that, your pay was docked. If you came back to your work station a couple of minutes late after your twenty minute lunch break, your pay was docked. A third absence in a year was automatic termination even if you had the West Nile virus. To make sure these rules were strictly enforced were crude, leering men who patrolled the floors, similar to the Gestapo Secret Police in Nazi Germany.

Very often you would hear passionate moaning or pig-like grunting, depending on who was doing the talking, coming from one of the storage rooms. One of the floor patrollers would soon emerge followed by a factory worker minutes later, and everyone would automatically know that a deal had been make for that particular woman to have a half a day off for one reason or another. That occurrence was as common as inhaling the raw sewage smell that often dominated the air from clogged pipes that were a century-old.

Things had suddenly changed for the Ramos family when some of the women who felt they were being taken advantage of started making noise about organizing a union to protect their rights. Mrs. Ramos quickly became an active participant, remembering how she herself was propositioned daily to have her breaks extended if *"the situation was right"* so to speak. The owner, a rich white South African, quickly squashed all the union talk by promptly firing approximately ninety women who he knew could be easily replaced in a matter of days.

Luis and his little sister still asked when their father was coming back home, never suspecting that their hardworking mother had lost her job. She would go out early in the morning and arrive back home sometimes eight hours later saying that she didn't work a double shift because things were slow.

179

Very soon the meat started disappearing from the family's meals, leaving only a pot of beans and rice, and maybe a piece of fatback.

Luis knew something was definitely wrong when his mother started cooking only two meals a day with, Mrs. Ramos very often saying that she wasn't hungry. He knew she wanted her children to have a somewhat full belly even if it meant that she herself had to do without for a while.

"Ma, you home?" Luis called out after coming home from school one afternoon.

"Yeah, I'm in my room. Run down the block and see if Mrs. Sanchez got that for me. Thank you dear," she answered from her room.

Luis threw his books on the table and flew out the door feeling better that his mom seemed to be in a good mood. A half a block away he turned around because he remembered that Mrs. Sanchez had gone away for a few days. He knew this fact because he and her son were in the same home room together.

"Ma, I forgot to tell you, she won't be back until the day after tomorrow because—" he stopped mid-sentence when he saw Mr. Frutose the fish store owner coming out of his mother's bedroom, and tucking his soiled shirt into his pants.

"How you doing, Luis?" was all the man said, not bothering to look the young man in his eyes as he quickly existed the stifling hot apartment.

Later on that night, the family of three feasted on broiled sea bass covered in roasted hot peppers and with what seemed like a mountain of succulent scallops.

Months flew by, and it seemed as if Luis was running into a different man every other night.

"Oh, he's just checking out the leak" or "He just came by to see if we heard anything about your father," his mother would tell him, creating excuse after excuse and sometimes reusing the same ones because she forgot that it had already been told.

Luis wasn't no way as gullible as his mother made him out to be. The food, clothes, extra money and sometimes expensive kitchen appliances had to be coming from somewhere. With their father still

Ice Cold Vengeance

MIA and his mother's back up against the wall, he knew that she was trading sex for the things they needed.

"No, motherfucker! You think I'm some kind of crack head who you can throw five dollars at? You better give me the rest of my money!" Luis heard his Puerto Rican mother yell one night when he had just come in after playing basketball. Luckily his little sister was away, sleeping over at a friend's house.

"You're just a no good whore! When I first started fucking you, you held your own. Now your cunt smells worse than the spoiled fish I sell to the damn niggers!" a man's voice spat out in a degrading tone of voice.

"Fuck you! You wasn't saying that when your tongue was pounding my pussy like a fucking jackhammer!" Mrs. Ramos responded with a mocking laugh.

Mr. Frutose was just about to backhand the grinning woman when Luis burst into the bedroom and rushed the overweight man. Frutose's speed surprised the young teenager when strong hands gripped his throat.

Luis, who had been brought up in almost every poor neighborhood in the Bronx where crime ran rampant, snatched out his switchblade and put the sharpened weapon behind the man's ear. "Let me go, you nasty piece of shit before I poke out your mother fucking brains!" he shouted, meaning every word of his threat as the tip of the blade sank just a little deeper.

"Okay, okay. Just put down the knife, son, and I'll be on my way," the fish store owner calmly stated while releasing his grip.

"Shut the fuck up! How much does he owe you, Ma?" Luis asked, while still watching the man closely who outweighed him by at least a hundred and fifty pounds.

"What?" his mother asked, surprised at how quickly things got out of hand.

"I said, how much does this pig owe you?"

"He's supposed to give me thirty bucks. Plus he owes me a twenty spot from last week," his mother said, tightening the robe around herself.

Luis made the man slowly take out his fake leather wallet and count out fifty dollars. "Now get the fuck out my house! If you want to come back, make sure you come correct!" Luis coldly stated and pushed the man out the door.

Right after that incident, his mother felt no stronger love for a birth child than she felt for him. "I will always cherish the love I have for you," she had told her young teenage son.

Luis soon had his friends and young girls around the way call him "Cherrish" from now on out of respect for his mother.

Cherrish began handling his mother's business affairs, collecting the money from her tricks and making sure no harm came to her. He soon earned the reputation of being a person not to be fucked with. If anyone crossed him thinking that they could get over because of his age, it proved to be a costly mistake on that specific individual's part.

It didn't take long for his pockets to be fattened up. With Cherrish's sharp new wardrobe he attracted an entourage of pretty high school girls willing to give him their money at any cost. During that time he met a younger Born who he considered his brother by another mother and schooled him to the game.

CHAPTER THIRTY-EIGHT

The dark blue unmarked police car was speeding through the residential streets of Queens, heading towards its destination. Detective Matthews and his longtime partner Kowalski had gotten a call about a possible homicide that might be connected to couple of cases they were working on. The sedan quickly came to a screeching halt and the detectives jumped out. A modest house located on the back streets of Liberty Ave was crawling with cops milling around and curious neighbors talking loudly amongst themselves.

"l hope that this is not another false alarm," Matthews stated as he walked under the yellow police caution tape. "Who's the primary on the scene?" he asked two uniformed police officers.

One of the red faced cops was about to question Matthews' authority until Kowalski walked up and stood next to his black partner.

"That would be Detective Wallace over by the front door," the cop answered in a polite tone of voice.

"I'm Kowalski, and this is Matthews. What have we got here?" Kowalski asked Detective Wallace when they approached him.

"We got a female DOA in the basement that we think might be that nurse, Rhonda Coleman who was abducted from Hands of Mercy Hospital by escapee... let me see. Oh! Nathanial Wilson a.k.a. Ice," Wallace stated after flipping over his overused note pad.

"What do you mean that it might be her? We have pictures of her and Ice posted in every stationhouse in the city. You couldn't do a visual ID from the picture?" Kowalski asked.

"We got her purse with her work ID card and her driver's license, but trying to identify the victim from a visual perspective is a different story altogether. Come on, I'll show you what I mean," Wallace replied with a slight smugness to his demeanor.

The three men started to enter the house when they were stopped. "Hold on. I think you might need one of these. Hey, somebody bring me over two more face masks!" Wallace called out.

A short, stocky female police officer ran over and handed the light-blue surgical masks to the detectives. Once the masks were firmly secured to all the men, they walked inside the death house. Seconds within the confined space, Matthews and Kowalski were hit with the unmistakable powerful stench of a decomposing body and rotting flesh. Wallace led the two detectives through the kitchen where there were other cops examining the crime scene, along with other departmental personnel.

"She's right there on the steps," Wallace said, stepping aside so the men could walk past him.

The detectives looked at the foul smelling corpse for a few seconds and walked back up the steps.

"Jesus! What the fuck happened to her face?" Matthews asked, not believing what he just saw.

What was once the nurse's face was now a deep bloody crater crawling with thousands of maggots, making the scene even more horrific. One eye was chewed to the socket bone, as well as the ears. Her once full lips were now shredded strings of tissue hanging down to her chin. The nose, along with bit and pieces of the fleshy cheekbones didn't fare much better than the rest of her facial structure.

"The owner of the house, it seems, had a few hungry cats running around," Wallace said, laughing at his own joke.

"Did the M.E. say what the cause of death was?" Kowalski asked, feeling like he wanted to throw up the raisin bagel that he had for breakfast.

"He found a deep, six-inch gash on the base of the skull, but it could have been a broken neck. He won't know more until they perform a full autopsy. He was sure that she had been deceased for about four days now. We should have the fingerprints back in a few hours to positively confirm who our dinner plate friend is," Wallace stated, again laughing at his own joke that on one else found funny.

Once all the detectives made it back outside to some much needed fresh air, Matthews asked, "What's the name of the owner of the house? And where's that person at now?"

"Her name is a Mrs. Doris Dillard. A couple of uniforms took her down to your station," Wallace responded.

"Okay, thanks. We'll catch you around," Kowalski said before he got behind the wheel of his car and he and Matthews raced off towards their precinct.

Neither man spoke. They were lost in their own thoughts as they make their way into the station house.

"There was a possible homicide on Lakewood Street, and the owner of the residence, a Mrs. Doris Dillard, was brought down for further questioning. You know where she is right now?" Kowalski asked the front desk sergeant when they arrived.

The sergeant flipped through his big detailed logbook and told the man that she was on the third floor.

"Hey, Jim, what room is Mrs. Dillard in; the lady who found the homicide victim this morning?" Matthews asked, desperately wanting to talk to her.

"You mean the lady who found her friend that looked like she was eaten by a pack of hungry wolves? What really happened, or was everybody just yanking my chain?" the young officer asked.

"Something like that. Where did you say she was?" Matthews asked again, not wanting to get into a useless conversation with the bored rookie cop.

"Oh, the paramedics took her away. Right in the middle of routine questioning she just flipped out and started screaming like she was having a seizure of something. They had to sedate her just to calm her down. All that medication they pumped her with, I think she might be out for a week!" the cop said, exaggerating.

"I have a strong feeling that's the nurse we been looking for. You think Ice murdered her when he found her no longer useful?" Kowalski asked, dropping quarters into the coffee vending machine.

"Of course. The name Ice fits him perfectly. Leaving that woman's body to rot like that, we need to get that animal off the streets as quickly as possible," Matthews strongly stated as he grabbed a steaming-hot cup of black coffee.

"I think she had to be in on the escape because—"

Before Kowalski could finish his statement a police officer walked up to the pair and said, "I've been looking for you two. We

185

picked up that kid Nature late last night at some seedy hotel by the Interstate. He used to work for Rizz."

The detectives quickly got the arrest report and walked into the interrogation room.

"Hi. How you doing? You need anything? Maybe a Coke or something?" Matthews asked as he took a seat across from the nervous Nature.

"Yeah, I'll take something to drink," Nature answered.

"You don't mind if I call you Nature, do you?" Matthews asked.

Nature shrugged his shoulders in an "I don't care" manner as he sipped on his cold drink.

"Well, I'm sure you heard how your boss, Rizz bit it. That's why you were found with an automatic handgun and a bulletproof vest on you. You figured that whoever took out Rizz was coming after the rest of the crew to make sure there wouldn't be any hidden surprises later on," The detective stated and waited for his words to sink in.

"Yeah so? I'm out the game now. I just want to do my own thing," Nature said.

"Boy, are you fucking stupid or what? You were caught with a loaded firearm and an illegal vest. That's two felonies right there. Now, just say the police never found those things when they rushed your room. You were caught in the act of beating a half-naked sixteen-year-old white girl. I'm sure the DA could rack up about ten felonies with just that one incident," Kowalski said, speaking the cold hard truth.

"I caught her going through my pockets when I was in the bathroom. Plus, I didn't know her real age," Nature said with beads of sweat popping out on his forehead.

"You think that shit means anything to a jury? The DA's going to put that sweet, innocent looking young white girl on the stand and have her say that you were pimping her out to all your scumbag friends. They're going to prove to the jury that when she got tired of having big black dicks rammed into her tiny cunt, you started beating on her, and that's when the police caught you in the act. Now, who you think the jury's going to believe? You or her? When the DA gets finished with you, they're going to have you connected to all the runaway teens in the area," Kowalski said, showing no trace of emotion.

"Okay, so I'm done for. What do y'all want from me?" Nature asked, knowing that his life was now an open sewer drain if everything the detective said was the truth.

"We want you to gather some information for us. We need to know who Rizz was with, and where he went before he was murdered. We also wanna know where your boy Universal is hiding out," Matthews stated, knowing that they had the scared young man by the nuts.

"I'm no snitch," Nature weakly said.

"Don't be as dumb as you look, kid. We could lighten up your problems if you play ball with us, otherwise, I'll personally see to it that my friend who's a judge, sits on the bench at your trial. And just for kicks, I'll make sure you have an all white jury," Kowalski stated, his pale-gray eyes causing Nature to start shaking.

"How do I know you for real about the charges?" Nature asked, knowing no matter what choice he made, he was in a no win situation.

"You can trust us. We're the good guys," Kowalski said, patting the man on the back.

"The only thing I could tell you right now is that the last time I saw Rizz, he left with some Spanish stripper from Foxxy Sista," Nature said, hoping they got off his back with that little information.

"What's her name?" Matthews asked.

"I don't know, but I'll never forget what she looks like."

Later on, the detectives had Nature poring over mug shots of women, hoping that she had been arrested before.

"Oh, and we're going to need you to keep your ears and eyes open about a guy name Ice," Matthews said.

"What do he got to do with anything?" Nature curiously asked.

"Don't worry about that right now if you wanna keep your ass outta jail!" Matthews shouted as he slapped a picture of Ice down on the table so Nature could get a good look at Ice's mug shot.

CHAPTER THIRTY-NINE

Ice was about to climb out of Chyna's Infiniti G35 in front of the apartment building, when he noticed a gleaming champagne-colored 600 SL Benz with twenty two inch chrome NC Forged Momo rims creeping slowly up to where he was parked. He automatically reached for his hammer, not knowing what was going down. Even though it was mid-afternoon, he knew people still got wet up in the hood no matter what time of the day it was.

He relaxed a little when he saw Chyna jump out the vehicle looking somewhat disheveled and tired, like she had been partying all night. Moments later, a spanish looking guy got out the driver's side and went over to Chyna. He talked to her for a few seconds, and then gave her a hug before pulling off. Even though Ice fucked his long-term friend only one time and there wasn't any type of commitment involved, he felt his chest swelling up like a jealous ex-boyfriend who didn't know when to let his girl move on.

"Chyna, what's up? You look like you been dragged through hell. You all right?" Ice asked as he caught up to the girl who was walking into the lobby.

"Oh, hi. I didn't even see you," Chyna responded in a low voice.

"Everything cool? You act like you got a lot on your mind," Ice stated while looking at the woman's wrinkled up clothes.

"You know how it is sometimes when things don't flow your way," she answered as they entered the elevator.

Ice wanted badly to ask her about the guy who dropped her off and if they were swinging something. He knew he couldn't push the issue because that would be the quickest way to turn off a female right from the jump. So he played the game quietly as they entered the apartment.

Chyna went straight to the bathroom without saying a word, and minutes later Ice heard the familiar sounds of someone preparing to take a bath. "Chyna, I'm about to blow. What's up with little man?" he asked, referring to four-year-old Anthony.

Ice Cold Vengeance

"My aunt's taking care of him for a little while. I'll see you later," she replied behind the closed bathroom door.

Something was definitely going on with Chyna and that nigga in the big body SL. But right now he had more pressing issues to deal with. He was supposed to meet up with Carmen to see what she was really about and who she was down with.

Also, his pockets were starving, and he needed some serious bank to let the stripper know that he wasn't just some fronting ass nigga flossing in an ill whip that had forty-eight car payments left. He needed to do a real robbery, not a juxx at some bullshit dice game.

Ever since that lame nigga, Rizz got sent back to the essence, the streets have been real quiet and on high alert status. The police were throwing rat snitches up against the walls right and left, and the hustling niggas were flying low under the radar but still getting that bread.

"Fuck them scary motherfuckers! Shit won't stop me from caking up!" Ice said to himself as he changed into his business wear—if you would call it that. He walked out the door wearing all black while Chyna was still soaking in the bathtub as if she was trying to wash away some sin that hot water, soap and a scrub brush couldn't possibly erase from her memory. He had on baggy fatigues, a black Yankee fitted, cap and a pair of black and white Air Jordan's.

Ice got in the car just as the sun was slowly starting to set, creating a grayish hue color over the city. He wanted a drink but decided against it because he knew he had to be on point. So, he settled on his pack of Newport's to relax him.

Thirty minutes later, he pulled the car over on a side street in the Woodhaven section of Queens and got out. He walked through the quiet, middleclass neighborhood and made it to a small but quiet check cashing store. He had been watching the spot for the past three days. There was an old guard in his mid-sixties who always sat on a tall stool. The old guard continuously chitchatted with the customers, who were just trying to take care of their business and be on their way. From what Ice could tell, the only thing the guard carried was an early twenties .38 pistol with a small brown wooden handle.

Ice pulled his hat down a little lower out of habit and walked through the front door.

189

"CD's, DVD'! I got the latest stuff. Whatever you looking for, I got it," a voice said that was thrown in Ice's direction.

Ice turned around and saw a Guyanese man grinning from ear to ear like he had the most prestigious job in the world. "I'm cool," Ice told him.

"Come on, man. I know you need something. I got that new 'Black Dicks and White Chicks Volume 5 DVD'," the persistent man said, holding up the porno DVD and walking towards Ice.

"I said I'm fucking straight!" Ice barked, not counting on this asshole being up in the store selling bootleg items on a cardboard box with a tablecloth draped over it.

Ice then walked over to a counter off to the side and started filling out a Western Union form while the man he had brushed off began mumbling something under his breath. "Damn! These papers are so confusing!" Ice said out loud so everyone could hear.

Just what expected would happen, the white guard limped over and said, "I know how you feel. A lot of people complain about these confusing forms."

"Okay, Grandpa, keep yapping like before and everything will work out!" Ice whispered as he poked his police-issued Glock nine into the man's protruding gut. Ice concealed the weapon with a few Western Union forms while he kept talking to play it off to anyone who might be watching.

"Okay, son! Take it easy! Don't do nothing you might regret!" the guard said, not taking any chances by making any sudden moves.

"Walk over to the window and say what you gotta say to get inside the office, or I'm gonna blow you kidneys out through your motherfucking mouth!" Ice growled.

As they slowly started walking to the main window, Ice glanced off to the side to see what the DVD man was doing. He was busy watching a movie on his ten inch DVD player that he kept around just in case a potential customer wanted to check out the clarity of his movies.

"Sara, I need to use the bathroom again. You know how those 7-11 Big Gulps always run through me," the guard said with a weak smile.

"Sure. I'll buzz you in," the woman behind the bulletproof window said as she hit the button.

Once Ice was sure the heavy steel door was open, he pushed the man inside and snatched his gun out of his holster.

"Who are you?" was all the woman got a chance to say when she found a gun being pointed at her right eye.

"Sara, it's all right. We're being robbed. Just give him what he wants so he could be on his way," the guard said, still trying to put on a brave front.

"Give me the loot like pops said, and I'll be out. Now hurry the fuck up!" Ice said and waved for the guard to get over in the corner.

The short, frumpy cashier opened the drawer and began taking stacks of cash out with her pale pudgy fingers.

"Oh shit! I forgot to bring a bag to put the dough in!" Ice thought to himself. He went over to a small garbage pail and dumped the contents on the floor to remove the bag that lined the pail. While he was emptying the can he mistakenly applied a little pressure on the trigger of his gun, causing a shot to go off.

"Blam!"

As soon as the already frightened woman heard the shot, she vividly pictured her teenaged son seeing her being carried out in a body bag on the eleven o'clock news. She dropped to the floor and balled up in the fetal position. She then began screaming hysterically at the top of her lungs and sending money flying in every direction.

"Bitch, shut the fuck up!" Ice spat out as he stuffed the money into the small garbage bag.

Meanwhile, the old guard took the minor distraction as an opportunity to play hero. He rushed Ice, grabbed him in a bear hug and said, "Give it up, son! You're not going anywhere now!"

All the commotion caused the Guyanese DVD man to start banging on the door and yelling, "What's going on there? Is everybody all right?"

Shit was getting out of hand real quick as the old guard held onto Ice for dear life, putting more pressure on his spine.

"Call the police! Call the police!" the guard yelled over the noise of the cashier who was still screaming her head off.

With the old man acting like he was an ex-wrestler, Ice knew that he couldn't break the man's vise-like grip. He had to do something and fast before the police showed up. Plus, the next door neighbors probably already dialed 911 after hearing all the commotion.

Ice's arms were pinned down tightly at his sides, so he decided to do whatever he could in this type of situation. He let off a quick succession of bullets into the guard's foot, blowing off two of his toes.

The hero guard dropped to the floor screaming like a woman in labor as he grabbed his mutilated foot.

Ice was vexed that the guard had the nerve to pull a stunt like that, especially since he had no intention of harming him or anybody else as long as they acted right.

The cashier was now rocking back and forth and praying incoherently as Ice pointed his gun at the man's forehead. The gun had somehow jammed when he tried to fire it, so he just swung the hard metal at the man's face, causing him to fly backwards. A deep ugly gash opened up on the guard's forehead. Ice then grabbed the rest of the cash out of the drawer and buzzed himself out.

As he ran out of the store, the DVD man was on the sidewalk talking on his cell phone. "That's him! That's him! Somebody stop him!" the guy started yelling and pointing directly at Ice, which caused people on the street to stop and stare.

Ice calmly walked up the block as the guy continued to yell, "Killer!" and "Thief!" at the top of his lungs. To the average person walking by, it would seem as if the man was deranged and just wanted attention.

Ice jumped into the Chyna's car just as he heard police sirens getting closer and closer. He pulled off very carefully so as not to draw any more unwanted attention in this quiet neighborhood. He wished his gun hadn't jammed, because he would have without question caught a body right there on the sidewalk.

Ice's mouth was cotton-dry and his heart doing back flips for almost getting trapped by the over-zealous security guard. "I guess maybe now his old ass is gonna retire now," He said to himself and laughed, thinking about how he let off a couple of good shots into the man's foot.

Ice Cold Vengeance

Once Ice was out of that particular hot area, he stopped by a Spanish bodega and copped a 40 oz of Old English with the wide mouth bottle. He didn't want to start on the liquor right now because he knew he was going to get lifted with Carmen later on tonight.

He drove to his next destination, which was a jewelry store that catered to niggas getting it in the hood. They specialized in big heavy pieces of flashy jewelry that go-getters often wanted to let the world know that it was all about them.

He counted his recently ill-gotten stash which totaled to over twenty one thousand dollars. It was nothing compared to what Rizz was holding—or used to hold.

Ice spent a little over an hour and a half in the jewelry store before settling on a hundred and twenty five gram 18-karat old eagle pendant that had diamonds attached to its entire body. The bird had its talons clutching a replica of the earth that also had diamonds embedded into heavy gold. He also chose a simple diamond ring to have something on his hand. He didn't want to blow all his money in one shot because cash was always needed first and foremost over jewelry any day of the week.

"Come see me again anytime, okay bro?" the Romanian salesman said, wishing more black men in the ghetto sold drugs so he himself could become richer off the blood money that he eagerly accepted.

Later on that night while watching the late news, the salesman would comment to his wife and kids after seeing a drug related drive-by that resulted in three deaths, one of which was an innocent bystander, "They need to burn down all those goddamn projects and build some real houses for decent folks like us. Animals like that should be taken out and shot like the dogs they are."

A few hours later Ice was taking a steaming hot shower and thinking about how everything was falling into place. But nothing was solid concrete as of yet. He definitely wanted to get out of hot-ass New York, but he definitely needed some major paper to make the correct moves. Everybody knew you needed money while on the run.

Ice dressed in a pair of Armani Exchange jeans with the frayed bottoms, and a crisp, light-blue Ralph Lauren button-down long-sleeve shirt.

Chyna was now in her room with the door locked and playing soft music like she didn't want to be disturbed, so he left her to do her own thing.

******

"Hello, Ice, this is Carmen. Change of plans. I don't want to meet at the strip club tonight," she said after Ice answered his cell phone. She told him where she wanted to meet at and at what time, keeping the conversation short and brief before ending the call.

******

Ice parked in front of the Blue Oasis Bar and Grill and waited for the stripper to show up while he smoked a cigarette.

Just like clockwork, Carmen hopped out of a raggedly cab, looking like a spoiled diva on the Sunset Strip.

"Damn! Shorty's looking mad good!" Ice thought to himself as he peeped the woman's gear.

She had on a pair of Norman Smitherman knee-high leather boots with a matching Saran Wrap tight short suede skirt. Her stiff, pointed nipples screamed for release from her low-cut Thomas Steinbeck silk blouse. The woman also carried a black and gold genuine python skin clutch bag that cost as much as the monthly rent on a three bedroom apartment.

"I'm over here," Ice called out to her while getting out of the car.

"Ooh, I like a man that smells good!" the woman said after walking over and giving Ice a friendly hug.

This was the first time Ice was wearing House of Creed cologne that he heard so much about.

The down-low couple entered the bar, which was somewhat crowded with the Wednesday night crowd getting their drink, on and hopefully their fuck on if their game was tight enough.

Ice and Carmen sat at the end of the bar and ordered their drinks. Ice had a Hennessy Sidecar, while Carmen had a Remy French 75. They really didn't talk much about anything. Ice just cracked jokes about how lame niggas always tried to push up on women who were way out of their league. These women would throw excuse after excuse to the desperate guys who couldn't take an obvious hint by saying things like, "Nah, I don't have a name." or, "I only fuck with chicks." or, "I'm not trying to meet anyone; I'm just out to have a good time."

Carmen knew just what he was talking about as she laughed enjoying herself.

Meanwhile, some bum guys were hating on Ice's glittering jewelry, while the dark skinned women were shooting envious looks at Carmen saying that she thought she was all that because she was light skin with long flowing hair that was obviously hers.

"I know her shit gotta be fucking weave," a woman who was rocking a thirty dollar flea market wig said to her girlfriends at the other end of the bar.

After the couple finished their second round of drinks, Carmen said, "Yo, let's get outta here. I'm tired of these people."

Ice knew it wasn't about the people, but it was about the horny woman's hormones on overdrive. He sped off playing a "Papoose Extra Clips" mixed CD and asked, "So, where do you wanna go?"

"It's up to you, playboy," she replied.

No more words needed to be said as Ice hit the gas pedal to get where he was going.

He was soon putting the key card into the hotel room door in silence. The newly formed couple hardly said a word to one another because they both knew what time it was.

Once inside the hotel room Carmen said, "I'll be back. Let me go freshen up." She went to the bathroom while Ice took out a pre-rolled joint that was stuffed with Sour Diesel. He then sat down on the bed and kicked off his shoes.

A short time later, he was laid up on the spacious bed in only his Polo boxer shorts, showing off his rippled six-pack stomach muscles and puffing on the blunt.

Carmen finally emerged from the bathroom wearing a two-piece crimson black lace bustier and matching panties set. She tip-toed over to the bed carrying her street clothes in a neat folded bundle and placed them on a chair.

She then crawled onto the bed like a cheetah stalking its prey, and began lightly kissing on Ice's chest and stomach while her tongue flickered over his nipples and bellybutton.

The woman quickly unsnapped her bra and practically threw her bouncing fluffy soft breasts in his face.

Ice barely had time to place the blunt in the ashtray as his mouth found the soft flesh. His hands tightly grabbed the woman's ass and kneaded it like he was handling raw clay.

Carmen began kissing on his neck as her perfumed panties flew across the room.

Ice didn't need any more bullshit foreplay, because as soon as the beyond sexy woman stepped from the bathroom, he was ready to handle his business.

The stripper was wet from day one, so it wasn't a big surprise when her pussy juice dotted the bed sheets.

Ice turned her over on her belly, but not before throwing on a Slip-n-Slide condom. He banged the fiery Latina chick doggy-style as if he was trying to tear the lining out of the pussy. By now Carmen was wetter than the rainy season in Cuba.

"Squiss! Squiss! Squiss!"

The loud, wet sex sounds could probably be heard by the occupants in the room next door. The sounds turned Ice on even more as the force of his powerful sex thrusts had the woman's head banging up against the solid cherry and oak hand-carved headboard. He didn't want to put her in a coma, so he eased up a bit.

Carmen's neck ended up being bent from pressed up against the headboard, But Ice could have cared less if she left the hotel room with a neck brace on. He wanted his at all cost.

The stripper was also enjoying herself, especially the way Ice was manhandling her. "Oooh! Aaah! Right there! Don't stop! Deeper!" she screamed out. She then took her hands and spread her fat ass cheeks wide apart so they wouldn't be in the way of the dick that was on the verge of making her cum a second time. Sweat from Ice's forehead dripped down on the arch of the freak's back mixing with her own sweat.

Ice dug into her rib cage while ramming the pussy back towards him time and time again, making sure she had nowhere to go to.

After Ice came, he plopped down on his back to catch his breath. He reached for the now half-empty bottle of Brazilian rum that they had purchased on the way over to the hotel.

Carmen laughed and said, "I hope you ain't done yet. Let me find out!"

"Hell motherfucking no!" Ice responded, regaining his energy at the insulting remark and throwing the girl's long legs on his wide shoulders. One hand played with the hot pocket while the other hand worked on sliding another rubber on. He didn't care on how bad the dancer looked or how good the pussy felt; he was going to keep it wrapped up. *"This bitch is super star material, but those are the ones who catch niggas sleeping on the AIDS tip. Then they would laugh about it thinking on how many stupid motherfuckers they infected with death,"* Ice thought to himself, knowing how most promiscuous women got down.

Ice soon had the flexible woman on her back with her knees touching her ears. He pounded away at the dripping wet pussy like it was going to vanish any minute. After twenty minutes of long-stroking the kitty-kat and hearing the woman yell out every curse word in spanish, Ice decided to throw her in the wheel barrel position. He had to let this hot stripper know who the boss really was. Seconds later Ice had her walking around the room with her palms on the floor and her legs wrapped around his waist for support.

Approximately two hours later, the couple was drinking from a pitcher of cold water to help replenish lost fluids. After they both drank a couple glasses of much needed H2O, Carmen reluctantly stated in a baby-soft voice, "Ice I want to spend the night with you, but I gotta go. You know how it is."

"Yeah, I know, but do what you gotta do," Ice nonchalantly responded back.

After they both finished dressing Ice said, "I'ma be real with you. I know you're not really feeling your man because he doesn't respect your potential. As you can see, I'm 'bout it 'bout it, so what's up?"

"Yeah, you're right. I'm getting tired of him making excuses on how to handle shit the right way," she said while twisting her face up.

"Well, I say we do it up right and stack some real paper," Ice said as they walked up to the car in the parking lot.

"Fuck it! I knew you was a real nigga from jump street. I'm down for whatever. I need a thug in my life who don't take orders or shit from anyone," Carmen said, thinking about how her man, Lite did everything Haitian Jack told him to do just like a little bitch. Just thinking about the whole situation caused the woman's stomach to twist up in knots. To make sure that Ice knew she was down with whatever program he had in mind, she gave him some quick head as they drove down the darkened streets of Queens.

A short time later Carmen walked into Foxxy Sista acting as if she had been there the entire time, and waited for Lite to pick her up.

She was totally unaware that somebody was making a phone call about her so-called clandestine rendezvous with the light skinned, green-eyed stranger.

CHAPTER FORTY

"Where the fuck you been at, nigga?" Universal spat into his cell phone after he found out it was Nature on the other end.

"After all that shit went down with Rizz, I decided to lay low for a minute. So are we gonna get them niggas or what?" Nature weakly asked.

"What's with you? You trying to get niggas indicted over the phone? I wanna kick it with you in person. Meet me by Brookville Park in two hours," Universal barked before ending the phone call.

After taking a strong pull of his Backwoods blunt, Cory asked, "Who was that?"

"Some lame nigga named Nature. Motherfucker's talking about he's ready to get busy. He ain't gonna do nothing but help carry a nigga's casket. I don't know why Rizz kept that fronting ass nigga around anyway," Universal said, meaning every word to the fullest.

"If I wasn't in that bullshit ass group home, I would'a been doing it up with y'all," Cory said, passing the weed to his friend.

Universal and Cory were sitting in the Jaguar, kicking ideas back and forth. Universal was a master at putting shit together, especially when things didn't add up on a scientific level. His father, an intelligent strong black militant, always instilled in his young son the art of elevating the mind at an early age. He constantly gave Universal reading materials thus expanding his young mind and making him see things for what they really were, and not as someone presented them to be.

Universal's father was arrested while trying to rob a Manhattan saving and loans bank with a few other men who thought the same as he did. They had been hoping to finance a movement of his that he had been planning for years. While at Rikers Island waiting for his day in court, both the father and son exchanged twenty page letters on a regular basis, which sharpened Universal's mind even more about the ways of mankind.

Before Universal had a chance to really build with his father, whom he considered a man ahead of his time, he was killed in an altercation with correction officers. Five burly white CO's in full riot gear had rushed an inmate in his cell for refusing to come out for chow. Universal's father couldn't stand by and watch the down-low KKK officers pound out a frail black man if he had any say so. His father tried to intervene, and the correction officers' racist wrath was suddenly turned on him. The correction officers took the intervention as a pure insult when trying to do their so-called job. They practically beat the man to death. The official cause of death in the Rikers Island report stated that Universal's father was asphyxiated due to a compressed chest cavity. To put it bluntly in ghetto terms, the police choked him to death while pounding his internal organs into jelly.

At his father's wake, Universal promised his dad that he would still keep reading while elevating his sense of awareness that the public schools failed to provide. He read extraordinary literature such as "Soul on Ice", "From Man to Superman", "Sex and Racism in America", "The Art of War", "The Autobiography of Malcolm X," etc., and the hood favorite, "The 48 Laws of Power" by Robert Green. For some reason, that particular book was seen as a threat by white officials, and was banned by numerous Upstate New State correctional facilities.

******

Hours later under the cover of darkness, Universal drove to the meeting place with his little man, Cory. They parked the Jag at the far end of the park where they could pretty much see any vehicle that came and went. Both guys had gats close by just in case. You can never be too on point when it came to dealing with anyone in the hood.

It was a known fact that best friends and partners in crime had the tendency to flip on each other in the worst way, and act like they were life-long enemies. It could start from something minute as a he-say-she-say rumor, or if somebody tried to throw little sexual innuendos at somebody else's girl.

Ice Cold Vengeance

Sometimes a hood rat female in the middle of the drama would be down with the program, and then would always flip the script towards her favor by acting like she had a halo floating above her head. One guy would end up dead while the other one would be facing murder charges, thinking he upheld the female's honor. Shorty bird would be off still doing her thing and telling her friends, "Fuck him! I didn't tell him to kill nobody." Life in the slums very seldom showed mercy to anyone.

"Beep, beep!"

A car's horn sounded, causing the occupants in the car to be on alert status.

Nature pulled up alongside Universal's Jaguar in a rented Dodge Intrepid.

"Yo, park your shit and let's blow," Universal stated.

Nature did as he was told and climbed into the back seat.

"So, what the fuck is going on, Nature?" Universal asked as he sped down the block.

"Whatchu mean?" Nature nervously asked, wondering who the guy in the passenger seat was.

"You know what the fuck I mean. You were the last person hanging out with Rizz before he died, so where did y'all go?" Universal asked, growing agitated.

Universal wasn't really concerned with Rizz's ultimate demise as he made out to be. What he cared about was what happened to all the cash Rizz had secretly stashed away somewhere. After Rizz found out that his number one wifey, Mia was stealing from him on the low, he murdered her and made a pact with himself to never trust another bitch with his drug proceeds again. Once Rizz started smoking his woolie laced blunts, his pact became void. When the highly addictive drug started stimulating and twisting his brain cells every which way, Rizz had the bad habit of bragging to one-night-stand chicken heads on how much money he was holding. Universal knew that it was only a matter of time before Rizz's reckless ways would catch up with him causing some female to set him up for a fall.

Universal knew that whoever got to his former boss came off with major paper but not everything. Rizz had a habit of stashing his money in different spots, but the million dollar question was where?

201

He suspected that the only person Rizz might trust with his dough would be his sister, but she seemed to be MIA Maybe she had something to do with her brother's death. When it came to that much money, people had a habit of flipping no matter how tight they were. They could have felt that they didn't receive their fair share, or maybe somebody had a hand in gassing that particular person up. He planned on finding out who killed Rizz's stupid ass, and maybe the rest of the puzzle would fall into place.

"We went to that whorehouse on Central Ave that Rizz was always bragging about. I took a cab back to my place, and Rizz stayed behind to do his thing," Nature replied, lying better than a rug. For some reason he didn't want to tell Universal that they were at Foxxy Sista, tricking. Nature practically lived at most of the strip clubs throughout Queens and Brooklyn. During his drinking, partying and spending crazy money, he came across a lot of shady money-hungry dancers who would go to any lengths to get that paper. Even though he had nothing to do with what went down with Rizz, he didn't want to take the chance of Universal or anybody else thinking that he could have somehow been involved with the gruesome setup.

"So, nigga, get on with it. What's the bitch's name?" Universal asked, hating the sight of the man every minute he was with him.

"It was a Filipino chick named Heaven. From what I heard she's top-notch and doesn't come cheap," Nature added, trying to throw in extra information to get on the man's good side.

"Did I ask you all that?" Universal spat, causing Cory to snicker out loud. *"Nature had to be telling the truth, because Rizz always went to the whorehouse when he didn't find a girl to his taste in the club or walking down the Ave. Not to mention the fact that he heard him mention Heaven's name on a few occasions,"* he thought to himself.

Universal cruised through the dark streets of Queens after dropping Nature off by his Dodge Intrepid. "Make sure you always keep your phone on so I could contact you anytime," he said to Nature before pulling off.

"So, what's the plan now?" Cory asked, feeling bored.

"We gonna check that bitch Heaven out right now," Universal answered with a sick grin on his face.

CHAPTER FORTY-ONE

"Hey Jenise, what do you think about me and you getting our own place together? I know this dude who'll give us the hookup on a three bedroom apartment," Trina said.

"What about Lilly? I don't want to just bounce and leave her with all the bills by herself," Jenise replied.

Both cousins were cooling out and talking in one of Cherrish's deluxe rooms.

Jenise had just finished sucking off a customer so good that he plain forgot about the dripping wet pussy that was waiting for him. He practically begged for another blowjob from the Arkansas native who took him up on his offer... for more money of course. A heavy tear came down the customer's cheek when he came, causing the man to leave a generous tip and the promise of leaving his fiancée of three years for her. Jenise was a natural born thoroughbred whore from day one who took dick as easily as waking up in the morning.

"That's your big sis and all, but fuck her! She's stuck in a motherfucking dead end job babysitting those wild juveniles," Trina threw out, causing Jenise to giggle a little bit. "Have you noticed how every time we step foot back in the crib she always has something slick to say about me and you being out? I ain't with the bullshit. I'm trying to stack that paper without all the small time hassle. I'm trying to move onto bigger and better things. Are you with me or what?" Trina asked, knowing the answer already.

"Yeah you know me, I'm down for whatever. So, when you wanna do this?" Jenise asked. She knew that her sister was living a boring life, going to work, coming home watching the set, and maybe going to the movies with her straight-laced boyfriend. She left countrified Arkansas behind to get away from those types of people.

Now Trina on the other hand, knew how to make it happen. Trina knew how to dress, kick it with people on different levels, and most importantly, she was about excitement and unlimited amounts of money. Even though she never imagined that she would be fucking leering strangers in New York for a pimp, it wasn't all bad. She even came a few times when she was high off coke and imagining that it was cute Cherrish who was banging her guts out.

"Sometime tomorrow afternoon, I'm gonna roll over to the apartment building and hook shit up for us," Trina stated as she pulled out a bag of nose candy.

Even though it was a slow process, Trinas's plans were gradually starting to materialize. A good portion of the customers used some kind of illegal drug of some sort when they partied with the women of their choice. If they didn't use, they did after coming back a few times. The girls would coach the customers into purchasing drugs by hinting that it made the sex more pleasurable for both of them.

Trina had found out through the talkative Heaven that Cherrish dabbled in the drug game, but only on a small level. Cherrish supplied his working girls with crack, weed, and cocaine for them to sell to the tricks. She knew that the house had the potential to make some serious bread.

Cherrish had what 90% in the world wanted: pussy or drugs. In his case the pimp had both. Trina wanted to open up a little something in the back of the house where motherfuckers who just wanted to get high could cop and then bounce.

She saw the way Cherrish operated and knew that he would never make her a partner because he saw her only as a whore to fatten his pockets even more. He had come to her a few times talking that good shit, saying that he had some special customers that only she could take care of. But Trina, being from the old school, knew that he was only spitting his game to get her on her back as well. She needed to get that nigga out of the way as quickly as possible so she could do her thing. But first she needed to keep working on Heaven's mental to help her if everything rolled according to her master plan.

"Jenise, Cherrish told me to tell you that he had a couple of spiders coming through in a minute who want the Beef Curtain," a woman said, swinging open the bedroom door.

Ice Cold Vengeance

"Yo, check this out; we're not in some barnyard. You knock first before entering a room," Trina spat out as she stood up to face the woman.

"First off, I don't have to do shit! You just came on board ship, and here you are trying to be the motherfucking captain or something! You must don't know who the fuck you talking to!" Kiwi replied, her eyes glowing, automatically disliking the white girl standing before her.

Both women sized each other up, after which Trina said, "Oh, you must be Kiwi. I heard about you. You been down with Cherrish from the jump. But after a while the high rollers kept passing you up, so Cherrish put you back on the street fucking nickel and dime motherfuckers and sucking cab drivers in the alleys for loose change," Trina threw out with a loud mocking laugh.

The statement Trina just made stuck in Kiwi's heart like a thousand red-hot needles, because the white woman spoke the cold concrete-hard truth.

******

Kiwi had met Cherrish when he had popped up at the real estate office where she working. Cherrish was looking for some property to invest in, and the two just starting talking and laughing like old friends.

Kiwi was a pretty, fresh faced twenty two year old with big expectations and trying to make it like everyone else in the hood. She had a nicely furnished apartment, a decent vehicle, and a boyfriend who promised that they would be together forever. They even had a little miniature Doberman pinscher puppy that ran around the apartment.

Kiwi soon found out that her man, who she trusted with every fiber of her being, was creeping around with some big-breasted college freshman slut whom he met at a fast food drive-through.

Kiwi soon became obsessed with trying to figure out why he would fool around with some ghetto bird bitch that made no more than a buck and change a week at Burger King, when he had somebody like her. She gave her man her check, her loyalty, and most importantly her undying love, which he took for granted. She began an obsessive pursuit of trying to find evidence of her man's infidelity, even though a five year old could see the obvious signs. The stress of following him around, examining his boxer shorts, and decoding his cell phone soon affected her work performance at the office. Cherrish was there for her when she was let go for the many unexplained absences and paperwork mistakes.

Two days later after she had come back from a fruitless job interview, she found that her boyfriend had packed his things and broke out. To make the situation even more intolerable was the fact that he had been pocketing the rent money for the past three months, causing a bright orange eviction notice to be placed on the front door for all to see.

When she went to Bank of America to withdraw money to keep a roof over her head, she heartbreakingly found out that he had emptied out their joint bank account, leaving her with a negative account balance. Kiwi was now broke, on the verge of being homeless, and still had a car note to look after.

Cherrish, being the good friend that he was, paid the back rent, gave her a stiff shoulder to lean on, and a sympathetic ear to pour her heart out to. "Don't worry; you don't have to pay me back right away. When you feel you're a little more stable, then we could talk about it." He had told Kiwi as he kissed her on the cheek and handed the grateful woman a little cash to help get over her hump.

Little did Kiwi know, she would be paying back more money than she would have ever dreamed of. How could she possibly ever say no to the man who helped her when her own family abandoned her in her time of need?

Soon Kiwi was out hustling on the strip, slinging that firm ass because Cherrish said that he needed a little more money to put down on one of his investments. No matter how much money Kiwi brought in, it still wasn't enough.

Years flew by like calendar pages blowing in the wind. The stress of working the unmerciful Big Apple streets began taking its toll on Kiwi's once head-turning good looks. She still had the tight body to attract drunk men passing by in cars, but wasn't up to status to work in Cherrish's expensive whorehouse.

******

Kiwi still gave herself some kind of hope that maybe Cherrish would let her run the house until Heaven slithered into his life. Now here was this white bitch and her half-breed cousin trying to bark on her like a motherfucking nobody after all the work she put in over the brutal years. "Okay, you got that, you white, dick loving, cum sucking bitch! We gonna see who has the last laugh when you spread out on the floor!" Kiwi shouted as she quickly retrieved a small straight razor that was hidden in the hem of her skirt. The anger was mostly motivated by Trina's beauty and her being white, which took the cake. Kiwi wanted to touch up the smirking face in the worst way.

"Come on now, ladies. Let's all take a second to exhale," Heaven said, walking into the bedroom and standing in between the two women after hearing all the commotion.

"I think you should let this bitch know how I get down," Kiwi said, speaking to Heaven as she walked back out of the room, not waiting for a response.

"That's the best thing you could'a done for your health!" Trina shouted out, wanting a piece of the washed up street walker who was hating on her.

"Okay, okay. Now that we got that out the way, Jenise, the man will be here any minute, so please get ready. I have somebody who specifically asked for me, so I gotta do my thing also. Bye ladies!" Heaven said, and smacked his shiny thin lips before heading back out the door.

"So, you heard about me? Well here I am," Heaven said with a dazzling bright smile as he slowly spun around so the person standing in front of him caught a view from every angle.

"Yeah. I heard you the person to get with when niggas want that little something extra," Universal replied while taking a look around the exotically decorated bedroom.

There was a large custom made heart-shaped bed in the middle of the room that sat on a specially made revolving device that was activated by the touch of a button. The bed was covered with expensive imported Indonesian silk sheets and matching pillowcases that were overstuffed with hand-picked goose down feathers that a grown person could fall asleep on in minutes like a newborn baby.

The room had three different colored light bulbs strategically placed throughout the lavender-scented bedroom, giving it a mystic sort of feel.

Close by the bed, Universal spotted a wide hanging glass case enclosed by a highly glossed cherry wood finish. The case held a variety of wild looking dildos and other freaky sex toys that he had no idea what they could be used for on the human body. But he suspected that Heaven was well acquainted with each one on a personal level.

"Well I hope your friend told you that my usual rate is six-hundred an hour, but for you I'll make it an even four-hundred," Heaven said in a soft but businesslike voice.

"You think a nigga like me is worried about small figures like that?" Universal replied, pulling out nothing but crisp hundred dollar bills.

Universal was feeling Heaven's mixed race looks. The way she carried herself with such confidence made her all that more appealing to the man. *"Pretty bitches in the hood thought they had a little class just because they wore underwear from Victoria's Secret and drank champagne at the club that some trick ass nigga bought hoping to tap the hot-box,"* he thought. Yeah, Heaven had the looks and the style to knock all those other slummy broads out the box. He was especially curious about what she did for the clients to charge so much, being that she was so close in the hood. He knew about the upscale white bitches charging a grip for businessmen and guys with too much dough on their hands.

But the main question on his agenda was finding out just how much this bitch knew about Rizz's murder, and if she was indeed involved. He had to admit that Heaven was definitely topnotch, so he could see why Rizz would spend all his time over here. But there was something different about her that he couldn't quite put his finger on it. *"Maybe I'm just being paranoid"* he thought to himself as he lit up a Philly blunt.

A short time later with the pungent weed vapors still swirling around the bedroom, Universal was laying on his stomach in the heart shaped bed, in his boxer shorts. Heaven was lightly sitting on his lower legs and rubbing strawberry flavored Motion Lotion on the now very much relaxed man's back and shoulders. The more the lotion was rubbed, the hotter it became while massaging the stressed out muscle tissue.

Heaven slowly inched down Universal's underwear, all the while still expertly doing his thing with soft, delicate fingers. Heaven turned the customer over after he was completely naked and began working on his exposed chest and stomach area. When Heaven's hands touched Universal's genitals his dick shot towards the mirrored ceiling.

Like a bootleg magician, Heaven produced a long string with silvery metal-like beads attached to it. Before Universal could react, Heaven had quickly wrapped the strings around his stiffened organ and nut sack. The next thing Universal knew was the beads began vibrating like a jackhammer on low, causing a sensation to flow through the man's loins that he never experienced before. His dick became harder than Chinese arithmetic right before Heaven's mouth tried to slurp him dry.

Universal hopped off the bed, snatched off the vibrating beads, and took a swig of the bottle of champagne on the nightstand. He was tired of playing these slow games. He wanted to fuck, and right now.

Heaven had been in the skin game long enough to know what the horny man wanted, so he slipped of his flowing Chinese robe.

Universal's mouth dropped open when he saw the unmistakable bulge in front of Heaven's panties. His eyes went to the medium-size, perfectly shaped breasts, and then back to the crotch area.

Heaven caught the look on the young man's face, and knew the next couple of seconds was a very crucial moment for both the parties involved.

Universal knew that the person standing before him in a silk panty and bra setup was a beautiful transvestite. His entire rational thinking process was thrown out of whack due to the fact that he felt that if he didn't cum as soon as possible, his testicles would be plastered around the room. At this point in time Universal would have put his dick in a blender if he thought it would help him get his nut off.

Heaven peeped the look on Universal's face and knew that his skills had prevailed once again. He slid into the middle of the bed and threw two fluffy pillows under his stomach while taking off his silk underwear.

Universal's mind convinced him that he wasn't getting in bed with a real man, and that the weed was controlling his unnatural actions.

A nanosecond before he was about to pound out some man's shit box, Heaven quickly placed a studded Rough Rider condom on Universal's penis, while his other hand smeared his anus with a glob of K-Y Extra Lubricating Jelly.

Universal was like an unbound savage on the loose as he pumped Heaven's ass while biting on his back. It took less than a minute before he released his shameful load. He then climbed off of Heaven like he had some kind of highly contagious disease and began getting dressed. He had his back to the transvestite as Heaven said, "That was good; probably the best I ever had. You gonna come see me again?"

Universal ignored the question and was in such a rush to get out of the room that seemed to have shrunk to the size of a shoebox, that he put his Polo boots on the wrong feet. He quickly bounced out the bedroom, throwing a thousand dollars on the floor and not believing that his hardest, most powerful orgasm was with a fucking man.

Just as he was walking out of Heaven's private VIP room, Trina was coming out of Cherrish's office. As Universal walked by with his head down, Trina said in a shocked voice, "Oh shit! That's the nigga that's getting crazy paper with Cory! He's freaking off with Heaven? What the fuck!" At the precise moment, an idea popped into her scheming mind on how she was going to get Cherrish out of the way so that she could live like God intended her to.

CHAPTER FORTY-TWO

Haitian Jack cruised the gritty streets of Queens in his shiny new olive-green Beamer, thinking about how he had this town in a WWE death grip drug-wise. He smiled to himself as he fingered the former drug kingpin's heavy diamond encrusted medallion that hung loosely from the car's rearview mirror. Jack knew that in order to stay on top of his game and maintain a well-disciplined loyal organization, he had to know the intimate in's and out's of everybody within his circumference.

He learned from his mistakes in Miami when one of his top lieutenants began gambling recklessly at underground dice and card games. The lieutenant would sometimes go in with shopping bags filled with cash, lose everything, and end up still owing a couple hundred thousand dollars more. He thought it would be easier to kill the owners of the illegal hood games instead of standing up and paying off his debts. It wasn't enough that Jack had heat up the ass from police trying to lock him up and competitors trying to giving him a dirt nap, but now his lieutenant was bringing unnecessary beef to the table with dudes who were just trying to eat like everyone else.

Once Jack diplomatically handled the situation with the gambling spots, he took care of his lieutenant in the most brutal way possible, sending out a clear message to the rest of the crew. Jack didn't mind if a nigga gambled or did whatever floated their boat, as long as their extracurricular activities didn't affect his business in any way. He himself had bet heavily on underground boxing matches and lost house money, but he was the boss so he had it like that.

Even before Lite and his girl touched down in New York, Haitian Jack was feeling uneasy vibes coming from Carmen. He had caught her on more than one occasion cutting eyes at him in the worst way. Once Jack and Lite had started making power moves in Queens, the bad vibes became more intense in feeling. Haitian Jack learned from experience that most crew leaders within the inner circle who began being at odds with each other was the result of a woman putting a bug in their ear: "You're the one who puts in all the work, so why you're not the one making the decisions?" or "You should start your own shit. We don't need them." Or the most frequently used statement, "You're the one everybody respects, so fuck that nigga! We don't need him." The comments could be endless in words, but all held the same meaning.

The bugs in the ears just didn't go for illegal drug crews, but also for rap and R&B groups as well, causing a member to think that they were the superstar above the group, and eventually causing a breakup. But in the dope game, breakups usually resulted in someone being wrapped in barbed wire and stuffed into an old Maytag refrigerator behind an abandoned building.

Being on point and trying to keep a close knit family—if you could call it that—Jack had somebody at the strip club watching Lite's girl from day one. And just as he suspected, Carmen was stepping out on his right-hand man, Lite, instead of keeping her ear to the streets like she was supposed to do. The phone call Jack received confirmed that the woman had quickly fallen prey just because her and Lite's relationship was going through some minor turbulence. Jack's informer didn't know where Carmen stepped off to or who she went to see, which disturbed him the most. You can never tell what a person might be thinking or predict what course of action they might take in any given situation.

Jack decided to look more closely into her activities and decide on how to follow up on what the sneaky woman was really doing. Haitian Jack compared his drug organization to a well-oiled machine. When a weak link in the machine was discovered, it had to be taken out as quickly as possible or it could ultimately disrupt the other components. Carmen was that weak link and had to go. But for now, his stomach was being pushed towards his spine and he needed some grub.

A little while later Jack was strolling through a small Haitian restaurant, wearing a perfectly cut crème colored Armani suit with dust free Benjamin Choo suede loafers. He had on a tight black T-shirt that showed off his sparkling thirty-karat plain diamond chain even more. Diamond chains that size were known throughout Miami as "The Ghetto's Guillotine". It was a well-documented fact that starving dudes in the hood wouldn't hesitate to chop off your head for the high priced piece of jewelry. In the slums it was considered the ultimate come-up. Haitian Jack also wore his brand new Breitling watch with the platinum face and custom made Ostrich skin band that he picked up from a well- known and respected Russian jeweler that same morning.

He had been trying to find a decent spot to get his eat on since hitting the Rotten Apple. He when finally got word on a somewhat good Haitian restaurant located on Merrick Boulevard between a hair salon and a 99-cent store. Jack sat at one of the three small tables that were covered by a cheap red tablecloth that had a slim metal vase with plastic flowers sitting in the middle.

"Hello. May I take your order?" a woman said after coming from behind the counter and wiping her hands on a stained apron.

Jack gave the woman his order and watched her walk away. She had on thick brown stockings and a long black cotton skirt that held her plump frame. Still Jack found himself staring and lustfully, thinking, *"Damn, I need some good pussy!"* He had been too busy setting his plans in motion on his dangerous climb up the ladder to think about women. His genitals still had the dull pain of the syphilis disease that was busy racing through his bloodstream.

Jack kept himself occupied by watching a large black and white television set that hung on the wall in the corner until the woman brought back the traditional Haitian dish of *lumbe* smothered in pepper sauce, with rice and peas, fried plantains and a large salad. He also ordered a bottle of red wine that was so dusty that the woman had to thoroughly wipe it down twice.

"So, how did you like your meal?" the lady asked as she removed the dirty dishes from Jack's table after he finished eating.

"It was good, and I'm definitely coming back," he replied with the utmost sincerity.

Jack was back in his vehicle listening to some music and feeling and nice after the old bottle of Haitian wine. He rode around the neighborhood just checking things out to see who was out and doing what. Jack felt like some female company since he had a little time to kill, not to mention the fact that he was still horny.

"So, you looking to do some partying, big boy?" a woman asked as she leaned into the window on the passenger side when Jack pulled over.

He looked at the way too skinny hooker whose skin on her face looked as if an unqualified plastic surgeon had pulled back the flesh too tight. He chuckled to himself when he also noticed that her generic curly fry wig was off center, causing it to be slightly tilted to one side. It gave the woman a clownish appearance. "I'm good," Jack answered while laughing, He then rolled up the power window in her face.

Just then out of the corner of his eye he noticed a girl talking on a cell phone. "Fuck all them other bitches! I'm stepping to that one!" he said out loud, driving closer to the woman that caught his attention. She was standing wide-legged like she just gotten off a horse, and her skintight 7 For All Mankind jeans showed the feminine curves of her vagina, causing Jack to lust even more.

"Hey, let me holler at you for a minute!" Jack called out after turning down the music. *"Yeah, that's just what a nigga like me needs,"* he thought to himself as the woman slowly walked towards the expensive car while showing the customer her fist-size pussy gap.

"We can go up the block to that hotel," the girl said as she jumped into the car.

Normally Jack would have flipped on anybody, man or woman for pulling a stunt like that, but for some reason he liked this chick who was so sure of herself. He studied the woman as he drove. The streetwalker had a cute face and a banging curvy body that would put a few video vixens to shame. But her eyes told the sad story of crushed dreams, dark endless tunnels, and total despair. Jack wasn't a social worker so he didn't really care if the woman was dying from cancer the next day; all he wanted was some juicy pussy to let out all his pent up tension into.

The woman could tell by the way Jack was looking at her that no matter what she charged, the man would cough up the dough.

Once the girl checked in and got the electronic key card, Jack asked, "So, what's your name?"

"You can call me Kiwi," she answered with a sexy smile as she opened the door to the room.

CHAPTER FORTY-THREE

"I never thought you were this way," Chyna said as she looked over at the driver.

"You know how it is when somebody throws a label on you. People tend to run with it without really getting a chance to try to know the person," Cherrish replied, speaking the truth.

Chyna knew exactly what he was getting at. During her late years in middle school and throughout high school, her classmates automatically assumed that all she cared about was books and studying. They placed that label on her just because she wore thick glassed, had braces on her teeth, and got good grades. In all actuality, she was just like everybody else on the inside. She liked the basketball games, the cut parties she heard about, and everything that went on during freshman week. But people assumed that she wouldn't be interested.

"I'm sorry I misjudged you. I should have never even listened to the haters," Chyna stated, leaning back in a more comfortable position on the soft plush leather. She and Cherrish were riding in the Benz after coming back from having a bite to eat, and talking about life for hours on end.

"Don't worry about it. As long as we're cool now. I'm glad you took the chance to get to know me," Cherrish responded, staring into the woman's chinky eyes. He then looked at her well-formed thighs that her short but tasteful skirt failed to hide. Being the person he was, or better yet like most men, he quickly imagined what style of panties she wore and how she kept her pubic hair. *"Was it bushy; the hairs going wild in every direction like an African tribal woman? Or was it neatly trimmed into a perfect V-shape? Or was it smooth as whipped cream?"*

He kept his urges in check because he didn't want to rush it and blow this bad money-making potential whore. When the time was shaped up for his specific qualifications, then and only then would he lay the supreme pipe game down, giving Chyna no choice but to submit to his selfish demands.

He knew his heavy dick game was no joke, because every once in a while he had to set a time schedule just to bang his chicks to keep everyone happy and his pockets on high octane. But he knew very well that wasn't all it took to control a woman, especially if she was a live wire without any instillations like so many ghetto chicks throughout the country.

Many pimps and regular guys alike made the mistake of assuming that all a guy needed to give a female was a good dose of big dick and possess a never tiring stamina, and he would have her on lock. It's true that some chicks may stick around for a minute, but Cherrish used verbal gymnastics and his skill at playing mental chess to snare unsuspecting women into his web of lies and deceit.

Cherrish had to hit Chyna from a whole new different type of angle, mainly because physically she didn't need anything from him. She had a nice little ride that some nigga was pushing at the moment, a decent apartment, and a wardrobe that the average girl would be envious of. For now he had to make this girl depend on him mentally, and play it by ear like true pimps often did.

"So, are we still going to see that black play? 'Your Arms Too Short to Box With God'?" Chyna asked when the car pulled up in front of her building.

"You know it. I've been dying to see it for a minute. I know a couple of the actors, so after the play we'll go backstage and I'll introduce you to everybody," Cherrish said in a friendly voice as he patted Chyna's thigh.

"Okay, and thank you for the meal," she said and attempted to lean forward and kiss Cherrish on the lips. He turned his face slightly and gave the girl a friendly peck on the cheek, throwing her off balance once again.

After getting out of Cherrish's car and riding in the elevator, Chyna began thinking about how much her life has moved at such a fast pace in such a short while. Her long term friend Ice, whom she grew up with, suddenly found her to be irresistible, when he could have had any girl he wanted. Then by fate and extenuating circumstances, she found her private parts being ravished against her will by a woman who had saved her from being sexually assaulted by crack heads only hours earlier.

Ice Cold Vengeance

What put her mind in a tailspin was that she never even came close to being attracted to another female no matter what she looked like. But on the other side of the coin, she came multiple times, draining her life's fluid.

Then, Cherrish popped into the picture as if by magic with his thuggish flattering charm.

******

"Is everything all right? I bounced right over as soon as I could," Cherrish stated when he arrived at the house the following morning.

Kiwi told him how everything jumped off at the club, and Cherrish flipped the fuck out like his little sister had been violated beyond belief. "What? I'm going to find those fuckers and make sure they on a slab of concrete before the weeks out!" he yelled, his face full of fake outrage.

Cherrish and Chyna had talked for hours; their conversation steering towards art, literature and life's conditions. She had never met a man like him before who was knowledgeable about so many various subjects. Cherrish sounded like an intelligent and articulate person who had graduated with an English degree. Everything she ever had with a guy was purely physical, but Cherrish stimulated her thought processes to a degree she never knew existed.

******

"Look what the cat done finally dragged in! What's up?" Ice said, thinking that Chyna's behavior had been suspect for the past couple of days.

"I'm cool. I've just been having a lot of things on my mind lately," Chyna replied while walking into the kitchen and pouring herself a full glass of apple juice.

Ice watched her movements, knowing that she was telling the truth by the blank look on her face.

"Oh Ice, I forgot to tell you that my mother wanted to talk to you about something important," she said, poking her head out the bathroom as she prepared to take a shower.

"That's cool. I'll drop by a little later to see what's popping," he replied. He hoped that Mrs. Teal had some street news about who put Rizz to sleep. Maybe that little information might put him closer Rizz's missing money.

Ice wanted to move light-footed today so he put on some fresh Fruity Pebbles high-top Air Force 1's, a pair of Red Monkey jeans, and draped his neck with the heavy Cuban link chain that had his new piece attached to it.

He was about to break out when Chyna came out of the steam-filled bathroom with a fluffy white towel wrapped around her and said, "Ice, I'm going to need my car back tonight."

"No problem," he replied as he left the apartment.

Ice's eyes were burning fire as he walked out of the lobby and jumped into Chyna's luxury Infiniti. He didn't know why, but he was mad at that spanish-looking dude whom he saw drop Chyna off. "That bitch ass nigga's probably putting shit in her head just so he could push the whip himself. That Benz is probably just a motherfucking lease so he could front. Something ain't right about that clown, and I'm going to find out," Ice said, again talking to himself. He had no real reason to believe that the man was living foul or up to no good, but the very thought of him fucking Chyna made his hatred for the stranger grow tenfold.

A little while later Ice pulled up to the bootleg liquor spot and parked. He rang the bell through the rusted metal fence. Seconds later a old, gray-haired man wearing a pair of dirty overalls like he still living in 1950's Mississippi hobbled over to the fence. "Whatcha need?" the man asked, his teeth looking like a row of baked beans.

"Yo, is Mrs. Teal here?" Ice asked.

The man looked Ice up and down through red, bloodshot eyes and said, "Hold up."

Mrs. Teal came walking out as if she was on her last leg. "Ice, I didn't know it was you out here. Come on in," she said, unlocking the gate. "You want a little something?" she asked, referring to some alcohol.

"No, I'm straight. What do you had to tell me? I'm kind of in a hurry," Ice stated, really wanting to get down to business.

"Okay, okay! I know how you young folks like to move around so quickly," she replied. She then began rifling through a drawer that was stacked with all sorts of meaningless papers. "Here you go. A friend of mind ran into you mother, and she passed this letter on to me to give to you," she said, handing him a sealed envelope that looked like someone had spilled coffee on it.

Ice took the letter, forgetting to ask the lady what was going on in the streets pertaining to Rizz. He rushed out of the house and tore open the envelope as soon as he was back in the privacy of the car.

Ice, how you doing?

I've heard that you've grown to a handsome young man. You definitely been living up to the name I gave you.. It's been a long time since I seen you, but I've been going through some problems for a while like everybody else in this rotten world. When I get my act together maybe we could talk face to face, which I will be looking forward to.

Anyway, I know you probably don't remember too much about your father, but he's getting sicker and sicker every day. I know in his heart that he would like to see his oldest son before he dies. Yes, you have a half-brother. I hope you two could be friends one day.

I have to go now. Here's your father's address.

Love, your mother

Ice read the letter a few more times before carefully putting it back into the wrinkled envelope. He sat in the car staring into space, not knowing what he was feeling. He had heard his mother speak countless times on how his father was a spineless jellyfish of a black man, and that's why he left his family behind. His mother gave him the nickname Ice so that he could have a heart like a block of ice, totally the opposite of what his dad had in his chest cavity.

He was still undecided as to whether he should go pay his pop a visit, which was close by in the neighborhood.

CHAPTER FORTY-FOUR

"**I** want some answers now, you fucking young punk!" Detective Kowalski spat out with his smelly cigarette filled breath polluting the surrounding area. His right hand was tightly squeezing a pair of extra sensitive testicles.

The unfortunate victim on the other end happened to be Nature, who could barely breathe must less answer the detective's question. His eyes were filled with water thinking that his most vital organ was about to burst any second now. Unbearable pain shot through his whole nervous system.

"Hey partner, ease up a bit so the motherfucker can speak," Detective Matthews spoke up with a slight chuckle in his words.

The three men were in the damp underground garage at the police station. After seeing the wild look in the black officer's eyes, Nature wished for a second time that he had left the city instead of meeting with the detectives. But he was more afraid of how much time the judge would slap him with for having sex and beating on an underage pure white girl, especially since Kowalski told him that her father was a well-respected businessman with connections.

Kowalski eased the pressure just a little bit, but not much just in case he got lame answers that he wasn't looking for.

"Okay! Okay! Please, just don't hurt me no more! Whatcha wanna know?" Nature asked after finally catching his breath.

"Don't fuck with us! It's been three days since we let you go. Whatcha got for us, or these little nuts are going back in the pressure cooker!" the detective stated, meaning every single word. Kowalski was especially serious today, because their captain chewed their asses out again. This time around he threatened to suspend both detectives for a week for dereliction of duty for not solving the murders of Rizz and his grandparents. It seemed that every angle they hit turned into a wasted dead end. He'll be damned if this piece of shit won't give him something to go on.

"The girl Rizz was hanging out with the night he went missing is a stripper who goes by the name of Miss Latin. People say she

220

might be down with some guys from outta town who might have had something against Rizz. That's all I know right now," Nature replied with no choice but to speak the truth as he gritted his teeth, still in pain.

Kowalski knew not to ask Nature the woman's real name because it would be a waste of time. Some guys may know a stripper for years, slip most of their pay checks into her thongs and still won't know her real name. "So, who are these guys and where do they hang out at?" he asked, wanting something more to go on than what the young man was giving him.

"Nobody knows too much about them, except that they're some Haitians from outta town who be pushing mad weight," Nature responded, hoping this answers were satisfactory so his nuts could be released from the redneck cop's vise-like grip.

Kowalski knew that the street hood (if you would call him that) was telling the truth, because they had heard the name Miss Latin mentioned a few times before since starting their investigation.

"She has to be the key to solving this gruesome murder mystery. Once we get our hands on this bitch, we can chalk this case up for the books," Matthews thought quickly.

"The only thing we gotta do is snatch up the girl at the strip club when she goes to work tonight. It shouldn't be too hard. Then I could spend a little time with some personal business that I've been neglecting," Kowalski thought to himself as he released the man's sweaty private parts.

"Now, what about this Ice character? Where the fuck is he holed up at?" Detective Matthews asked, jumping into the mix of things.

"I haven't heard anything about him," Nature replied, taking a step back and leaning against the elevator.

Without warning, Matthews roughly backhanded Nature like he was his bitch who came up short after coming back from her hoe stroll.

"Whap!"

The sound echoed throughout the parking structure, causing a couple of uniformed police officers who were just getting out of their vehicle to quickly turn around. Once they spotted the two detectives standing with the black youth in baggy street wear, they

221

automatically knew what time it was. They were used to seeing suspects sometimes getting the shit beat out of them before being taken upstairs to be processed by the arresting officers.

"I'm not sure, but I think that Ice guy be fucking with them bitches that be selling their ass in that big white and green house by the church under the trestle!" Nature quickly replied as he grabbed his bruised cheek like a female would do after her boyfriend had slapped her up.

"I know the place you're talking about," Matthews said, a little more relaxed now that he had something to look into concerning where Ice might be hanging out.

Kowalski looked at his partner, thinking that Matthews must have something personal against Ice. He wasn't that far from the truth, because when Detective Matthews first met Ice years ago in the interrogation room at the precinct, he viewed the young man as the scum of the earth. Back then, Ice was being accused of murdering his ex-girlfriend and then dumping her nude body by the railroad tracks like old debris.

Matthews' own daughter, who strikingly resembled Ice's ex-girlfriend, was herself brutally beaten and murdered. The case was never solved, and when he saw the pictures of the dead woman, old painful memories just floated back to the surface.

Then when the DA prosecuting Ice on the homicide case decided to drop the murder indictment because of a lack of physical evidence, Matthews almost flipped out. He knew that Ice killed that poor girl and was getting away with the crime, just like the animal that killed his only baby. Now years later, Ice had murdered the nurse from the hospital.

"How many more women must die at the hands of this unthinking monster?" Matthews thought to himself, remembering the sadistic smirk on Ice's face when first trying to get him to confess to the heinous crime. No way was he going to let him get away with his devilish deeds again.

"Okay, get your ass outta here and stick close by. We might need you again," Matthews barked.

Both detectives had agreed that once the case was over and done with, Nature was going under the jail with the rest of the slime.

Ice Cold Vengeance

Nature slithered away, knowing that he just told the detective a bold faced lie about Ice being at the brothel. He had to give the crazy men something or his balls might end up like crushed egg shells. *"Fuck that nigga! I don't know him!"* Nature thought as he left the underground police garage.

******

Later on that night while working late, the detectives were preparing to go down to the Foxxy Sista strip club and snatch up Miss Latin for questioning, when Kowalski's cell phone rang. He picked it up and spoke for a few minutes. After a brief conversation he said to his partner, "I have a little family situation at home. We could pick the girl up tomorrow night."

"Okay, no problem. I hope everything works out," Matthews said, not wanting to pry into the man's personal life.

An hour later, Detective Matthews was sitting at his kitchen table, drinking a triple Jack Daniels on the rocks. He was staring at his dead daughter's picture that was in a solid, sterling silver frame.

Half-way through the liquor bottle his wife appeared at the kitchen door, wearing her housecoat and said, "Trevor, its late. Are you coming to bed?"

Matthews just ignored her. He was lost in his own thoughts.

Walking up behind him and softly massaging his neck and shoulders she asked, "Is it that case you're working on involving that Ice guy?" Matthews's wife knew she had to be careful when her husband was in one of his strange moods that had something to do with a certain case.

"How could the system be so blind that they would let a person go who just killed a beautiful girl?" he asked, referring to when Ice wasn't charged with the murder. But he was really talking about their eighteen-year-old daughter.

"You can't let it get you down. We just got to pray and be strong," she answered wishing that her husband would stop drinking.

Just then a thought popped into Matthew's drunken mind. *"If I go to the strip club and pick up Miss Latin, we could hurry up and finish the case with Rizz and his grandparents. Then we could fully concentrate on finding Ice."*

Even though the snitch, Nature told him where Ice gets his dick wet, he didn't want to take a chance of going to the whorehouse alone. Matthews knew from experience that when raiding a whorehouse, anything unexpected could jump off. He vividly remembered a rookie cop getting stabbed in the neck by a prostitute high on speedball. The cop never fully recovered from the surprise attack because the knife had damaged important nerves causing paralysis on one side of his body.

"I gotta go take care of some important business," Matthews said grabbing his suit jacket along with the bottle of Jack Daniels.

"Be careful, dear!" his wife called out, following the man to whom she'd been married to for over twenty two years. She watched her husband drive off in their personal car knowing he was off duty. "But where could he possibly be speeding off to?" she asked herself.

******

"Raise your hands," the bouncer at the strip club ordered in an attempt to search the customer.

"Out of my way, asshole, or I'll lock your ass up for obstruction of justice!" Matthews yelled as he flung open his wallet revealing his badge. He then roughly pushed his way past the beefy man.

The doorman quickly stepped aside because he didn't want any type of altercation whatsoever with the police because of his parole status. Officially he had a curfew of being home at 9:00 o'clock, and working at the strip club until the morning was an instant violation that could send him back to the penitentiary for another unwelcomed stint.

Being a seasoned, street wise detective, Matthews scanned the crowd and found a spot at the end of the stage. "How you doing tonight, honey? What can I get you?" a brown skinned waitress with a firm body and wearing too much purple lipstick asked.

Matthews looked at her large breasts that were spilling out in all directions from her tiny bikini top. "Let me get a Jack Daniels on the rocks. As a matter of fact, bring me the whole bottle," he said, wanting to keep his strong buzz running. He watched the woman walk away with her long legs reaching up to an ass that the tiny boy-shorts failed to fully hold in.

"That will be a hundred and fifty dollars," the woman stated after returning with the liquor bottle and a glass, and setting them down on the table.

"I don't think so," the cop said as he flipped open his police-issued wallet, revealing a detective's shield.

"I don't care if you the fucking president, you still gotta pay your bill!" the woman shot back over the loud music.

"Bitch, do you know who the hell you talking to?" Matthews shouted out as he stood up toe-to-toe with the waitress.

Just before the woman was about to say something that she would later regret, a man approached and asked, "Is there a problem?" It was Paul Garney a.k.a. Silk, the owner of Foxxy Sista. He automatically disliked the stranger who was about his age.

"He ordered a full bottle of JD, and when it came time to pay, he showed me some kind of police badge saying he don't have to pay. I don't know who he is. For all I know he could have gotten that shit right off the Internet," the waitress said, getting herself more hyped up.

Silk waved his hand for the woman to shut up, when Matthews asked, "Who are you?"

"I'm the owner of this establishment," Silk responded in a professional manner.

"I'm Detective Matthews from 113th Precinct. I'm working on a case involving one of your dancers, a Miss Latin. What can you tell me about her?" he asked.

"She started working here about a month ago. She pretty much keeps to herself," Silk said, knowing that the man standing in front of him was definitely a cop by the way he carried himself with the overwhelming confidence that no one or anything could ever challenge his authority.

Silk smelled alcohol on the detective's breath. He knew that along with the cop's rotten attitude were the perfect ingredients for trouble. But what could he do?

"Where's she at now?" Matthews asked.

"She was scheduled to work tonight, but I haven't seen her for a couple of days now. She sometimes comes in late. What's she gotten herself into?" Silk asked.

"I'm not at liberty to discuss an ongoing investigation," Matthews stated as he poured himself a fresh drink.

"Well anyway, the drink's on the house. If you should happen to need anything else, just ask for me, Silk." he said before walking away.

******

Nutmeg, who was giving a customer a three-song lap dance red light special, ear-hustled and heard every word between Silk and the undercover detective. *"I knew that Spanish bitch was living foul!"* the woman thought to herself with a satisfied smirk.

Ever since Miss Latin had humiliated and played her out in front of every dancer at Foxxy Sista by stealing her regular customers, Nutmeg was hell-bent on finding something incriminating on the new girl. "Now my chance to bring that bitch back down to earth." Nutmeg was thinking. When Miss Latin had stepped off with that little drug dealer guy, and then left with that green eye guy the other night, she had been acting paranoid and jumpy ever since.

"Now here was the motherfucking police asking about her sneaky ass," Nutmeg was thinking, trying to put two and two together. *"I'm sure that whatever the police is looking for her for, it has to have something to do with those two guys,"* she thought with a cunning, calculating mind.

"You act like you got something on your mind," the guy who was getting the lap dance stated after he noticed the faraway look in the stripper's eyes.

"What, you expect me to be all up in your face when you smell like three day old funk?" Nutmeg spat out as grabbed her bikini top and walked off.

******

Meanwhile, detective Matthews was still drinking heavily watching the show and everyone around him.

Ice Cold Vengeance

The DJ was playing Outkast's classic hit song, "I like the Way You Move" at full volume. The dancer onstage was in full money-making mode, sliding upside down on the slippery, bacteria stained pole. Matthews had to admit that she was attractive and well put together woman to say it bluntly. The stripper strongly resembled the Indian princess Pocahontas. She had two long swinging pig-tailed braids and prominent cheek bones so Silk gave her the stage name "Stroke-A- Hontas." The wild horney patrons threw bill after bill at the woman as if she was a goddess reborn.

"Yeah, shorty! I know you probably taste like honey!" a man called out as he attempted to lick the sweat off the dancer's back. Stroke-A-Hontas was on all fours making her ass cheeks clap resembling loud gun shots. He managed to get in maybe a half a stroke of his tongue when shovel-sized hands roughly snatched him up by the collar. Buttons flew in every direction while his two friends laughed as the bouncers began giving the man crippling body shots. One hard powerful kick with a sturdy steel toed boot actually ruptured the man's spleen. In the ghetto there was an old saying: *"Sometimes you get more than you bargained for."*

Once their partner began getting the dog shit beat out of him, his buddies reasoned, "I came here to watch butt naked ass freaks and get my drink on, not get into a pointless brawl with guys who are twice my size!"

"It's nothing but fake boobs and real ass holes up in here!" Matthews said out loud and drinking straight from the bottle now as he watched the one-sided beat-down.

"You looking kind'a bored. You want a dance?" a bronze-colored girl who had to be no more than nineteen asked with him a bright smile.

Matthews took a good look at the girl through the hazy cigarette smoke. She had a cute oval-shaped face with big brown eyes and long eyelashes that had to be fake. Her hair was tied in a neat ponytail with the sides slicked down in a baby doll type of style. "Why not?" he found himself saying.

"I knew you would," the smiling girl said while sliding her slender body onto his.

Matthews' dick did all the talking, causing him to pay for a five-song dance at ten dollars a pop. His hands also took on a life of their own as he gripped the girl's small, perky breasts like a teenager out on his first date. He felt his penis being bloated beyond belief. The detective didn't want to cum in his pants like some slime ball degenerate.

"You wanna go somewhere more private?" the girl whispered in his ear while feeling the organ straining against the thin suit fabric.

"I got a wife," Matthews said, wishing for the first time that he didn't.

"You got a dick too," the dancer said, grabbing a handful of solid stiff cock.

Matthews gently lifted the willing girl off of his lap and threw her a little something extra for making him feel like a young man again.

"Fucking faggot!" The girl mumbled under her breath as she wiggled away, showing off her skintight black Juicy Couture body suit that accentuated her perfect ass. She was not used to men turning her down.

Matthews stumbled out of the club with a massive hard-on. "Fuck it! I'll check out the whorehouse and see what they know about Ice," the man said out loud while searching for his car keys.

"I heard you say earlier that you were looking for Miss Latin," Nutmeg said, running up to the detective. She had waited all night for the cop to leave so that she could talk to him in private. She didn't want to take a chance of her nosy coworkers seeing her chitchatting with the detective. She would automatically be labeled a snitch, which in any situation would have dire consequences. If a person working at the club was to get locked for any reason, your name was sure to come up, being that you had the snitch tag on your resume. It wouldn't matter if you were involved or not.

"What do you know about her?" the detective asked.

"I don't want to talk here. Can we take a drive somewhere?" the eager stripper asked as she walked over by the passenger side door of Matthews' car.

"Come on, get in," Matthews ordered.

Nutmeg threw her bag into the back seat and climbed in. She lit up a Virginia Slims cigarette as she watched the rain come down in a slight drizzle.

Ice Cold Vengeance

"So what you got for me?" Matthews asked, slurring his words.

"I knew that Miss Latin was into some wicked shit when she first started working here. I told Silk to keep an eye on her. You know how them Spanish bitches get down. I remember one time when—"

Before Nutmeg could continue, the detective screamed, "Can you get to the fucking point? What do you know?"

"I saw her leave with a few guys a couple of times. What, did she rob them or something? I knew she was a thief," Nutmeg said taking a drag of her cigarette.

Even in Matthews' intoxicated state, he knew that the girl didn't know anything about Miss Latin. It was obvious that they had some kind of personal beef going on. "Have you seen this guy around?" he asked, taking out a mug shot of Ice.

"Oh shit! I think I heard her call him Ice," Nutmeg replied, vividly remembering the man who had dissed her in the VIP room. *"Yeah, both their asses can go down for all I care!"* the spiteful stripper thought with a wicked smile.

Matthews grew excited, because he knew the woman was telling the truth. "Tell me everything about the motherfucker!" he yelled, adding speed to his Toyota Solara coupe as he turned a sharp corner on the wet pavement.

At that exact moment and making the same turn was Rufus, a local truck driver making a long return trip from Texas. He was feeling good because he had a pocket full of hard earned cash. His big butt girlfriend who was an expert at giving blowjobs was waiting for him at the apartment that they shared. Rufus was on his fifth can of beer from the six pack so he could be good and ready to give his woman the all night drunken dick.

"Crash!"

Metal met metal as the semi-truck crashed head-on with Detective Matthews' personal vehicle. The Solaris crumpled up like used tin foil mixing fragile flesh with sharpened, jagged pieces of steel and iron.

Matthews' last thought was, *"I'm finally gonna get you, Ice!"*

Nutmeg's last thought was, *"Yeah bitch, you going down now! Let's see how well you shake your ass in jail!"*

The coupe turned into their own personal coffin, while the stunned Rufus tossed the remaining empty beer cans under the seat along with a full bottle of Kentucky Black Hills whiskey.

CHAPTER FORTY-FIVE

Universal tossed and turned all night, thinking about the episode he had with exotic looking she-male, Heaven. It had to be the liquor or weed that made him act other than himself. *"Why didn't I choke the motherfucker to death when I first found out he was a fucking dude trying to trick a nigga?"* he thought highly disgusted at himself.

When he got back to Cory who was waiting in the car for him, he couldn't even look his young friend in the face.

"What's up? You look like you just fucked your mother," Cory said in a joking manner when Universal climbed in behind the wheel looking real strange.

"Everything's cool. That bitch, Heaven wasn't even there, so I just banged out some shorty since I was there," he answered, still avoiding eye contact.

"Damn! You should'a let me live too. I peeped a couple of bad bitches going in," Cory replied, thinking about how good the women looked.

"You ready to fuck with my peoples from BK so we could stack this paper," Universal stated, trying to shift the subject away from sex.

Later on Universal woke up with a massive hard-on that would make a stallion's organ look puny by comparison. He was beyond angry at how the transvestite conned him into cumming with such force that he wasn't used to.

He jumped into a cold shower to cool down his body temperature from the night's strange, enticing dreams. He put on a pair of fitted ripped Seven jeans, threw on a Champion hoodie and rocked the new Carmelo Anthony 860 patent leather sneakers. He completed his outfit with some expensive platinum jewelry and headed towards the door, but not before tucking his gun in his waistband.

Cory wasn't in his room, but his father was downstairs in the living room. As usual he was sprawled out on the musty couch and watching "Jerry Springer" with a bottle of Wild Turkey on the floor next to him for easy access.

"Hey, kid, let me borrow a couple of bucks," the father said when Universal walked by.

"What you need it for?" Universal asked.

"I don't have to tell you shit! You staying in my house doing God knows what!" the father shot back.

What could he say? The man was right. Universal needed a down-low spot to rest his head until he managed to get the beef under control and towards his favor. He didn't want to take the chance of staying in hotels when the residents were always yapping about who moved in. The few relatives he had were smoked out, and they were sure to snitch him out for a couple bags of crack rocks to whoever killed Rizz. "Here you go," he said, handing the man five twenties before leaving the alcohol-fumed house.

Soon Universal was peeling off in the Jag. He knew exactly where he was going. He turned on the radio to clear his mind a little before he reached his destination.

He soon pulled up to a neat, clean looking apartment building located on Hillside Avenue. He punched in the code, got on the elevator and rode it to the floor he was looking for.

"What's up? Come on in," a girl said after hearing the doorbell.

Universal slowly walked in and plopped down on the sofa.

"Can I get you anything?" Chyna asked, sitting down on a matching lounge chair next to the couch.

Chyna and Universal had met in high school during her senior year. Even though Universal considered the girl a nerd, he still saw something else behind the heavy books and glasses. From his experience, the chicks who rarely dated or went out were the most freakish ones. They had a pent-up sexual frustration just boiling over.

Their first night out he banged Chyna every which way 'til Sunday. He at first was there to get the nappy dugout and then bounce, but he ended up really liking the quiet girl.

Right after Chyna graduated from school, she found out that she was pregnant by her boyfriend, Universal. Everything was flowing at picture perfect mode throughout the whole pregnancy and a little while after their son was born.

Then things slowly started to change between the couple when Universal started hustling and running the streets. Once he started raking in the chips and getting a rep in the streets, he felt he needed to step his A-game up a notch or two.

Chyna was his baby's mother and cute, but she was very dark skinned. It was an unwritten rule in the hood that the most livest dope boys had to have the ill, pretty red bone females riding around with them in their luxury cars. Just like in the suburbs, a rich couple often had a Ferrari or a Bentley just sitting in the three car garage, never being driven. They were their status symbols only. The lighter the chick, the higher your status as a baller rose.

The more money Universal made, the less he stayed home. He paid Chyna even less attention, hardly making love to his girl anymore. Approximately three months later he informed her that it was time for them to move on, but he'll still take care of their son.

Chyna understood very well the psychological make-up of a lot of black men in the ghettos across the country. They were still suffering the mental effects of slavery passed on to them from generation to generation. Some guys would date a girl for no other reason than she was fair skinned, or a straight up snow bunny. Like she was the invisible woman, Chyna herself was passed up by guys who went straight to the much lighter females on numerous occasions. These girls could be butt-ass ugly and/or have abnormal features, but the guys only saw skin color. Universal fit into the pattern of self-hate perfectly.

"Come over and sit by me," Universal said.

"I'm good. So what you been up to?" Chyna asked, noticing the look in her baby's father's eyes.

Universal wanted some pussy right now, but he usually wanted some ass from his baby's mother when he was high or couldn't get with one of his freak bitches at the moment. "Just doing me. Why are you so far over there? I ain't gonna bite you," he said, catching a whiff of her Ocean Rain body mist spray that was turning him on even more.

Chyna saw no harm, so she went and sat by her ex-man. They talked a few minutes about their son and about the new horror movie that just came out.

Universal began rubbing Chyna's bare thigh and staring at her like a lovesick boy. She pushed his hand away and said, "Come on! Stop!"

"What's the matter? You act like you ain't with it," he stated, feeling insulted.

"Why don't you go to one of your half-white girlfriends?" Chyna responded, meaning every word.

"What? I came here to chill with you for a minute, and you try to shit on me. You talking about half-white motherfuckers? What about that piss-colored nigga with the green eyes who was laid up in here when I came by the last time?" Universal stated as he stood up.

"That's my friend I grew up with," she answered.

At the same time the ex-couple was arguing in the living room, Ice was taking a long, much needed shit in the bathroom. He had the shower radio on full blast, so he had no idea what was going on twenty feet away from him. He reached under the bathroom sink and found a strong air freshener and sprayed the bathroom like he was at a toxic waste dump site.

While he was washing his hands, he started thinking about Chyna and the time they spent together. He really cared for her and had feelings that he never had for any woman he came across in his life. He momentarily daydreamed what his life would be like if he and Chyna had a baby together.

Ice then made up his mind that he was going to get Chyna pregnant and cut out all the gangster shit once he finished up his business. Just in case anything happened to him, he wanted a son to carry on his name. But there was one problem he had to take care of first.

Ice found out that the guy who had dropped Chyna off in the shiny Benz was the local pimp who ran by the name of Cherrish. A rage grew inside him as he imagined the man trying to turn his future baby's mother the fuck out. Ice wanted badly to empty a full clip into the pimp's dome piece.

Ice finished washing his hands and walked out to the living room.

Universal turned and looked at Ice before he left the apartment, slamming the door.

"Who the fuck was that?" Ice asked Chyna. His eyes were full of hate at the stranger's presence.

"Oh, that's just Universal. He's—" Just then her cell phone went off so she said, "Excuse me. I'll talk to you later." She then headed towards the privacy of her bedroom.

Ice stood there putting two and two together. *"That must be one of that faggot pimp's boys. He's trying to go hard body on getting Chyna to be another one of his hoes. He's the same nigga who came over before looking for Chyna. Both them niggas gotta go!"* he thought to himself. The wheels of vengeance were turning in his head.

******

Universal was equally as mad as he rode the elevator down to the lobby. "That light skinned nigga must be laying the pipe game on Chyna for her to turn me down like that," he said to himself.

Even though Universal and his baby's mother weren't together anymore, he still hated the thought of his ex-girl fucking another guy. *"She probably be sucking that nigga's dick while my son is in the other room sleeping!"* he started thinking as he bit down on his bottom lip.

He had already made up his mind to take Ice out on the low, but the real reason he stopped by Chyna's apartment was to confirm that he was still a man and attracted to women. But when Chyna turned down his sexual advances, his mind told him that maybe her sixth sense kicked in and suspected that he was bi-sexual.

"What if Heaven was to tell someone that I fucked a man and enjoyed it? I would lose respect, my dignity, and nobody in the hood would want to fuck with me on any level."

Universal then made up his mind to get rid of Heaven as soon as possible also.

CHAPTER FORTY-SIX

"Okay, motherfucker! Go ahead and leave!" Lilly yelled.

"What the fuck you think I'm doing? Just let me bounce in peace!" Trina shouted back equally as loud.

"Just so you know, I went down to the precinct and put out a warrant on you for stealing my money! I hope they lock your ass up for good!" Lilly stated as she twisted up her face in a hateful grimace.

"Whatever!" Trina threw out as she placed the remaining clothes in a large duffel bag.

Just as Trina was placing the remaining bags in the trunk of the Altima, Lilly called out from the doorway, "And don't call me when you're all fucked up again in your bullshit street life, and need some more help! I hope you burn in hell a thousand times for getting my sister mixed up in your shit!"

"Well fuck you and your lame ass lifestyle!" Trina spat back before peeling off at breakneck speed. She lit up a pre-rolled joint to relax as she drove to her new residence.

"My sister's really on some other shit. I don't know why she acts like that," Jenise said, grabbing the blunt and taking a good pull.

"Well I'm glad you're nothing like her. She's gonna be an old hag, still snatching crumbs off the table trying to get ahead in life. Fuck that! Nobody's gonna give us shit. We gotta go out and get ours like everybody else," Trina said.

She was soon parked around the corner from the newly built Edgewood Towers on Hillside Avenue because all the parking spaces in front were taken up.

Both cousins were soon out of the car and walking up to the front double doors while carrying arm loads of bags stuffed with clothes and everything else that a single woman would need.

As they rode the elevator, an older man eyed them suspiciously and with open lust. Trina stared the bowtie wearing, grandpa-looking man up and down with an expression clearly saying, *"Old fart, you could never even come close to getting a piece of this unless you sign over your social security checks for the next five years!"*

The embarrassed man looked away and pressed the button to his floor, even though it was already lit up signifying that it had already been pushed.

Jenise giggled as the man made a quick getaway with his head down and wondering what he was ever thinking.

The women stepped out on the third floor, dragging their bags.

"Here we go!" Trina said with a smile. She found the key under the welcome mat just as the person said it would be. She was very much surprised when they stepped inside the apartment and looked around. Her hook-up had told her that the last tenant had gone to jail and left all his belongings behind. Since he had no immediate family to take possession of his property, it became the property of the corporation that owned the building.

Trina and her cousin Jenise looked around the spacious apartment that that had shiny, hardwood floors. There was a three-piece coca-colored velvet sofa sitting in the middle of the living room. The only other thing in the room was a tall potted plant and a couple of cheap oil paintings hanging on the wall.

Trina noticed a few scuff marks on the floor in front of the couch where a floor model television would have been, and figured that her connect probably took it.

The women walked throughout the three-bedroom apartment checking everything out. Except for a couple of plastic bags filled with trash in the kitchen, everything was clean and looked brand new.

"I see y'all made it here already," a male voice said, causing the cousins to turn around.

"Yeah. It's cool, but I didn't think it would be this nice. Oh, this is my cousin, Jenise," Trina said.

Even though Jenise was attractive, the man never took his eyes off of Trina. His small, black lizard looking eyes roamed over the woman's body like she was a succulent piece of meat ready to be devoured.

Trina had on a tight, cocaine-white one-piece body suit by Triple S. The outfit hugged every curve of her eye-popping voluptuous body.

The forty-something man who ran Edgewood Towers was known throughout the building as Tito. Trina had met him a few years ago with one of her friends who sold Hawaiian Ty weed to the man. After their first encounter, Tito openly lusted after Trina and said how he would love to ride her like she was a prize winning horse or something.

Then just recently, Trina had run into him again. He told her that he was the super of an apartment building. The news couldn't have come at a better time for Trina, with her cousin Lilly flipping out every day like she didn't have any sense. It so happened that Trina was wearing, her shortest bend-me-over-and-fuck-me skirt that day when she told Tito that she needed an apartment right away.

"We already have a two year waiting list. It's damn near impossible to get in right now," he had flatly stated.

"Oh, that's too bad. Well, here's my number. Put me on the list," Trina replied as she began going through her pocketbook and acting like she was looking for a business card. She dropped her Coach bag and gave the wide-eyed Tito a bird's eye view, letting him know that she wasn't wearing any underwear as she clumsily attempted to pick up her pocket book. Now, what you were saying about some list?" she asked with a smile and breaking the horny man out of his trance.

"Oh, I think I might have something for you. I just remembered," Tito replied, already vividly imaging going up to the woman's apartment on the late night creep and fucking her raw dog.

Trina and Tito sat on the sofa filling out the lease forms while Jenise went to gather the rest of their bags. Trina signed a one year lease agreement, giving the man a fake name. She then gave Tito fifteen hundred dollars, which was first month's rent that burned a hole in her pockets. She wasn't worried though, because the way she had this man drooling all over her, it would be the last time she would be spending another dollar on rent; not to mention the fact that she had major plans for this apartment.

"So, whatchu doing later on?" Tito asked, ready to cash in on his favor right away.

Ice Cold Vengeance

Trina looked at the short Latino man who always seemed to smell of old sardines and other unknown offensive odors. She had dealt with all kinds of men on all sorts of levels, but for some reason this man sitting so close to her turned her stomach. "I'm kinda beat right now. You know how it is with the stress of moving and shit. Maybe once I get settled, we could do something," she replied, giving the man false hope. If worse came to worse and he kept stressing her, she would get Jenise to suck him off real quick to get him off her back for a while.

Later on, Trina sent Jenise to Walmart to get some sheets, pillows, covers, and a queen size air mattress for her to sleep on. The previous resident had left a king size bed with a large wooden headboard carved into the shape of two dolphins coming towards each other, along with a small nightstand.

Trina planned on getting some more furniture to accommodate her soon to be horny customers.

Later that night as Trina drifted off to sleep, she smiled to herself. This apartment was just a first in a series of steps towards her thought out plan to make some serious money off the strength of Cherrish's name.

CHAPTER FORTY-SEVEN

Haitian Jack sat cross-legged in the middle of his bedroom floor. He was totally nude while going through one of his many sacred rituals. He had about twenty ragged mountain incense sticks burning intensely throughout the room, giving it a hazy look and feel. Closer to him were two twelve-inch solid black candles burning brightly. They were hand carved in the shape of the Madonna. Jack mumbled incoherently for a few minutes, and then stuffed a handful of undigested grass from a goat's stomach into his mouth to produce good luck.

A short time later he was splitting a fresh cow's heart down its center. He carefully wrote down a name on a piece of plain white paper, placed it into the animal's bloody heart, and covered it with some very old strong tobacco. He then wrapped everything up in a clean white cotton cloth and tied it firmly with some black cotton thread.

In order for the spell to be at its full effectiveness, Jack had to place the hex in his enemy's backyard within forty-eight hours. That wasn't a problem for him because he paid a good piece of change for that particular information.

Next, he cut the heart out of a live turtle and gobbled it down while it was still warm. Looking at Jack eating the raw meat while totally nude, you would come to the conclusion that he was a savage running around the darkened hillsides in search of food. He then washed it down with some hot silvery liquid that had parsley flakes floating in it to complete the spell of being protected from harm.

Much later after Jack fully rested up physically and mentally, he sat comfortably on his bed in a pair of sweat pants. "That's peace. I'll be by to pick up the money and bring you some more shit," he said into his cellphone, talking to one of his soldiers who was holding the fort down.

Once he gave Lite, his number one man, a couple bundles of crack, weed and dog food to take down to the spot, he decided to settle some unfinished internal business. "Hey Carmen, let me holla at you for a minute," he said, walking into her bedroom.

"What's up?" the woman asked suspiciously.

Jack looked at her long flawless legs that met up with a pair of skimpy French cut Fredrick's of Hollywood red panties. But sex was the last thing on his mind as he asked, "What's going on between you and Lite?"

"What do you mean?" she asked, putting herself on the defensive while grabbing a pillow to cover herself.

"I've been noticing how you been acting kind of shifty towards Lite the last past couple of weeks," he flatly stated while looking directly into Carmen's eyes.

"First off, it's none of your fucking business what goes on between me and my man. Second, who do you think you are, busting in my room and asking personal questions like you my goddamn father!" she spat out, letting it be known that there was no love lost between the two of them.

"Watch who you talking to. I'm not one of your tricks from the club," Jack calmly responded, trying to hold down his growing anger out of respect for Lite. If there was any other person, man or woman who would have talked to him in such rude and disrespectful tone of voice, their major organs would be liquefied. It was a technique he learned from his uncles in the old country.

"In order for a corporation to be successful, all of its top people have to be on point and thinking straight at all times. Lite doesn't need any type of distractions or having his mind focused on anything other than getting this paper," Jack stated, hoping that Carmen read between the lines. His fixed piercing gaze let the woman know that he knew what she's been up to, and that she was treading on dangerous grounds.

"I'm sorry I blew up on you like that. It's that time of the month again. You know how females can act sometimes when we get our friend," Carmen said with a sad puppy dog look, hoping to curb the fire in the man's eyes. "As far as me and Lite go, we're all right. I'm just trying to get used to New York, that's all," she then stated barely above a whisper, and thinking about how, just a short while ago, the man standing before her had mutilated a young man to death and fed his genitals to the neighbor's dog.

"You never know who's watching what," Jack stated, ending the conversation on that note as he turned around and headed back to his room.

A little while later Jack called Kiwi as he fixed himself a strong lean drink.

"You have reached Kiwi, but I'm not available right now. You can leave a message and I promise I'll get back to you as soon as possible. Bye!" the woman said in a flirty voice and then blew a seductive kiss for her clients.

Jack's face showed a slight sign of disappointment because he really wanted to set up another round of sex with the always energized woman. Even though he met Kiwi while she was out hooking, he felt some kind of weird emotional attachment to her. After slamming the pussy, they laid up while Jack talked nonstop, even though he had to pay for the extra time. In the cash strapped ghetto, everything was up for sale, including a person's time. Just thinking about her had him stroking his already hard penis.

Kiwi was so skilled in the age old art of fellatio that Jack knew for a fact that the woman could probably suck the copper off a roll of pennies. Before he knew it, he was steadily pumping his dick to a full-fledged, no holds barred orgasm. In less than five minutes a stream of hot semen mixed with an unnatural amount of a yellowish fluid stained the bed sheets. The syphilis still ravishing Jack's body didn't stop the man from doing his thing even though every time he came, it felt as if red hot razorblades were shooting though his penis.

Later on Jack was discussing business with his second in command. "Hey Lite, I got everything prepared. I need you personally on this one. You know what to do," he stated, and handed Lite a wrapped package.

"No problem. You know I got you." Lite replied.

Once this important business was finished, Jack planned to have a long talk with Lite about his girl. But for now, he needed the man clear headed and on point. "Call me when everything's done," he called out as Lite stepped into his Lex Jeep and drove off into the midnight air.

******

Ice Cold Vengeance

"Why did it have to happen to him? He was such a good man," Matthews' wife said between sobs as she rocked back and forth.

"Sometimes the worse things happen to the best of people," Kowalski replied in a low voice as he held a strong arm of support around his former partner's wife.

They had just come back from the city morgue where Matthews' wife officially identified the remains of her late husband.

Kowalski had seen many dead bodies in his twenty plus odd years on the force, but to be up close and personal with a corpse that used to be his good friend was a different matter. Matthews's corpse was charred over 85 percent of its body that reeked of a stomach turning, nauseating foul odor. His face was frozen somewhat into a sick grotesque smile that only he knew the secret to. Kowalski didn't have the heart to tell the grieving widow that Matthews died along with a woman who was a stripper and a known prostitute.

"I knew something bad was going to happen to him that night. As soon as he left I prayed all night for his safe return. Why did he have to go out?" she asked while wiping away slimy mucus that was running out her nose and down her chin.

"I promise you, I'm going to look into the entire matter if it's the last thing I do. Here, have some more tea," he said and handed the crying widow the cup that had a splash of liquor in it to help calm her rattled nerves.

As she sipped her herbal tea, her housecoat come slightly apart revealing full ample breasts that a pair of newborn twins would have loved to attack, as well as a full grown lusting man. Detective Kowalski was no exception as he felt the unmistakable twinge flowing through his genitals, causing him to get a mild erection.

Matthews's wife began sobbing more heavily and deeper now, so he gave the woman a full hug. His wide-shouldered frame pressed firmly against her chest as he took in her pleasant scent. "Don't worry. Everything's gonna be all right. Call me anytime, day or night if you just wanna talk," he whispered into the crying woman's ear as his lips brushed lightly against her earlobe.

Kowalski knew that he had the grieving and heartbroken woman under his thumb when he slowly began caressing her lower back and offered no resistance whatsoever. He planned on stopping by his late partner's wife's house a few more times on the pretext on seeing if she was holding up all right. Then he would go in for the kill. He would bring over a bottle of wine and tell her a sad sob story about how he just lost a close relative, and he knew exactly what she was feeling and going through. The end result would be that both people would comfort each other through unbridled, unrestrained passionate sex. Kowalski wasn't a stranger to this type of tactic of getting easy pussy. He did it twice to fellow officers during his career, and countless times to victims of various crimes who needed someone to share in their pain. Not only will the conniving Kowalski give the woman a sympathetic ear, but also a stiff dick.

A half hour later as he drove his car heading home, he smiled to himself thinking about how his partner's wife's pussy would taste after she came a couple of times. Yeah, Kowalski was ready to split the dark wood.

The detective finally made it to his quiet neighborhood with neatly trimmed lawns and entered his house. After putting a Hungry Man TV dinner in the microwave and fixing himself a double Bourbon on the rocks, he heard a strange noise coming from his backyard. He peered through his window blinds and saw a shadowy figure digging into the soil. His first thought was that maybe it was some neighborhood kid playing a prank, until the moonlight hit the person's face. It was a full grown man, and a Negro at that.

Kowalski grabbed his departmental issued Glock nine and crept out the back door as he was trained to do. "Okay, motherfucker! Turn around slowly and raise your hands!" the detective said in a stern voice.

The dark figure rose from his crouched position and turned towards the voice.

"What the fuck are you doing in my yard, and whatcha got in your hand?" Kowalski asked, pointing the gun at the much bigger man.

"This right here!" Lite responded, and threw the cursed cow's heart at Kowalski.

The wrapped up heart hit Kowalski flush in the face temporarily blinding him, but that didn't stop the gun from letting off three quick rounds shattering the quiet night air. Kowalski braced himself for a lunge attack not knowing if he hit the man or not, until he saw his supposed attacker lying on his back.

Ice Cold Vengeance

Lite was holding on to his neck where a bullet hole made an acorn sized hole. Blood was oozing through his fingers like slow moving molasses. Dark rich blood was bubbling from the corners of Lite's mouth as his terrified eyes said that he didn't want to die. Kowalski also noticed that the man's left ear was completely gone, leaving a bloody stump caused by one of the bullets. Lite's legs twitched for a few more minutes, and then stopped altogether. Kowalski then slowly called 911 to report an intruder at an officer's house.

Kowalski quickly rummaged through the dead man's pockets and began stuffing handfuls of cash into his own pockets. His cop vibe told him that the incident that had just transpired was somehow connected to the case that he and Matthews were working on. Somebody from the ghetto knew where he lived, and he was going to find out who at any cost.

CHAPTER FORTY-EIGHT

Senior Detective Kowalski sat in his stationhouse waiting for the slain man's fingerprints to come back from the National Database. On his fifth cup of straight black coffee and stale plain donuts, a uniformed officer walked over and handed the detective some paperwork. Kowalski quickly scanned its contents. It read:

Name: Fritz Guillaume, Age: 29, Illegal immigrant from Haiti
Aliases: Lite, Red Dog.
Last Known Address: Miami Florida
Priors: Assault, reckless endangerment, assault with a deadly weapon, aggravated battery and assault, drug possession with intent to distribute, attempted murder, criminally negligent homicide.

"It's a miracle that this piece of shit wasn't deported back to his shit hole of a country a long time ago," Kowalski said out loud.

Minutes later he walked into Captain Frank Saveni's office looking worn out.

"How you holding up? I know it's been a rough couple of days with Matthews dying unexpectedly in the middle of a tough case, and now you had to put up with some gang banging nigger trying to put a hex on you or something," the captain said before lighting up a Cuban cigar.

"What do you mean, Cap?" the detective curiously asked.

"Well, it seems that our friends in the Anti-gang Crime Unit have come across this type of thing before. The Africans, Haitians and other blacks from coon countries make it a practice to bury pieces of dead animals on their enemy's property to bring about harm or bad luck. Go figure these people out," Saveni explained as he puffed on his fat cigar.

"Cap, I have a feeling that Matthews was onto something that night at that strip club, and he was bringing a potential witness down when he was killed. My gut instinct tells me that the strip club, the

246

murders of Rizz and his grandparents, and this black nigger voodoo bullshit are all tied in together somehow," Kowalski flatly stated.

"You need to wrap this case in a nice tight little bow real quick before these niggers start thinking that it's okay to show up at an officer's home and do what they want. I'm assigning a good man, a Detective Mendoza, to help assist you in a tactical operation to bring these animals in. We need to resolve this problem right away," the man in charge said, starting to breathe heavily again whenever he started getting himself worked up.

******

"Crash!!"

The door to Cherrish's money making brothel flew halfway off its reinforced hinges when a heavy steel NYPD battering ram did its work. The muscular doorman was quickly and expertly thrown to the floor while guns were pointed at his head. The twenty or so police officers were part of the highly trained FRAT (First Response Assault Team) were dressed in all black tactical riot gear complete with shatterproof helmets. They descended like hungry fire ants throughout the surprised house.

Kowalski and his new partner, Detective Mendoza, opened the door to one of the bedrooms. A short man of Mexican descent with long shiny black hair in a ponytail was so engrossed into eating a woman's pussy that he didn't even notice that a couple of cops had noisily entered the room. He was naked and on all fours while holding the prostitute's long legs tightly on his broad shoulders. The highly intoxicated customer was happily lapping up cunt juice like his life depended on it. The man was so eager to taste the pussy that he failed to see the open Herpes simplex 3 sores that covered her groin area.

Four months later once the incurable disease was securely implanted in the man's bloodstream and cells, his wife would be affected also due to his creeping on the low with prostitutes of every race. The wife would routinely break out with painful embarrassing sores on her lips and tell her co-workers at the hotel that it was caused by eating hot pizza too quickly. She later on would lose her job of six years with her supervisor giving written notice stating that her appearance made customers feel uncomfortable.

247

"Shh!" Mendoza whispered while holding a finger up to his lips as he tiptoed towards the bed.

"Whap!"

A three and a half pound steel police flashlight made direct contact with the Mexican's exposed dangling nut sack that was swinging back and forth like church bells. He hopped up like someone splashed ice cold water on his back and began running around the room and screaming like a wounded animal.

The woman, being a veteran to raids, knew very well how the police got down, so she quickly threw on a see-through nightie before a pair of hands roughly grabbed her arm. Usually the cops would take you to jail with whatever you happened to be wearing at the time. In her case since she was completely nude, they would handcuff and prance her around in front of every leering and joking cop before finally handing her a robe or something.

Meanwhile both Kowalski and Mendoza were laughing deep laughs that came up from their bellies at the man's pain before they finally snatched him up. They soon led the couple away.

"Don't put you filthy hands on me, you dirty fucking pigs!" Heaven shouted in a high pitched voice. A big overweight police officer with a receding hairline had the struggling Heaven in a tight bear hug. He smiled his widest grin at his fellow cops while grabbing handfuls of chemically induced breasts. His expression clearly said, "Check it out! I got the cutest chick!"

"Hey, Bob, I hope that you know you're getting your rocks off with a fucking man. I personally arrested him myself a couple of times," his fellow officer said, causing everybody in the immediate area to break out into a boisterous mocking laugh.

The cop ceased his molestation and quickly slapped on a pair of handcuffs on the still cursing transvestite.

Just as the police were stuffing the johns and the women of the night into a crammed police transport van, Trina was turning onto the block. "Oh shit! The police done ran up in Cherrish's spot!" she said out loud, watching all the activity and flashing lights.

"We're lucky we came late. If we hadn't stopped by that bar, we would've been jammed up too," Jenise said.

Ice Cold Vengeance

Trina made a quiet U-turn and thought, *"Yeah, the jump-off couldn't have come at a better time. Now it's time for me to get my shine on.*

******

At the exact same time that Cherrish's whorehouse was being rushed, police officers from another FRAT tactical unit were loading women from the strip club Foxxy Sista in different police wagons. Carmen had the misfortune of going back to the club to pick up her clothes from her locker when everything went down. She was hustled and arrested along with the rest of the dancers in various stages of dress and undress, depending on who was doing the looking.

CHAPTER FORTY-NINE

Ice sat in the triple black Infiniti whip, drinking straight out of a large Patron bottle and getting himself hyped up by the minute. His mind was speeding in every direction at once, like an out of control souped up race car that had just hit an oil slick. He was staking out the Palm Springs Motel where major activity going on. Anybody living in the hood for more than one month could easily tell that the individuals coming and going were straight up dope fiends, crack heads and stank pussy ghetto birds willing to give some mean head just to get their high on. Judging by the current flow, whoever was running the spot was definitely holding mad cash and product alike.

Ice spotted a guy who appeared to be about eighteen years old open the door when a pizza deliveryman made his late night delivery.

It wasn't hard for Ice to find out from the streets who had the banging ass kicking dope, because one thing that crack heads do more than smoke up was gossip about the happenings around town. Ice had known this one crack head snitch who blabbed so much and so long that the detectives had to actually smack him and say, "Okay! Shut the fuck up already! We didn't ask you all that!"

Ice was waiting for the right time for the flow eased up a bit so he could make his move. He wasn't interested in drugs where he was going. He planned to rob the drug spot and ask Chyna if she wanted to move out of state with him and her son. He knew that Queens was a hot spot for him to keep running around in, and it was only a matter of time before the police caught up with him and put his lights out.

"I'm really starting to feel Chyna," he thought with a satisfying smile as he took another drink. That smile quickly faded as he thought about that bitch pimp nigga and the other guy who stopped by Chyna's apartment. To make the situation even more critical, Ice wanted Chyna to have his first seed, and here were these niggas trying to turn his soon to be baby's mother out.

Ice Cold Vengeance

Just then the unmistakable silver Benz with the mirror tints pulled up and came to a stop. Ice's heart almost dropped when he saw Chyna climb out the ride and laughing up a storm. She was wearing a short red skirt that revealed the imprint of a G-string, and a pair of Nancy Geist open toe high heels that made her tight firm ass bounce up and down even more. Cherrish was walking next to her and smiling his signature smile that seduced many a women in his time.

It took all of Ice's self-control and willpower to keep from jumping out and killing the man on the spot.

Once the couple was inside the dope spot, Ice noticed that he had gripped his gun so tightly out of pure rage that his palm was beet red with imprints of the weapon's handle imbedded deep in his skin.

******

Cherrish and Chyna casually walked toward the drug spot, never realizing that they were being intensely watched by Ice, who had murder on the agenda.

"What's up? You got some more of that fish scale?" Cherrish asked once he was inside the messy hotel room that was littered with empty food cartons.

"You know it! And I got that scag too, if you want some more," the young teenager replied.

"Yeah. My girls been working hard, so I gotta throw them a little treat every now and then," Cherrish said when he caught Chyna's look that said, "I hope you don't fuck with heroin."

Cherrish's usual spot where he picked up his much needed drugs was shut down, from what he'd been told. But it took him less than a day to find out who was slinging some real high quality shit. Once he shot the highly addictive drug into his veins, he knew at once that he had a winner. After snapping back out of his nod, he realized that his dick was unnaturally hard, and he had unconsciously scratched his arms until they bled. "I have to cut down just a little bit," Cherrish said to himself after regaining his composure.

"Okay, playboy, here you go," Haitian Jack's young but well-trained street soldier said, handing Cherrish exactly what he came there for.

"Man, if I had your hands, I'd cut mines the fuck off," the second guy replied as he hungrily looked Chyna up and down, but mainly focusing on her medium size perky breasts that stood out like missiles.

Cherrish just looked at the guy stone-faced and not bothering to respond as he nodded that it was time for them to make tracks.

Earlier, Cherrish had taken Chyna to his apartment building after the black play "Your Arms Are Too Short to Box with God."

******

"You live in this apartment building?" a wide-eyed Chyna asked as the straight laced doorman greeted the couple shaking Cherrish's hand with his starched white gloves.

Cherrish ignored the comment, taking it as a disrespectful and ignorant statement from someone with a limited vison on life. "Most of these ghetto bitches think only a white motherfucker could live in luxury," *he thought. He then started thinking about how there were countless guys riding around profiling in the hood with expensive whips, chromed out rims, drop down TV's and imported Hibachi sound systems, but still lived in their parents' damp basements.*

"What would you like to drink?" he asked Chyna, who still had her eyes wide open, looking around the beautifully decorated apartment and knowing she could never afford anything like this in her lifetime. Most of the time, all it took was for a female to take a quick glimpse at his apartment and their panties would end up dripping wet.

"I'll have whatever you recommend," she responded, not wanting to offend the man even though she drank almost a half a bottle of wine not too long ago.

Cherrish brought back two glasses and a bottle of Timeless Courvoisier from his well-stocked, hand-carved imported Swiss bar and sat next to the impressed girl. "So, whatcha think about me now? I know you was kind of skeptical about hanging out with me, but a nigga like me has gotta show a choice female of your caliber the finer things in life," he said in a smooth voice. He then hit a button on the remote control causing a fifty-two inch flat screen three dimensional plasma TV to emerge from a hidden wall panel.

Ice Cold Vengeance

"Like I said before, people are gonna always say something shady about a guy who's making moves like you. I knew you were doing your thing by the vibes you gave off when you first approached me. The reason I acted the way I did was because I was stressed out, going to school, working, and trying to provide for my son. So don't think I was trying to dis you," Chyna responded back in a soft voice.

"Fuck it! That's all behind us now. I'm all for a beautiful young woman trying to do something with herself instead of trying to live off the next nigga," Cherrish said as he refilled her glass.

With the liquor running through her system making her a little bolder, Chyna asked, *"I noticed that you have a lot of women around you who look up to you. So, what do you really do to acquire all of this?"*

"I'm really a promoter. I'll promote anything that I think I could make a decent profit. Every now and then I might have a girl or a stripper who wants me to set something up for them where they could make some quick easy cash."

"If that's all you do, I wouldn't mind being down so I could live too," she said with a huge smile as she sank deeper into the plush Moroccan leather sofa and took a sip of her Courvoisier.

"For sure. With your looks and intelligence you could be living just as well as me if you put in work," Cherrish said, gassing her up on an empty tank.

He saw that she was momentarily daydreaming, probably about her future riches, so he hit another button on the remote. A crystal clear picture popped up on the wide screen showing Cherrish steadily pile driving a thick, dark brown girl from the back. The moaning girl had a couple of large fluffy throw pillows under her stomach, making to the pussy more assessable to Cherrish's dick that seemed to have a life of its own. While he had the bent over woman with her eyes rolling into the back of her head, his right hand was doing a little work of its own. He had three manicured fingers sliding in and out of a white girl who held her long legs up by her thin ankles. The woman had a look of pure ecstasy on her freckled face as sticky cum slid down Cherrish's wrist.

Chyna's mouth dropped open as she stared at Cherrish's long tree trunk thickness, not believing that God could make such a monstrous looking penis on a human being. As sat there fascinated with the unrestrained X-rated scene, Cherrish had secretly put some Scream Crème on the tips of his fingers and slid them inside of her panties.

Scream Crème was a special scientifically designed concoction that one of Cherrish's friends had picked up in Thailand. The clear looking lotion was made to cause a woman's clitoris to be overly stimulated and extremely sensitive beyond normal.

Chyna became too embarrassed to look over at Cherrish as she spread her legs even further apart feeling the effects of the powerful crème. Her breathing became heavier like she just ran the Boston Marathon as she continued to watch the homemade X-rated video.

Meanwhile, Cherrish began flicking his tongue on her delicate earlobe and kissing her neck at the same time.

Raging hormones became too powerful for Chyna to ignore. The girl couldn't hold back any longer so she finally screamed out, "Please fuck me now! Do me like you doing those girls on the TV screen!"

The horny woman then tried to release Cherrish's penis from his jeans, and to her surprise the man spat out. "Nah, shorty. You can't have the dick right now until you prove yourself worthy of being in my company." Cherrish then told the shocked Chyna to straighten her shit out and make a run with him.

******

Cherrish and Chyna walked towards the Benz, with the pimp smiling to himself knowing that he was going to have Chyna snorting up some high quality fish scale cocaine with him.

******

Ice watched the couple climb back into their vehicle as he started up the Infiniti. He planned to murder the pimp at least a good ten blocks away from the drug location, because he didn't want to make it hot with homicide detectives. He didn't give a fuck about some niggas he didn't know losing business; he just wanted to rob them and kept it moving without all the police presence.

Ice Cold Vengeance

Right before he was ready to pull away from the curb to follow the Benz, a police car pulled up in front of Ice's car, blocking him in and shining a bright spotlight directly at him. There was a van directly in back of him, and to make matters worse, he forgot to put the clip back into the gun when he checked it to make sure he had it fully loaded. Both police officers got out of their vehicle and started walking towards him with their hands on their guns.

(CHAPTER FIFTY)

"Come on, Cookie. You've been in that dump for as long as it's been open. You probably know every piece of scum that comes through the door. I wanna know what you heard about that drug dealer, Rizz and the murder of his grandparents. What do you know about Lite and his crew, and how they're connected to those deaths," Detective Kowalski asked, getting more stressed out by the second.

Kowalski had been up for more than twenty four hours, drinking stale coffee, chain smoking Marlboro cigarettes, and running himself ragged. His head was throbbing as if there were tiny people stomping on his brain with concrete boots on.

"I just mind my business and go home. I don't even know why ya'll dragged me down here. I was—"

Before the stripper could continue, Kowalski's new partner, Mendoza barked, "Listen bitch! You probably sucked off half of the neighborhood, so we know you know more than what you're telling us. Who is behind this black magic crap they were trying to pull on my partner?"

The two detectives and the woman were in the hot stuffy interrogation room of the 113th Precinct, trying to put together the puzzle that was still missing some major pieces. The station house was in total chaos, with strippers and hookers talking loudly while police officers tried to maintain some sort order from the two surprise raids.

"Who the hell you think you talking to, you fucking redneck, limp dick peckerwood? I should—"

Before the woman could continue her fiery tirade, Mendoza grabbed a handful of the stripper's bleached blond hair with the intention of snapping her head backwards to let her know who was running the show. But before he could do it, he suddenly realized that he was holding a cheap wig in the palm of his hand.

The pair locked eyes with one another, and before Cookie could utter another word, Mendoza with lightning fast reflexes, gave the woman a hard heavyweight shot to her midsection, doubling her over. He then wrapped his huge paws around the woman's exposed throat. "Now, I want some fucking answers before I crush your goddamn windpipe! Who is this bitch Miss Latin, and how is she tied to everything?" he screamed, spraying the teary eyed woman with dry spittle. Kowalski was busy closing the blinds from prying eyes.

"I heard from another dancer that Miss Latin might have set that young kid Rizz up for his loot. She's that half-white Spanish girl wearing the light-blue tennis skirt who y'all brought in with the rest of us," the dark skinned woman quickly stated, looking up at the man with her blue contact lenses.

"Okay, now we're getting somewhere," Mendoza said, releasing his death grip. He remembered the beautiful Hispanic woman who was now in the bullpen with the other lowlife women.

Kowalski just looked at his new partner and admired the man's style, which evidently produced some results.

"Get your shit together," Mendoza growled as he kicked the wig that had fallen into some spilled coffee towards woman.

Cookie tried to piece together her shattered dignity as she picked up her hairpiece and shook out the caffeine droplets. She then placed the wig back on her brown stocking capped head and slowly adjusted it as best she could under the circumstances.

The detectives had barely enough time to open the interrogation room door when a loud commotion diverted their attention.

"I told you white motherfuckers already, you're not gonna keep putting your goddamn hands on me and pushing me around!" Heaven shouted as he held onto a long, sharpened No. 2 pencil.

Standing a few feet away from the outraged transvestite was a uniformed officer holding his punctured hand where Heaven had stabbed him. Heaven had his back up against the wall by the fingerprinting station. He dared any person, man or woman, to approach him.

"Okay, Miss. Just calm down. Nobody wants to hurt you or to get hurt," a skinny, red headed cop said while pointing his service weapon at his target.

All the police officers in the immediate area had their guns drawn in a firing stance as if they were facing a mass murderer or public enemy number one instead of a petite five-foot transvestite. The remaining cops had quickly ushered all the civilians back into their holding cells. They quickly came back and waited for their co-workers' next move.

"Fuck you! You come near me, I'ma stab you in your motherfucking throat!" Heaven yelled, meaning every word. His eyes were dancing wildly from side to side like a scared trapped animal.

"Where are you gonna go? Look around you. There's no way out. Let's end this in a peaceful manner. See, I'm putting my weapon away," the red haired officer stated as he put his gun back in his holster.

While he was steadily jibber-jabbing and trying to gain Heaven's trust and confidence, a barrel chested plain clothes cop was inching his way closer and closer to Heaven's blind side. The cop tried to lunge a surprise attack at Heaven, but the transvestite caught the movement out of the corner of his eye and reacted immediately. Before the officer could wrestle the wooden weapon away from the prisoner, Heaven violently sank the pencil into his meaty collarbone, severing major blood vessels. The pencil was so embedded into the screaming cop's flesh that Heaven didn't have time to pull it out as a whole army of cops rushed him. The sounds of their colleague moaning in agonizing pain only intensified their brutal beating of his attacker. Instead of trained New York City police officers, they acted more like a 1920's Mississippi unstoppable blood thirsty lynch mob. They beat Heaven with their guns, flashlights, steel handcuffs, and even a heavy brass table lamp. When a couple of cops started slipping and sliding on slippery blood is when they eased up on their unmerciful savagery.

"Hey, Sarge, I think somebody ought to call an ambulance," one cop stated as he stood up and looked down at the carnage that he and his fellow co-workers had produced.

Heaven's once pretty, delicate face was now a bloody swollen mess of unrecognizable tissue that bled from every orifice. Both of his arms were at an unnatural angle, with a grayish bone protruding at the elbow on one of them.

Ice Cold Vengeance

All the officers involved in the struggle—if you would call it that—began slowly backing away. They knew that they had participated in beating a man to death in under three minutes.

Two months later after a whitewashed watered-down police investigation, four of the cops were awarded the Mayor's highest commendation medal for bravery in the line of duty for their role in the beating death of the defenseless Heaven.

"Come on. Let's go find this bitch so we can straighten this shit out," Kowalski said to his partner as he started walking towards the back bullpens where the women were being held. Once both detectives arrived at the cages, they looked over all the women and asked them questions like they were mindless cattle or something.

"Where's the Latina girl with the long black hair that was taken from the strip club?" Kowalski asked the female police officer on duty.

"Which girl you talking about?" she asked with a slight attitude because she had to babysit a bunch of foulmouthed strippers and hookers.

"Oh, are you talking about Miss Latin? She bailed out about twenty minutes ago. Do you know if my man came up yet? My name is—" a woman began talking who was also arrested at the club along with Miss Latin.

Kowalski cut the woman off and yelled, "Shut the fuck up!" Then he directed his complete attention to the overweight black female officer. "Did y'all release any prisoners we brought in tonight?"

"Yeah, we released two women. What's the problem?" the officer asked.

"What's the problem?! I gave specific orders that no one was to be released until me or my partner interviewed each and every one and gave the say-so!" Kowalski screamed, turning red in the face.

"Well excuse me! Nobody told me anything. They might still be in the property room getting their things though," the woman said, placing her hands on her hips with as much attitude as she could muster up.

Kowalski and his new partner rushed toward the property window, passing EMT workers just arriving on the scene. One

259

woman was still being processed so Kowalski told Mendoza to detain her while he rushed out the front door of the police station.

Just as Kowalski was looking up and down the street and hoping that maybe he could spot Miss Latin, Haitian Jack was already a block away with Carmen a.k.a. Miss Latin in the passenger seat of his BMW.

CHAPTER FIFTY-ONE

As the two stern faced cops walked closer and closer to Ice, he knew his back was basically up against a brick wall. There was no way he could throw the clip back into the Glock and blast his way out of his trapped situation. If he was to make the slightest move that the cops perceived to be threatening, he would be filled with bullet holes in a matter of seconds.

Even if he didn't have a weapon or was reaching for something, once the shooting victim was deceased, the police representatives would contact the local newspapers about the so-called suspect's past. They would go into detail about how he had been arrested for drug possession, assault on an elderly person, weapons possession, etc. Then the public would automatically form a biased opinion saying, "Oh, he was a criminal so he had to be up to something."

If the murdered person had an unblemished record and was simply reaching for a wallet or some sort of paperwork when he was killed, the NYPD would throw another type of spin on the encounter. They would give a formal statement praising the officer in question, saying how he had been decorated in the line of duty such-and-such amount of times.

Then, most of the time the news articles would end with some long drawn-out rhetoric editorial saying how New York City police officers have one of the toughest, most difficult jobs in the world. They would go on to say how many times a cop was killed or grazed by a bullet, even though the innocent victim wasn't even armed, much less a threat. Most times they would give the standard excuse of the NYPD when they shot or killed an unarmed civilian: "Our dedicated police officers have to make split second decisions every day."

Ice had very limited options, so he dropped the gun on the floor of the car and kicked it under the seat. If the cops decided to search the car, which they always did in the hood, that would be the first place they would look. No matter what a person had in their possession, whether it be alcohol, drugs or a weapon, throwing it under the seat was everybody's first response when they see the police lights flashing at them to pull over.

"Sir, is there any reason why you parked in front of a known drug location?" the cop asked while looking at Ice in a suspicious manner.

"I just got here a moment ago. I was waiting for a friend. He should be out any minute," Ice responded, giving the officer his brightest smile.

"No, you've been here for a while. There are about ten cigarette butts by your door," the cop stated as he looked around in Ice's car for any signs of what he really might be up to.

"Okay, to tell you the truth, I think my girl is running around on me with some dude that stays over here. You know how it is sometimes," Ice responded, hoping to appeal to the officer on a lovesick boyfriend level.

"Enough of the bullshit. Let me see some ID," the officer flatly stated, looking at Ice intensely and thinking that he wasn't the type of guy who would stalk some chick who was whoring around on him.

"I ran out without grabbing any. I guess I wasn't thinking," Ice said as a drop of sweat rolled down the side of his face.

"Sir, could you please exit the vehicle?" the cop asked in a stern voice while taking the latch off his gun holster.

Ice knew it was an automatic trip to the police station for not having any type of identification on his person. Once they took him in and ran his fingerprints, which was standard procedure, they would find out that he was wanted for the murder of a New York City police officer. His only hope was to snuff the nosy cop when he got out and make a mad dash for it on foot, and pray that he didn't catch a bullet in the back like so many other black men in the hood.

"Francis, come on! We just got a call about a double shooting on Hollis Avenue!" his partner called out. He wanted to have another felony arrest on his record instead of some lame misdemeanor charge for not having any ID... or so he thought.

"I'm going to let you off with a warning this time. Next time carry some identification. And if I see you around here again, I'm going to lock you up for loitering," the cop said before he quickly walked back to his patrol car to join his partner.

"With a faggot name like Francis, no wonder that cracker is a fucking asshole!" Ice said to himself as he pulled off.

As soon as he was a couple of blocks away from the hot zone, he put the clip back into the Glock and chambered a round. "The next motherfucking cop that runs up on me, I'm definitely gonna give his ass something he won't be expecting," Ice said dead serious, as he lit up a fresh Newport.

Ice decided to try and hit the drug spot some time later on in the week. It would be a bad move on his part if he tried to stick up the spot so soon since there was a double shooting maybe even a homicide in the immediate area. Ice knew police would be crawling around like roaches snatching up every black male trying to gather information.

Ice decided to head back to the apartment to get some sleep so he could better figure out his next plan of attack. Surprisingly he found a good parking space directly in front of the apartment building. He wanted to get off the streets as quickly as possible because of his run of bad luck and almost getting knocked.

But bad luck still clung to Ice like crusty drawers on a sweaty fat woman, because he never noticed a ski masked figure walking quickly towards him with a sawed-off shotgun in his leather gloved hands.

CHAPTER FIFTY-TWO

"**I**'m your cousin. You know I would never lie to you. That motherfucker lied to me and tried to use you from the get-go," Trina stated.

"Word? You said he was good peoples. Why would he flip the script like that?" Jenise asked. She then took a shot of straight Bacardi Wolf Berry. The women were relaxing in their new apartment.

"Nah, that nigga Cherrish is a low down snake. He told me in the beginning that the only thing you were gonna be doing was watching out for the girls. Then, he turned around and had you fucking every creep that slithered in the door. And to top it off, he tried to turn you into a fucking dope fiend!" Trina said, faking on overly amount of concern and momentarily forgetting that it was she who gave her cousin her first hit of coke. "Yeah, he sold both of us a dream. I say we do our own thing and get this paper the right way. But you remember what we talked about? It's the only way," she continued and refilled Jenise's plastic cup to the top with more liquor.

"What if someone was to find out?" Trina's country cousin asked.

"Fuck that scary shit! You see how all the scary, wanna be solid citizen motherfuckers are always the ones with nothing but lint in their pockets? Well, I got everything already in motion. All you have to do is sit back, relax, and watch the money just roll in," came the hyped up ghetto speech that Trina often used when she was trying to manipulate someone.

"Okay, I'm with you. Fuck that lame ass nigga, Cherrish!" Jenise shouted as she grabbed her jacket and the half-empty bottle of Bacardi.

Trina had a hidden sick grin on her face as she followed Jenise out of the door, thinking how easy it was to move her cousin like a pawn in a chess game.

Ice Cold Vengeance

Soon Trina was pulling into a twenty-four hour gas station not too far from where Cherrish's whorehouse that was raided the night before. "Just chill out and finish your blunt. I'll take care of this," she told Jenise, as she climbed out of the rental car that was now reported stolen for non-payment.

"I need a large gas can and twenty dollars' worth of gas," Trina said to the skinny, bifocal wearing attendant behind the thick glass.

"Did you run out of gas or something?" the man asked, happy to be talking to someone, especially a pretty woman in the middle of the night.

"What's wrong with you? You see my car parked right over there. I thought geeky nerds were supposed to be smart," Trina spat out.

"I was just trying to make small talk," the attendant replied, feeling a little embarrassed and wishing he hadn't spoken in the first place.

"What you need to do is press the button on that machine so I can start pumping my gas. Then you can go back to reading insect books or whatever you do," she continued, humiliating the man even further as she slid a fifty dollar bill into the metal slot.

The geek did as he was told and handed Trina a bright red gas can and her change.

Trina had to look at the man one last time before laughing in his face at his discomfort.

As she walked back to her vehicle, a flicker of recognition flashed into the attendant's mind. *"A white girl talking and acting like that in the hood... I know I've seen her somewhere before,"* he thought to himself. He racked his brain as Trina peeled away from the station.

******

At 3:15 a.m., Trina pulled up the block from Cherrish's brothel, and cut the Altima's lights off. "You ready?" she asked Jenise.

"What if someone's still inside?" Jenise nervously asked.

"You seen how everything went down. The police took everybody to jail. They probably snatched up Cherrish's ass earlier

265

on or something. Come on, we don't have all night," Trina said as she reached in the back seat, grabbed the filled gas can and handed it to Jenise. "Remember where I told you to pour it at," she reminded her cousin.

Jenise got out of the car and looked around to make sure no one was watching what she was up to. As she was pouring the last of the gas around the back of the house, she lit up a cigarette and took a strong drag.

"Whatcha doing back here?" a voice called out, scaring the already nervous woman. "I said what the fuck you doing back here sneaking around?" Cherrish's brother, Born asked again as he reached out to grab Jenise's arm.

"Nothing! Let me go!" she responded growing more frightened. She pushed the drunken Born away and attempted to make a hasty getaway.

The unexpected shove caught the man off guard. He slipped on some spilled gas and fell backwards. Jenise's lit cigarette also fell, causing the gas to ignite and illuminate the dark night air.

Jenise ran back to the car as fast as she could as the fire started to spread like a California brushfire. "Drive! Drive!" she yelled in a frantic voice as she jumped into the passenger seat.

Trina had already pulled up to the front of the house and was ready to pull off, when they heard a loud thump against the side of the car that caused both women to scream out loud.

"Ahhhhh! Help me! Help me! Call an ambulance!" Born was completely engulfed in hot flames as he screamed at the top of his lungs, causing the neighbors' lights to flicker on. His clothes started to melt to his body, causing his inhuman screams to intensify.

Trina just stared at the man whom she once loved and would do anything for, including selling her body which she did all too eagerly. She snapped back to reality and screeched off without a second thought as Born fell to the cold sidewalk, writhing in agonizing pain.

About a half an hour later, the once still night was flooded with fire trucks, squad cars, ambulances and a host of neighbors looking and talking amongst themselves from behind the yellow police caution tape.

******

Ice Cold Vengeance

Wilbert, the attendant from the gas station with the extremely thick glasses, was also there with the crowd so he could have something exciting to talk about tomorrow with his customers.

Then it hit him where he recognized the white girl from. He had been to Cherrish's whorehouse every Friday for the past three months straight. Since he was such a regular customer, Cherrish would sometimes give him credit, charging him only twenty percent interest until he got paid.

When Wilbert saw the beautiful, full-bodied Trina for the first time at the spot, he had to have her at any cost, even if it cost him his entire paycheck. Hoping to impress the new woman, he asked her if he could take her to the VIP room. The white girl just laughed in his face just like she did at the gas station.

It was no coincidence that she bought a full can of gas, and a little while later Cherrish's brothel was burning down to the ground. Cherrish would definitely want to know these peculiar facts about the rude ass white girl. "He might give me six months of discounted pussy for this information," Wilbert said to himself with a smile as he got a massive erection through his tight, dirty slacks.

CHAPTER FIFTY-THREE

Haitian Jack sat in the living room of his rented house, sipping on his usual codeine-laced drink. When his most trusted, loyal right-hand man, Lite didn't check in from the simple mission, Jack knew that something was definitely wrong.

He lit two white Mardet candles wrapped in pitch-black plastic rosary beads and patiently waited for an answer. His suspicions were finally confirmed when the swirling gray smoke and the shadows dancing wildly on the darkened walls let him know that his boy was dead.

Then, Lite's woman, Carmen called Jack and told him that she got locked up during a surprise raid at the strip club. She told him that he had to get her out as quickly as possible before they ran her fingerprints and found out that she had several warrants on her in a few Florida counties. So Jack hustled his high priced lawyer that he kept on retainer out of his bed and down to the stationhouse in his fourteen hundred dollar George Jensen micro crafted silk pajamas.

After the smooth-talking, highly paid attorney pulled a couple of strings, he called Jack to inform him that the girl would be released in a half an hour, so Jack drove to the stationhouse and picked her up.

Carmen told Jack that the police rushed the strip club probably on a citywide crackdown on bitches slinging pussy.

Jack then told her about Lite. He couldn't tell her the exact details, but just said that her man was murdered while handling some important business.

"Who did it? Let's go get the motherfuckers right now! Are you sure he's dead? I want to go and see him!" she screamed in total despair.

"Whap!"

Jack gave the hysterical woman a rough, open-handed slap to bring her to her senses. "Now calm the fuck down and chill out. I got everything already worked out. You just relax and let me map shit out the right way. You know he was my man, so I'm gonna make sure things are handled properly," he said in a take charge manner as he pulled up in the driveway. He then rolled up an overstuffed Philly blunt that was sprinkled with a little coke, hoping that it would relax Carmen, who was now in a cold, silent mode.

The next day, Carmen was still in her room as Jack prepared to handle his business. Even though Lite was gone, he still had a growing empire to run and more money to make. Jack made a call to the motel where his no questions asked young soldiers had the game on lock on that end.

All the other spots were up and running smoothly, so he decided next to call Miami to see when his cousin was coming up to join him in his new Big Apple venture. "What's up, nigga? You know who this is. When you supposed to be touching down?" he asked, talking into his cell phone.

"Probably in a couple of days. I'm just tying up a few loose ends. How's everything flowing up there?" the caller asked.

"I'm still doing me, but Lite went on an extended vacation last night," Jack replied, speaking in code to let his cousin know that Lite was murdered.

"Yeah, I feel you, but niggas still gotta make moves," the caller coldly stated, already used to hearing about this or that person who had gotten themselves killed in one way or another.

"Anyway, give me a shout out when you touch base," Jack said before ending his brief conversation.

Now that Haitian Jack was finished with his business, he wanted to relieve some pent up stress, and the only way to do that was to make one final call. "What's up? This is Jack. Can you make it happen right now?"

"I'm kind'a in the middle of something at the moment. How about later on?" Kiwi said, letting her newest customer know that she was already laid up or preparing to get down for her money.

"Fuck that shit! You know how I do. There's a little something extra in it for you if you meet me at the usual spot in forty minutes," he responded. He was not used to people—especially women—putting him on hold.

Kiwi laughed, liking the man's "take control" attitude. Before hanging up she said, "Okay! Okay! I'll be there!"

Jack jumped into a hot shower and found himself unconsciously stroking his massive hard-on while thinking about how the very energetic Kiwi rode him like a seasoned cowboy trying to break a wild bronco just a couple of nights ago. He had to force himself to stop because he didn't want to waste his sperm down the shower drain. He wanted every drop of his babies to end up in the bottom of Kiwi's stomach or soaking up her pussy walls.

When he finally finished in the bathroom, he splashed some Cool Water cologne on his scarred body. He then slid on a pair of dark blue Versace slacks, a white cotton button-down shirt, and a pair of D&G camel skin slip on shoes. He completed his outfit with a pair of Devo pitch-black shades, and a pair of bottle cap size canary-yellow diamond studded earrings.

Exactly thirty-nine minutes later, Haitian Jack was beeping his horn at Kiwi who was in front of a Metro PCS cell phone store, and loudly popping pink bubble gum with her thick lips. She walked slowly to the vehicle letting Jack get a good look at her wears. She had on a short army camouflage skirt with loose strings hanging at the hem in a stylish urban sort of way. She also rocked a tight green and black camouflage belly T-shirt that hugged her melon sized breasts. A pair of large gold bamboo earrings completed the look.

Jack wasted no time getting to their usual fuck spot. He floored the gas pedal, and Kiwi laughed to herself, knowing that she had the man pussy whipped.

A short time later Kiwi emerged from the hotel's bathroom in nothing but her high heels and her unmistakable, irresistible sex appeal, according to Jack. She had lubricated her vagina with K-Y Strawberry Scented Warming Gel so that her money trap could be hot and slippery for her new best trick.

In less than ten seconds, Jack had her bent over the cheap nightstand table, pounding the woman out raw-dog trying to make every stroke count.

Kiwi had to bite down on the hotel's Bible just to keep from crying out. Jack always gave her an extra three hundred dollars to let him fuck her without a condom. Greed always won over common sense and safety issues with the woman saying to herself, "He has plenty of dough, smells good, and always comes to see me fresh dip. What could he possibly have?"

Ice Cold Vengeance

******

At the same time Jack was down-stroking the closed eyed Kiwi on the bed, Carmen was making a series of phone calls. "This is Carmen again. I want to make that power move that we talked about. Call me back as soon as you get this message," she said, leaving a message on Ice's voice mailbox.

She felt deep in her heart that Jack had something to do with her boyfriend, Lite getting killed. Maybe Lite stood up to him and wanted more money for the both of them. Maybe Lite found out that Jack was up to some foul shit behind his back. Whatever the reason, she hated Jack now more than ever and wanted him taken out for the count. The same way Jack tortured that poor young kid Rizz into revealing where his stash was, is what Carmen planned to do with that bitch ass nigga.

Carmen's face became a mask of pure evil and hate as she dialed Ice's number once again, hoping to reach him.

CHAPTER FIFTY-FOUR

Universal, his little man Cory, and the always nervous Nature sat in the pecan colored Jaguar with the custom made goose down headrests, just patiently waiting. They all were puffing on some high grade Jamaican Sugar Haze weed; each person pretty much lost in his own thoughts. They were parked in front of Universal's baby's mother Chyna's apartment building waiting for his Infiniti G35 coupe to pull up. Universal had given Chyna his car to ride around in because she had blown out the engine on a previous vehicle he had purchased for her. Also, he didn't want his little son, Anthony riding with his mother on the train or bus with the rest of the losers.

Since Rizz made him second in charge, it seemed like the money was just falling into his lap. He didn't want to be talked about like other hustlers who were rolling hard, but their peoples had hoopties or just simply had to bum rides from whoever to get where they were going.

Now folks in the hood were talking about some light skinned nigga pushing and flossing around in Universal's Infiniti that he bought for his baby's mother. The haters who weren't getting as much loot as Universal started throwing extra mud in the game to spice shit up. Some of them were saying: *"That nigga, Universal is letting another dude fuck his chick and drive his whip."* And, *"Yo, I heard Universal's baby's mother was giving some light skinned nigga wop (blow jobs) while his seed was in the back seat asleep. That's some real foul shit!"*

Since everything that's been going on with the gruesome death of Rizz and his once powerful drug crew being scattered about, Universal had more important shit on his mind to worry about. If he wanted to get back on top of the game, first had to squash all the rumors before people started thinking that he was soft ass baby shit and wouldn't respect him on any level.

Then to make the situation even worse, when Universal tried to push up on Chyna for some quick pussy, she turned him down cold like he had the Hong Kong Hives or something. Then strolling out the bathroom like he got it like that was the same green eyed slim guy who had answered the door before.

Even though Chyna wasn't officially his girl anymore, Universal still felt that he had a lifetime pass to the pussy (so he thought) due to the fact he had a child by the woman. The very thought of another dude running up in his baby's mother and then being seen throughout the hood driving the car that he paid for put undiluted hatred in Universal's eyes and heart.

Universal couldn't tell his boys that he wanted to murder somebody just because his baby's mother was being dug out properly by some pretty boy thug. So instead he threw salt in the game by lying, saying that Ice was the one who set up Rizz to get bodied. Universal further stated that the green eyed stranger also had a hand in setting up their number one money making spot to get robbed.

"So why is that nigga driving around in the whip that you bought for your baby's mother?" Cory asked, feeling that there was something definitely missing from Universal's story.

"Come on, man. You know how them black chicks in the hood get down. As soon as a pretty motherfucker with light eyes gives them a little attention, they don't know how to act. They think they came across some hot commodity or something just because a motherfucker's a red looking nigga. Plus, he only got close to Chyna just to find out shit about us. You know how dumb ass, color struck bitches can run their mouths not realizing what they saying." Universal spat out his game, convincing the rest of the occupants in the car that he was telling the truth.

Cory had to admit that what Universal just said had a ring of truth to it. He had known firsthand how females be setting up dudes for the loot. Or sometimes bitches just talked too damn much not realizing what they're saying, especially after a long night of good fucking and a good bag of Piff.

"So why I gotta go by myself? Why don't we all just rush him when he pulls up?" Nature whined, wishing and praying that the black Infiniti would never show up.

"Listen, you scary motherfucker! Ever since you got with us, I never once saw you get down for your crown! Now, I'm about to build shit back up again, and I want to see you put in work with my own eyes!" Universal shouted as he blew weed smoke in Nature's face.

Before Nature could whine some more, Universal said, "Everybody get on point. Here comes the car right now. Hurry up before he goes into the building." He watched as Ice slowly got out of the Infiniti across the street.

"Boom!"

The sawed-off shotgun in Nature's shaking hands went off with sparks flying out of the short barrel. The shot was way off its mark as metal shotgun pellets struck the Infiniti's back door.

The Patron slowed Ice's reflexes down a bit, which could have cost him his life if Nature wasn't so nervous and unsteady on his feet. Ice whipped out the stolen police issued Glock nine and pointed it at his mysterious would-be assassin.

Nature froze like a timid deer caught in a car's bright headlights. He backed up a few feet and slipped causing the shotgun slid under a parked car.

As Ice pointed his weapon at the wide eyed man's forehead. He had to smile to himself as he stood over the bitch ass, so-called hit man.

"Pop! Pop! Pop!"

"Bloc! Bloc! Bloc! Bloc!"

Two different types of guns were being fired at Ice by a couple of guys trying to finish the job that their friend had failed at.

Nature, who was now a half a block away, had gotten up on his feet and ran screaming like a deranged person who had just escaped from a mental institution. A woman couldn't have screamed in a higher pitched voice than he did. *"Fuck everything! I got niggas wanting me to commit murder, crooked DT's putting pressure on me to become their number one snitch, and guys getting bodied everywhere I turn. I'm outta here!"* he thought to himself as he turned the corner and knocked an elderly woman flat on her ass.

When Nature first got down with Rizz's drug operation, all he wanted was a fly whip, some shines and some easy pussy from top choice females with dump truck asses. But now, he was headed for the first thing smoking out of New York.

"Pop! Pop! Pop! Pop!"

Ice Cold Vengeance

Ice shot back at the two guys who were trying to take him out for the count.

Universal spun around and fell back into the Jag as a hollow-point bullet ripped into his side.

Police sirens became louder and louder as Ice and Cory took a few more shots at each other before getting back into their own cars.

Universal had already climbed into the back seat as Cory jumped behind the wheel and peeled off.

Ice sped off in the opposite direction, but not before getting a good look at both of the guys who were trying to murder him. He remembered the taller guy—who he thinks he might have hit—as the one who visited Chyna's apartment the other day. He had to be connected to that pimp that pushes the 600 Benz.

The shorter guy who seemed to be around sixteen or seventeen, Ice had never seen before. But he seemed like he had something extremely personal against him. Ice burned the guy's face in his memory bank.

The third guy with the shotgun who ran away screaming like a bitch at a rock concert, Ice doubted that he would ever see him again in the hood.

"Them niggas gotta go, and like right now! Chyna's gonna tell me where they rest at whether she wants to or not," Ice said out loud as he parked the car away from the shootout and lit up a cigarette.

CHAPTER FIFTY-FIVE

"Okay. Come back and see us again," Trina said with her widest smile as a customer walked out the front door drained from a wild sex episode.

Business had been booming the last couple of days since Cherrish's house got raided and then burned down. It was too bad that Born, her long term off and on pimp got caught up in the mix of things on her come-up. "Fuck it! Some people just get the short end of the stick fucking with the game," she reasoned with herself.

The next morning after Trina had her cousin burn down Cherrish's brothel, she had five thousand business cards printed up. The cards had a black glossy finish with the edges trimmed in gold. There was a gold silhouette of a shapely woman wearing a thong, high heels, and her flowing hair was hanging down her back. The lettering, which was also in shiny gold tone, read: *"International Delights. Massages for All Occasions. Women Also Welcome"*. She had two cell phone numbers placed at the bottom next to a weed leaf, letting people know that they could get more than pussy if that was their thing.

Trina had hit all the spots where she knew guys always hung out: Barber shops, pool halls, car washes, street corners, etc.

Running from place to place, she also threw out the rumor that Cherrish's spot was burned down by neighbors who got fed up with all the comings and goings, and just took matters into their own hands. She tried to cover her tracks and divert attention away from herself just in case Cherrish started putting two and two together. It wouldn't take a genius to figure out that Trina would be the only one to profit from the man's loss, especially since she decided to strike out in the seedy skin game herself. Trina didn't come out and say it directly, but to a few regulars that she ran into, she kind of hinted that she was still down with Cherrish.

It didn't take long for Trina's cell phone to start ringing off the hook with guys making inquiries about her new business venture.

Ice Cold Vengeance

Trina also took care of Tito the apartment manager, so he wouldn't be a pain in the ass later on when people started coming through all hours of the day and night to get their freak on.

She gave her cousin Jenise very specific orders that when fucking Tito, not to make him cum too quickly. Therefore, Jenise slowed her now expert moves down a bit when she felt the man was about to reach an orgasm. When Jenise finally decided to let the horny man bust that nut, he nearly passed out. When Tito was about to cum, Jenise snatched the dick out her vagina and quickly placed it in her mouth. She then roughly milk his organ, slurping down every drop while her free hand roughly twisted his balls. Afterwards, Tito began breathing so heavily that Jenise jokingly asked him if he wanted to borrow her asthma inhaler.

"So, is everything all right?" Trina asked after the last of the tricks left with a look of pure satisfaction on his face.

"Yeah, everything's cool. That motherfucker wanted the Brazilian 68 blowjob special. The bastard had the nerve to try and get on some cheap shit," a female nicknamed Tyra Spanks replied with a *"How could a nigga be so lame?"* look on her face.

Cherrish had given her the tag name Tyra Spanks because she could have been the identical twin of the famous former runway model, Tyra Banks; except that her forehead was slightly larger.

Her curiosity getting the best of her, Trina asked, "So, what happened?"

"What do you think happened? After he got my paper right, I sucked his little dick so hard that the bed sheets got sucked up his ass like a Hoover vacuum cleaner!" Tyra replied with a hearty laugh as Trina gave the woman a high five.

Trina looked at the tall, slim woman who was wearing a short, transparent, sexy latex raincoat with a lime green Secret Embrace underwear set underneath it. Trina had recruited the girl after she came out of jail from the raid at Cherrish's crib. *"Maybe in another lifetime she could have been somebody special,"* Trina thought to herself as she admired the woman's beauty.

"The way shit is starting to boom, I might have to get another apartment," Trina said to herself as she counted a pile of money at the kitchen table.

******

"What?! Are you sure?" Cherrish asked as he leaned against his car, drinking straight out of a hundred and fifty year old bottle of Scandinavian scotch whiskey called King's Ransom that he specifically ordered off the internet.

"Yeah, I'm a thousand percent sure. It was that thick white chick who I saw at your house a couple of days before," Wilbert, the gas station attendant said with a look of hurt on his face because his favorite spot for buying pussy was now a condemned gutted-out shell.

"So who else was she with?" the angry pimp asked.

"I couldn't really tell how her face looked, but I know there was another female riding in the car with her. And I'm sure she did that foul shit, because now she's been handing out business cards all over town and talking about giving dudes good deals on massages," Wilbert said, as he handed Cherrish one of Trina's cards.

"Okay, cool. I'll look out for you again later on once I take care of this here business," Cherrish replied, giving the man a crisp hundred dollar bill after carefully reading the newly minted cards.

Wilbert's only thought was how he was going to get his rocks off with the money he just made.

Cherrish was soon behind the wheel of his Benz lost in his own thoughts as Chyna sat in the passenger seat, not knowing what to say or do. "I'ma make a couple of moves, then we gonna head to your place where I can map shit out," he said before he took another swig of his strong, highly expensive liquor.

He was dying to shoot some heroin into his veins so he could have a clearer head on how to handle everything that had been going on in the last couple of days. He couldn't go back to his luxury apartment because his lawyer informed him that the police had fugitive warrants tagged on his name.

A few of the women had made incriminating statements to the vice squad detectives, saying that they were coerced into selling their bodies for him. The women already agreed to turn state's evidence against Cherrish with the promise of having their charges dismissed. Coincidentally, one of the women had an out of state warrant for passing bogus checks, and another girl was found with cocaine and Percocet's in her handbag. The police agreed to make those pending charges disappear if they cooperated in the ongoing investigation against Cherrish.

Cherrish's lawyer also informed him that the police found heroin and cocaine on his property, and that the DA also added drug distribution to the long list of crimes that they were looking for him for.

"So, that fucking white bitch thinks she could set me up with the Jakes and then take food out my mouth! Motherfuckers gonna see how I really get down!" Cherrish said out loud, blaming the raid and everything else connected to his downfall on Trina. He really didn't care that his play brother was laid up in the Cornell Burn Center near death with burns over 80% percent of his body. He figured that Born got what he deserved since he was the one who brought Trina and her cousin to him in the first place.

It was a cold world living in the ghetto.

CHAPTER FIFTY-SIX

Cherrish sat on a closed toilet seat in a cheap hotel, wearing nothing but a wife beater and a pair of silk boxer shorts. He had just finished shooting up the very much needed powerful black tar Blanco heroin in between his toes. There was no way was he going to fuck with his arms, leaving track marks for the world to see.

After coming out of his dope fiend nod and leaving long red scratch marks on his thighs, Cherrish was ready to handle his business. He splashed some cold water on his face before returning to the bedroom.

Chyna was lying on the bed in the heated hotel room. She was butt ass naked, smoking some Hydro weed and watching the reality show, "For the Love of Hip-Hop". "You coming back to bed? You been in the bathroom for over an hour," she said while her chinky eyes hungrily roamed over Cherrish's fit and lean frame.

The on the run couple had been sexing all afternoon and into the midnight hour. Chyna never had a man freak her in so many wild positions, and with unmatched sexual stamina. Cherrish had hit erotic and sensitive spots that she never knew existed. And for the first time in her life she allowed a man touch the "brown eye". She never even let her son's father have anal sex with her after all the times he begged her with pleading eyes and soft kisses. Chyna previously thought that chicks who let guys fuck them in their asses were either porn stars who were getting paid a grip, or straight up nasty smut buckets who would end up catching some embarrassing disease sooner or later.

But with Cherrish, he made everything seem so natural and pure. When he began rubbing his already fully erect penis down with Vaseline, she was literally scared to death. She envisioned the man's monstrous looking organ ripping her in two like an ancient Samurai sword. At first she felt that she couldn't take another inch, and now here she was, secretly praying that he give her some more back door action. Chyna never guessed in her wildest dreams that her asshole had so many pleasurable nerve endings. In her book, the man was a God.

Chyna had already told herself that she wouldn't fuck with any other guy except Cherrish. She was past the point of caring that he had other women willing to do anything and everything for him. The nude, naïve woman believed that if she gave the pimp that extra mile, he would eventually make her his number one chick. Then, she could convince him to invest his money in a legitimate venture and leave the street life and all those skank ass hoes behind.

"Bitch! You don't question how long or why I do something! What you need to question is how soon it's gonna take you to stack my paper!" Cherrish screamed. He hated for anyone to question him, especially a female. "And put some goddamn clothes on! We got moves to make!" he barked as he went over to the worn, chipped wooden dresser and took out a .40 caliber gun that held steel jacketed hollow-point rounds made especially for shredding through internal organs like wet tissue paper.

"I know he's normally not like this. He's just under a lot of stress with all the bullshit that's been jumping off," Chyna said to herself as she proceeded to get dressed.

An hour later Cherrish walked to his car wearing a dark gray Azure sweat suit with the hood covering the long braids that Chyna had braided for him. "You drive," he stated, as he threw the keys to her.

Chyna climbed in and adjusted the memory seat to fit her height. "Where to?" she asked.

"Over to your place. What did you think? I was just gonna let shit slide? I should slap the shit outta you for ever thinking on that level concerning me!" the man responded in his harshest tone of voice.

The couple rode the rest of the way in complete silence until Cherrish ordered, "No, park around the corner!"

Chyna did as she was told and parked the car around the block from her apartment building.

As they rode the elevator up to Chyna's floor, she nervously tapped her foot.

Cherrish found out through his street contacts that Trina and her cousin, Jenise had actually opened up shop a couple of doors down from Chyna's apartment. "That bitch really thought she was gonna get away with crossing me," he said out loud to himself as he sat on the couch in Chyna's apartment.

Meanwhile, Chyna was calling her aunt/babysitter to see how her son was doing. "I promise I'll pick him up tomorrow morning. Yeah, I know it's been two days, that's why I'm going to throw something extra to you. Okay, okay! I'll see you in the morning. Tell Anthony Mommy misses and loves him," she said before ending the call.

For the next hour and a half Cherrish looked through the peephole watching the flow of human traffic coming and going from Trina's apartment. He even saw a few of his steady customers going there to get serviced, which made him grow even more heated by the minute. When he noticed things slow up a bit he said, "Come on. It's about that time. You remember what I told you?"

Chyna took a big gulp of her double shot of liquor and reluctantly said, "I'm ready."

******

"Hello. I heard about your spot through one of my homeboys, and I was wondering if you might need another girl up in here," Chyna said in her most friendly, sincere voice.

Tyra Spanks' pussy being overworked and pounded on by freaky customers all night thought the stranger looked pretty enough to take some of the weight off of her. She unlocked the door and said, "Well, you gonna have to speak to—"

That was all she got to say before Cherrish burst into the room. He pulled down his sweat hood and quickly looked around the room.

Jenise was sitting on Wilbert's lap and rubbing his nappy chest hairs. Trina was in the kitchen wiping down the counter after somebody spilled a pitcher of some kind of sticky red liquid.

"Oh shit! Cherrish! What are you doing here?" Tyra asked with her eyes as wide as two hard boiled eggs.

Trina, keeping a cooler head said, "What's up? I've been all over town trying to track you down. I heard what happened to your place. That's some real fucked up shit. Anyway, what brings you by?"

282

"I just dropped by to see how you were doing. Well, it seems that you doing all right," Cherrish responded as he closed the front door.

"Cherrish, are you gonna open up a new spot? You know I'm down with you for whatever," Tyra stated, sensing that trouble was brewing in the air and trying to get on the man's good side.

"Sit your fucking ass down and keep quiet," Cherrish responded while he still kept his eyes on everybody in the room. "Hey Trina, get out the kitchen and come talk to me," he boldly ordered.

Trina walked out of the kitchen and stood inches away from the pimp. She was still acting calmly, but getting caught off guard like this had her mind racing a mile a minute.

"Okay, I'ma give you a chance to tell me what you know about my place getting raided and burned down the next day," he said, trying to control his mounting anger.

"Why you coming at me like that? I ain't one of your motherfucking hoes!" she spat out. She was not about to be intimidated like everyone else in the room.

"Bam!"

Cherrish punched Trina in the face like she was in a heavyweight title fight, knocking the woman to the floor.

Knowing that the situation was getting out of hand, Wilbert lifted Trina's cousin, Jenise off of his lap and got up. "Whatever's going on is between all of you. I got nothing to do with it, so I'm outta here," he said, walking towards the front door while buttoning up his grease stained work shirt.

"Sit the fuck back down before you end up like this snake white bitch!" Cherrish barked as he whipped out his gun. He disliked the man immensely because he was trying to play both sides of the fence.

Trina finally got back to her feet with blood running freely out of her broken nose and onto her brand new Nicole Miller dress.

"Come on, Cherrish. You didn't have to hit my cousin like a fucking man," Jenice said, still not realizing the danger they all were in.

With natural adrenaline and heroin pumping through his veins, Cherrish viciously hit the girl with the steel barrel of the gun, cracking her cheekbone. Jenise fell backwards with an ear shattering scream, clutching her damaged face.

"It was her idea to burn down your house. She was telling me about how you get all the money while all she gets is a sore pussy. Born put me onto you. Why would he do that if he thought I would ever flip on his brother?" Trina said, trying to divert the man's anger away from herself and more on her cousin, who was now crying in a fetal position on the sofa.

"Bitch! What do you think, I gotta flower pot for a head or something?" he shouted not, feeling Trina's bogus story.

"I can prove it. Let me get a cigarette first," Trina said as she slowly walked over to the couch where Jenise and Wilbert were. She picked up her Coach bag that was in the corner by the couch and began searching its contents for her pack of Newports.

Tyra Spanks started trembling uncontrollably and said," Cherrish, please can I go? I promise I won't say anything."

Just as he was about to backhand the begging woman, Trina pulled a silver .25 automatic out of her bag and pointed it in Cherrish's direction.

"Cherrish, look out!" Chyna screamed as she tried to push the man out of the way just as the determined Trina began firing. The unlucky Chyna was hit just above the bridge of her nose and in her throat, splitting her voice box which resulted in her dying a silent, bloody death.

Tyra Spanks was already up on her feet and out the front door, banging on the neighbors' doors and screaming for help.

Cherrish reacted with the swiftness, and fired his own weapon at the woman who was trying to kill him.

"Blam! Blam! Blam! Blam! Blam! Blam!"

Jenise was still in a curled up ball when a couple of powerful slugs tore into her back and shattered her spine into fragmented pieces.

"Oh shit!" were the last words Wilbert would ever say as a bullet broke his thick glasses, entered his right eye and lodged firmly in his brain.

Trina was running towards the back bedroom still shooting her weapon while Cherrish continued shooting also.

"Blam! Blam!"

Ice Cold Vengeance

Bullets splintered the wooden door frame above Trina's head as she ran into the back bedroom.

"Someone call the police! Oh my God!" an old woman with pink curlers in her graying hair shouted.

The doorway was filled with neighbors awakened by all the commotion. They were staring down at all the bloodshed and bodies sprawled about.

Cherrish calmly put the smoking gun back in his waistband and pushed his way past the crowd that quickly moved to the side. He took the stairs, and when he couldn't hold onto the railing, that's when he noticed that he had been shot in the arm.

Meanwhile, Trina was out of the bedroom window and rushing down the fire escape, trying her best to make it as far away from the bloodbath as possible. "Fuck New York and everybody in it!" she said, breathing hard as her bare feet hit the cold pavement.

Cherrish was speeding away in his car to visit a female doctor friend of his with the hope of getting fixed up, and turning her out in the process as well. Yeah, a true pimp's mind was always fixated on that paper no matter what the situation was.

CHAPTER FIFTY-SEVEN

"Beep-beep!"

Ice blew the horn on Chyna's bullet-riddled Infiniti for Carmen to get in.

Carmen had finally got in touch with Ice the next evening. She informed him that her boyfriend's boss, Haitian Jack, was a foul type of nigga who probably had something to do with her man getting killed a few days ago.

Ice didn't give a fuck about who got murdered and for whatever reason. The only thing he wanted to know was if this Haitian Jack character had Rizz's dough, and where was it stashed at.

"I'm almost sure he keeps most of the money and dope in the house where we stay," Carmen responded.

That's all Ice wanted to hear as he sped off into the night with the Latina woman sitting next to him. He was smoking a blunt while he drove, hoping that the woman was real about what she was kicking. Soon they pulled up in a quiet, nice looking neighborhood and parked.

"That's the house and his BMW," Carmen said in a whisper, as if Jack might be able to hear her. She quietly climbed out the vehicle wearing an extra-tight Lady Godiva sweat suit and a pair of cute pink Puma track sneakers. She was also rocking a pair of extra tinted Chanel sunglasses.

Ice was wearing all black jeans, an LG sweat hoodie, and a pair of tightly laced up black Ugg boots. A fitted Raiders cap was pulled low over his face. He still didn't trust the sneaky conniving woman, so he kept a close eye on her and the surrounding area.

Ice already had his gun out at his side, prepared for anything as the stripper quietly unlocked a side door. They entered through the darkened kitchen with Ice trying to peer through the darkness.

"Shhh! He's in the bathroom!" Carmen whispered as they tiptoed up the carpeted steps leading to the upstairs hallway.

Ice Cold Vengeance

Ice slowly pushed opened the cracked door with the gun in his steady hand. A cloud of steam escaped from the bathroom. Ice saw a figure washing itself through the clear plastic shower curtain. Without warning, the shower curtain was yanked to the side and Ice was hit flush in the face with hot water from the spray nozzle.

Haitian Jack leaped from his once relaxing shower and rushed his would be attacker. He tackled the surprised Ice down onto the wet tiled floor, tightly gripping his wrist that held the Glock.

Ice tried in vain to wrestle the much stronger nude man, but his soapy, wet and slippery body kept making it extremely difficult for him to gain any type of hold.

Just when the much determined Jack was bending Ice's wrist to the point of breaking the fragile bones and having his weapon taken from him:

"Crash!"

A heavy porcelain flower vase came crashing down on the top of his exposed head. Jack rolled off of Ice and fell to the side with a slight thud and muffled moan.

Carmen stood over her one time friend as Jack's eyes and facial expression said, *"You set me up! I always looked out for you. Why? What did I ever do to you?"*

Meanwhile, Ice had jumped to his feet, outraged that he was caught sleeping like an amateur. Just as he was about to pistol whip the man up close and personal, Jack grabbed for the gun once again, causing it go off accidently.

The nine millimeter bullet entered under Haitian Jack's chin and out through the top of his head. He fell backwards and died with dark red blood trickling out of the corner of his mouth. His hateful eyes were still locked on Carmen's grinning face.

"Damn! I wanted to find out where everything was first. Now this bitch ass nigga can't tell us shit," Ice said out loud as he stood up and kicked the dead man in the ribs.

"Come on. I know he got shit stashed in his room somewhere," the woman said, motioning for Ice to follow her.

When they entered Haitian Jack's bedroom, Ice had to admit that the man had his own type of decorating style than what he was used to seeing in the hood. The first thing he noticed was a full grown stuffed cheetah in a protective stance by the bed. With the animal's fangs fully exposed and its piercing black eyes defiant, you would think the wild beast is about to attack you at any moment. The taxidermist was definitely skilled at what he did.

Haitian Jack was told as a youth by his grandfather that cheetahs protected the sleeper from harm and unwanted evil spirits that are most powerful after midnight.

Directly over the king size bed was a beautiful portrait of a glistening dark skinned woman. She was taking a swim in a river somewhere with, flamingos all around. Across the room was a large antique mirror surrounded by a variety of old curved swords and daggers, some with custom made ivory and wooden handles. On the far side of the master bedroom was a beautifully decorated hundred gallon fish aquarium that held ferocious looking red-bellied piranhas.

"Let's do this," Ice said to the woman while still holding onto his weapon, not willing to take any more chances with unexpected surprises.

Carmen spotted some of Haitian Jack's jewelry lying on an antique, hand carved Portuguese coffee table that had lion's paws for legs. The stripper quickly stuffed what items she could fit into her pockets.

Meanwhile, Ice saw Rizz's heavy chain with the custom made diamond medallion, along with a chromed out .44 bulldog gun on the bed. He scooped up both items.

After about twenty minutes of tearing the dead man's room apart, he said, "Come on, we out." He had found a pillowcase stuffed with cash and some drugs that were hidden in the hamper under a pile of dirty clothes. His gut feeling told him there was more loot around somewhere, but his street instincts also told him to break camp with what he had and keep it moving.

While Carmen was talking excitedly about how Jack finally got what he deserved, Ice was still deep in his own thoughts. He still had the letter in his back pocket that Mrs. Teal had given him from his mother. His mother had written that his father, who jumped ship when he was little, was now living in South Side Queens.

His mother also told him that he had a half-brother on his father's side who was around seven or eight years younger than Ice. Ice always wanted a little brother with whom he could kick it with and show him the ropes like older brothers often do. He was going to show his little brother that it would be best to finish school and make something out of his life instead of being caught up in the thug life. He was going to show first hand examples on how ghetto hood rat bitches, quick money, and so-called friends who don't give a shit about you, will always lead you down a dead end street without any options. You will eventually end up six feet under in a cheap pine casket, or doing a football number bid somewhere in one of the many Upstate New York penitentiaries, playing the age old game of "I used to have this or that." And, all the bad ass females you thought you had on lock when you were hustling and giving them anything they wanted will be the first ones to put a block on their phones when you try to call collect from jail.

Ice would prove to his half-brother that when you get murdered being caught up in some hood beef, or got bodied after being set up during a drug deal, your boys going to your wake will be real upset that you got killed at such an early age. They will pour some liquor out in your memory and say out loud so everyone can hear, "We're not going to let niggas get away with that shit!" But a week later you would be forgotten like yesterday's news, and life would go on like you never even existed.

Ice hoped that maybe he could have some kind of relationship with his father also.

"Are you listening to me? What are we gonna do now?" the woman riding next to him asked.

"Yo, I gotta make a few stops," he responded while thinking, *"Why is this bitch talking about 'we'? I'm not giving this chick a chance to stab me in the back the first chance she gets."*

Ice kept driving when he saw a whole squad of police cars, two coroner's vans, and a Channel 5 news truck in front of Chyna's apartment building. *"I can't get trapped up trying to see Chyna,"* he thought to himself as he made a wide U-turn almost running over a curious spectator. He couldn't shake the eerie feeling that somehow the entire scene was somehow connected to Chyna and that sleazy pimp guy he saw her with.

Ice had seen it too many times. When a good girl goes bad, she never comes back, or never arrives back to her previous status. He badly wanted to scoop Chyna and her son up and start a new life somewhere, but he didn't want to get locked up for life trying to do so.

As far as the Carmen was concerned, Ice had planned on getting rid of the woman the first chance he got. There was no way he was going to roll with a female who, when she thought someone did her wrong, would go to any and all lengths to get even with that person. Ice had seen firsthand how she got down and dirty with Haitian Jack without the slightest hesitation.

Ice was soon on the South Side and pulling up to a rundown looking house. This was the address that his mother had told him where his father lived. Even though it was late at night, he wanted to see his dad again, because life in the slums was never guaranteed.

Ice and Carmen walked up to the front door and knocked. A moment later the door swung open and a man who looked much older than his actual years said, "Yeah, whatcha want this late at night?"

"I'm looking for a Mr. Wilson," Ice replied.

"Yeah, that's me. Who are you?" the man said, eyeing the couple very suspiciously.

"I'm your son, Nathanial, but everyone calls me Ice."

The man looked at Ice for a split second, and then his eyes lit up as if by magic. He gave Ice an unexpected hug for a couple of seconds and then said, "Come on in! Come on in! You look so good. Is this your girlfriend? She's very pretty," he said with pride in his voice.

"No, she's just a friend," Ice responded.

Ice and his father talked for about twenty minutes. They were catching up on life when Ice finally said, "Mom told me that I have a little brother. When can I meet him?"

Before Ice's father could respond, Cory entered the kitchen through the back door and walked into the living room where the three people sat talking. His eyes locked with Ice's. The shocked Cory just stood their wondering why this man, who he was just trying to kill the night before, was sitting in his living room, talking to his father.

As soon as Ice recognized Cory as one of the three-man hit team who tried to kill him, he stood up and emptied his gun in him. The only thing Cory could do was throw up his hands in a helpless, defenseless posture as slugs tore into his young body. Ice hit the boy in his chest and stomach.

"Nathaniel! What did you just do?" his father asked, running over to his fallen son and clutching his head in his lap.

"This nigga tried to kill me last night. He probably followed me here to catch me sleeping," Ice said, wondering why his father was crying over someone he didn't even know.

"This is Cory, your half-brother! Why, why, why?" his father was saying while still holding his dead son.

"Come on, Ice! Let's get the fuck outta here! Somebody probably called the police after hearing the gunshots!" Carmen yelled in a panicky voice.

Ice just stared at his father and his recently deceased half-brother that he would never get the chance to know and teach him about all the pitfalls of being associated with the streets. His kept hearing the words, *"Your half-brother... Your half-brother,"* over and over in his shocked mind as he stood there frozen in place and unable to move.

"Do what you want! I'm out!" Carmen shouted as she ran out the front door and sped off in the charged up Infiniti with the money and drugs.

As soon as she jumped on the highway, the song "Super Woman" by Alicia Keys came on the radio. She gave a deep laugh knowing that the song was about her.

She was the only one who made it out untouched in this hellhole of a city that they call New York.

THE END

SNEAK PREVIEW

White Girl's Paradise

Black Man's Grief

An Urban Tale by DeJon

Chapter 1

The soft milky white hand tightly gripped the big black penis that grew and became thicker by the second. Grayish blue eyes stared in fascination at the humongous male sex organ that seemed to have an unnatural life of its own as it vibrantly pulsated like a beating heart inside of the small delicate looking hand. The white girl stared at the dark penis with it's bulging veins in a hypnotic trance as if she just discovered the 8th wonder of the world, or if she was looking at something extraordinary out of the prehistoric era. The owner of the hand belonged to 19 year old Jessica Ryan who was sometimes called Jessy by friends and family alike.

Jessica was always amazed at how her slender fingers could never full touch each other when she held on to the dick which caused her pussy juice to drip just a little harder damping the fragile transparent panties. But what really caused the young woman's heart to beat faster was the obvious danger she was putting herself in by creeping on the low with this thuggish African American gangbanger. It was close to midnight, and here she was sitting in his car on a well lit public street right across from one of Baltimore's most dangerous housing projects giving her secret jump-off some mean head.

Jessica had been told and threatened by one of his baby's mamas that if she was ever seen around this part of town again, she would cut up Jessica's face making it look like an overused jigsaw puzzle. Jessica heard vivid stories on how almost every project ghetto girl carried razor blades, (sometimes hidden in their mouths) or some other sharp cutting instrument. These girls were quick to use the weapons with little or no provocation. Also during that one particular altercation, the baby's mama friends threw in their crude threats as well. "I'm tired of these Marsha Brady looking white bitches coming down to our hood trying to steal our men." Fuck this talking shit! Let's jump the bitch!" A broad shouldered heavy set girl with buttery yellowish teeth had called out. Jessica was saved that time by a slow cruising police van making it's rounds steadily looking for someone to lock up trying to meet the precinct's quotas.

"Oh Jessy, oh Jessy please don't stop! I love your sweet mouth. I'm about to cum!" A voice called out hoarsely. "How many times I told you not to call me Jessy. My father calls me Jessy and plus it makes me sound like a little girl." Jessica snapped as she gave the man a pissed off look. She wasn't really all that upset that he called her Jessy, what bothered her was that by talking, he broke Jessica out her trance like daydream.

In reality, Jessica was giving a blow job to a good looking 29 year old white man who happened to be a successful downtown attorney. Furthermore it was mid-afternoon, nowhere near any type of project but in a safe respectable area. The area happened to be in the parking lot of her father's steak and seafood restaurant.

"Well do you think I'm a little girl?" Jessica asked as she frowned a little. "No of course not. You know how I get carried away sometimes', the man responded while trying to

2

catch his breath. "Ok then stop talking and let me finish. I'm already late for work", Jessica spat out as she began pumping up and down on the lawyer's penis praying that somehow that it would grow just a little bit bigger. In fact his member was almost hidden in her hand, with only the pinkish head being seen. Jessica expertly took him in her mouth again. To the young woman it felt as if a small gold fish was swimming around in her mouth. Jessica wished for the thousandth time that it was some negro's cock banging against her soft tonsils. A few seconds later, a spurt of low quality semen dampened the insides of her mouth. Jessica imagined that when a black man finally did bust off in her mouth, she hoped that his hot tidal wave like cum would damn near drown her.

All Jessica's waking hours and intense fantasies were centered with various detailed scenarios on how a screw faced black man would take her in one way or another. She imagined the man to be like one of those broad chested rough looking African slaves living on the plantations during the 1800's when sexual relations between the races were considered taboo and illegal, (at least on paper it was.) From what Jessica was led to believe in high school, the black man would be well built, unnaturally endowed, and if given the chance to be with a white woman would without mercy pound the pussy into oblivion like a sexed crazed jungle animal.

An involuntary but wishful pleasing smile crept across Jessica's flushed face. Little did Jessica know that in less than two days, she would be hanging out down in Baltimore's most infamous black ghetto nicknamed "The Bottoms" The white girl would soon be known as Paradise to the thugged out residents while she lived out her most shameful and secret fantasies.

AVAILABLE SPRING 2016

3

DeJon, the Donald Goines of the new millennium, takes you on yet another fast-paced adrenaline run that will have you eagerly anticipating more.

After being sexually assaulted by the aunt's bi-sexual girlfriend, Pumpkin, a pretty, naïve teenage girl fresh out of high school, gets hooked up with Goldmine, a stunning, conniving stripper.

Goldmine wastes no time introducing Pumpkin into Atlanta's cold seedy underworld of quick money, tarnished dreams, and exotic dancing. Pumpkin soon finds herself caught up in the middle of a brutal drug war between New York gangsters, run by Knowledge, and Atlanta's local drug dealers, who will stop at nothing to protect their territory.

AVAILABLE NOW

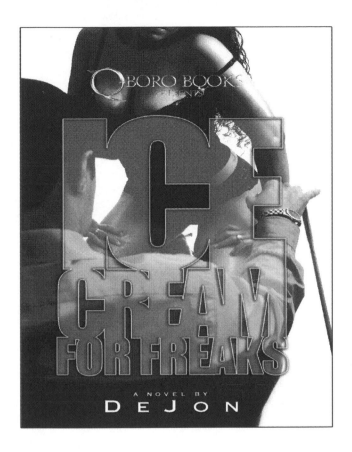

A NOVEL BY
D E J O N

In the tradition of cult literacy icon Donald Goines, *Ice Cream For Freaks* is written with a realness that accurately depicts the bleak conditions of the story's urban backdrop.

Nathaniel Wilson, better known in his middle class Queens neighborhood as Ice, has a reputation for being a brutal and daring stick-up kid. A seemingly well-planned robbery proves deadly to Ice when the victim happens to be Supreme, a rising star in a violent New York drug cartel. The robbery ignites a backlash of unpredictable murders, rapes, and mayhem throughout the streets of Queens.

When Ice lands in an upstate New York prison, his reputation and his manhood come into question after an unforgettable and terrorizing encounter in his cell with a prison homo thug.

AVAILABLE NOW